DATE DUE

Between Heaven and Mirth

Also by James Martin, S.J.

The Jesuit Guide to (Almost) Everything: A Spirituality for Real Life

A Jesuit Off-Broadway: Behind the Scenes with Faith, Doubt, Forgiveness and More

Becoming Who You Are: Insights on the True Self from Thomas Merton and Other Saints

Lourdes Diary: Seven Days at the Grotto of Massabieille

My Life with the Saints

Searching for God at Ground Zero

This Our Exile: A Spiritual Journey with the Refugees of East Africa

In Good Company: The Fast Track from the Corporate World to Poverty, Chastity and Obedience

Edited by James Martin, S.J.

Celebrating Good Liturgy: A Guide to the Ministries of the Mass

Professions of Faith: Living and Working as a Catholic (with Jeremy Langford)

Awake My Soul: Contemporary Catholics on Traditional Devotions

How Can I Find God?: The Famous and Not-So-Famous Consider the Quintessential Question

Between Heaven and Mirth

Why Joy, Humor, and Laughter Are at the Heart of the Spiritual Life

James Martin, S.J.

HarperOne
An Imprint of HarperCollins*Publishers*

HarperOne

Imprimi Potest: Very Rev. Myles N. Sheehan, S.J.

HarperCollins books may be purchased for educational, business, or sales promotional use. For information, please write: Special Markets Department, HarperCollins Publishers, 10 East 53rd Street, New York, NY 10022.

HarperCollins website: http://www.harpercollins.com

FIRST EDITION

Library of Congress Cataloging-in-Publication Data is available upon request.

ISBN 978-0-06-202426-8

11 12 13 14 15 RRD(H) 10 9 8 7 6 5 4 3 2 1

For my mother and father,
who taught me how to laugh;
for my sister and brother-in-law,
who laugh with me;
for my nephews,
who make me laugh;
and for my brother Jesuits and friends,
who remind me to laugh at myself.

Contents

Introduction

Excessive Levity

Mike is one of the funniest people I know. A Catholic priest in his mid-sixties, he regales his friends with clever stories, boasts superb comic timing, and has perfected an inimitable deadpan look. Today Mike is a popular professor at Fordham, a Catholic university in New York City, where his lighthearted sermons attract crowds of students to Sunday Masses. It's nearly impossible to be downhearted or discouraged in his presence.

But Mike's contagious humor wasn't always valued. And forty years ago the Jesuits—the Catholic religious order to which Mike and I belong—had an odd custom that made this clear. At the time, the young Jesuits in training were required to publicly confess their "faults" to the men in their community as a way of fostering their humility. This had been a long-standing practice in many religious orders, especially in monastic orders. (It sounds strange but, as the saying goes, the past is a different country. And the past in religious orders is a different world.)

So, for example, at a weekly gathering of the priests and brothers, a young Jesuit might confess that he hadn't said his evening prayers. Or that he had nodded off during a particularly dull homily. Or that he had said uncharitable things about another person in the community. This was supposed to help the young Jesuit become more humble, more attentive to his shortcomings, and more eager to correct them. On top of that, each young Jesuit was supposed to confess things privately, to the head of the community.

One day Mike, who was known for his high spirits, felt guilty. Earlier in the day, during Mass, he couldn't stop laughing about something that struck him as hilarious. He felt he had been acting silly and undignified. So Mike walked into the office of the head of the Jesuit community, an elderly priest with a well-earned reputation for seriousness.

Mike took his seat and prepared for his admission of guilt.

"Father," he said, "I confess excessive levity."

The priest glowered at Mike, paused, and said, "*All* levity is excessive!"

In some religious circles joy, humor, and laughter are viewed the same way the crabby priest saw levity: as excessive. Excessive, irrelevant, ridiculous, inappropriate, and even scandalous. But a lighthearted spirit is none of those things. Rather, it is an essential element of a healthy spiritual life and a healthy life in general. When we lose sight of this serious truth, we cease to live life fully, truly, and wholly. Indeed, we fail to be holy. And that's what this book is about: the value of joy, humor, and laughter in the spiritual life.

This book had its genesis a few years ago when I began to give talks based on a book called *My Life with the Saints,* a memoir telling the story of twenty saints who had been influential in my spiritual life. In a short while I noticed something surprising. Wherever I spoke—whether in parishes, colleges, conferences, or retreat centers—what people wanted to hear about *most* was the way the saints were joyful people, enjoyed lives full of laughter, and how their holiness led inevitably to joy. To a degree that astonished me, people seemed fascinated by joy. It was almost as if they'd been waiting to be told that it's okay to be religious *and* enjoy themselves, to be joyful believers.

Still, many professional religious people (priests, ministers, rabbis, and the like) as well as some devout believers in general give the impression that being religious means being dour, serious, or even grumpy—like Mike's superior. ("Um, uptight," Mike said recently, when I asked what the guy was like.) But the lives of the saints, as well as those of great spiritual masters from almost every other religious tradition, show the opposite. Holy people are joyful. Why? Because holiness brings us closer to God, the source of all joy.

Why am I so concerned with joy, humor, and laughter from a spiritual point of view? Why have I written an entire book on the subject? The reaction of those crowds is not the only thing that encouraged me to take up this topic. There was another phenomenon, equally persuasive, that I continually ran across: these virtues—yes, *virtues*—are often sadly lacking in religious institutions and in the ideas that good religious people have about religion.

A little background may be in order. I've been a Catholic and a Christian my whole life, a Jesuit for over twenty years, and a priest for over ten. So I've spent a great deal of time living and working among those whom you could call "professionally religious." Especially over the last twenty years I've met men and women working in all manner of religious settings—in churches, synagogues, and mosques; retreat houses, religious high schools, colleges, and universities; rectories, parish houses, and chanceries; parish adult-education programs, interfaith meetings, and religious gatherings of every stripe. And I have known, met, or spoken to thousands of religious people from almost every walk of life. In the process I have come across a surprising number of spiritually aware people who are, in a word, *grim*.

Not that I expect believers to be grinning idiots every moment of the day. Sadness is a natural and human reaction to tragedy, and many situations in life require, even demand, a serious approach. But I've met so many religious folks with sour faces that it makes me wonder why they seem to believe that the absence of joy is a necessary part of their spiritual lives.

Many years ago, for example, a friend of mine lived with a Jesuit finishing his doctoral dissertation. One morning, when my friend greeted him, he replied glumly, "Please don't talk to me. I don't talk to *anyone* before lunchtime. My writing is just too stressful," and walked away. But being joy-challenged is not just the province of Jesuit priests and brothers (most of whom are cheerful sorts). Joylessness is nondenominational and interfaith. "My minister is such a *grump*!" a Lutheran friend told me a few months ago, explaining what led her to search for another church. Last year I gave a talk to a large group of Catholics. After the talk someone said approvingly, "You know, I actually saw our bishop laugh during your talk. I've never seen *that* before." She had been working with the bishop for five years.

A certain element of such joylessness is probably related to personality types; some of us are naturally more cheerful, optimistic, and upbeat. But after encountering the same brand of dejection over and over for twenty years in a wide variety of settings, I've reached the unscientific (but I think accurate) conclusion that underlying this gloom is a lack of belief in this essential truth: faith leads to joy.

Moreover, this morose spirit has wormed its way into the culture of too many religious institutions. That is, it goes beyond the personal and moves into the communal realm. Why has this happened? A few reasons come to mind.

First of all, our understanding of God is often one of a joyless judge. More about this later in the book, but suffice it to say that when you consider the grim spirit that pervades some church groups, it's no surprise that one of the most influential American sermons is Jonathan Edwards's eighteenth-century tract "Sinners in the Hands of an Angry God." In it, Edwards thunders, "There is no want of *power* in God to cast wicked men into hell at any moment." Quite an image of God—enough to wipe the smile off any believer's face.

Second, and related to the first reason, the aim of religion is sometimes seen as one of overriding *seriousness*. We are to be concerned with our relationship to the Creator of the universe, our obligation not to sin, our adherence to a set of divinely ordained religious regulations, and, depending on terminology, our personal salvation, the last of which is worked out, as St. Paul said, "with fear and trembling."[1] These are hardly laughing matters, say some.

The Flames Do Now Rage

If you need an example of the historic grimness of American religion, check out this excerpt from Jonathan Edwards's famous 1741 sermon "Sinners in the Hands of an Angry God":

> They [sinners] are now the objects of that very same *anger* and wrath of God, that is expressed in the torments of hell. And the reason why they do not go down to hell at each moment, is not because God, in whose power they are, is not then very angry with them; as he is with many miserable creatures now tormented in hell, who there feel and bear the fierceness of his wrath. Yea, God is a great deal more angry with great numbers that are now on earth: yea, doubtless, with many that are now in this congregation, who it may be are at ease, than he is with many of those who are now in the flames of hell.
>
> So that it is not because God is unmindful of their wickedness, and does not resent it, that he does not let loose his hand and cut them off. God is not altogether such a one as themselves, though they may imagine him to be so. The wrath of God burns against them, their damnation does not slumber; the pit is prepared, the fire is made ready, the furnace is now hot, ready to receive them; the flames do now rage and glow. The glittering sword is whet, and held over them, and the pit hath opened its mouth under them.

Third, many religious organizations sometimes seem more concerned with *sin* than with virtue. Some religious leaders may believe that it's up to them to point out all the ways that their followers might fail, rather than to suggest the ways that they might flourish.

Thus the seemingly endless stream of "Thou shalt nots" overshadows the "Thou shalts."

Fourth, some religious organizations seem to reward the more *serious types;* they rise to the top because their dour attitude is perhaps seen as proof of the seriousness of their intent. I often wonder if those selected for ordained ministry are chosen on the same basis. Whenever someone says to me, "Boy, I've never met a funny *priest* before," I cringe a little. Is that because they have never known many priests or because their past experience with the clergy leads them to equate ministry with melancholy?

Fifth, much of what priests, ministers, rabbis, and imams deal with on a daily basis is *in fact sad*—suffering, illness, death, and so on—and ministering to those *in extremis* is naturally seen as more urgent. When the choice is between celebrating the birth of a child with a parishioner at home and visiting a parishioner dying in the hospital, which will win out? The pastoral choice is not difficult for the overworked minister, but this may mean that the minister becomes more burdened with heaviness of spirit than uplifted with lightness of heart.

Sixth and finally, there is a fundamental *misunderstanding* of the place of lightheartedness in religion in general—which is the main topic of this book.

Let's start with the encouraging fact that it's not hard to see the positive effects of excessive levity. You don't have to be a sociologist or psychologist to do so. All you have to do is look around. And sometimes, it helps to look *outside* the walls of the church, to the stuff of everyday life, in order to better appreciate the value of joy, humor, and laughter.

Funny enough, when I think about laughing, I often think about the mother of a good friend and a particular phrase from almost thirty years ago. When I was in high school and college in

Philadelphia, my best friend was a fellow named John, who came from a large Polish-Italian family. His mother was a lively, diminutive woman who always seemed delighted by life. John's father had worked in a factory for many years, but after setting aside some money, his family had bought a small house by the Atlantic Ocean in southern New Jersey—"the shore," as Philadelphians like to say.

On some summer weekends I would go "down the shore" with John and his family, seven or eight of us packed into a simple cottage with two or three bedrooms. At night John and I would go drinking (this was college, after all); then in the morning we would sleep late and spend the rest of the day lounging on the beach or going "crabbing" with his father, that is, catching crabs in a nearby bay on the family's ramshackle boat. ("A boat is a hole in the water into which you pour money," said a beat-up wooden sign on board.) In the evening there was always a huge pot of spaghetti or crabs or sausage that John's mother had whipped up.

Life was fun at the shore. I could have stayed for weeks on end. Of course we were all on vacation, but there was an unmistakable joie de vivre that continually drew me there.

John's mother had an interesting turn of phrase that John and I used to mimic playfully. Whenever describing an enjoyable family get-together or party, she would invariably end her long story with the same two words. "We *laughed,*" she would say several times, smiling, as if to indicate that this was the highest of compliments for any human interaction.

And it is. So why does it seem that religious men and women seem forget that so often?

Perhaps I'm reacting to something that is foreign to your experience. Maybe you belong to a religious community where people do nothing but laugh and enjoy one another's company. Some megachurches, for example, are distinctly joyful places, but what about other mainstream churches? Is Sunday a fun day for you? It should be. Humor, for one thing, can be balm for a troubled soul.

My father, who died several years ago, had a lively sense of humor. Some of my favorite childhood remembrances are memories of listening to his long, spun-out jokes, which he often brought back from the office and shared with my mother, my sister, and me over dinner. Even more enjoyable for him was telling a joke in front of a larger audience; the bigger the crowd, the more lavish he was with the joke's details. Sometimes, before the joke ended he would anticipate the ending and become helpless with laughter, almost unable to finish. How wonderful to remember this about my father, who had something of a difficult life in his later years.

While he was on his deathbed (literally, the hospital bed he died in, from lung cancer), my sister brought him a DVD of the movie *Young Frankenstein,* which she played on her laptop computer. Mel Brooks's comedy was one of his favorite films; his favorite scene featured the "monster" (played by Peter Boyle) doing a tap dance with Dr. Frankenstein (Gene Wilder) in a top hat and tails, the two of them belting out the song "Puttin' on the Ritz." He smiled even as he was dying. Humor enlivened my father's life and eased his passing from this world to the next.

Speaking of my family, one of the most beautiful sounds I've ever heard comes from my two young nephews. Their laughter—clear, untroubled, bell-like—always makes me smile. Is there anything more wonderful than a child laughing? Every time I hear them laugh, I think the same thing: this child, who a few years earlier did not even exist, is now expressing his boundless joy in life. Hearing them, I am grateful for this double gift: the child and the laughter. And just recently I shared with my twelve-year-old nephew one of my father's favorite jokes, and when he burst into laughter over the dinner table, I felt a profound connection between my late father, me, and my nephew—three generations now connected by laughter.

Finally, let me tell you about another Jesuit I know, Andy, who is probably the funniest person I know. (It's a tie between him and my friend Mike.) A few summers ago, I was on an eight-week retreat (the first half silent; the second half not) with Andy and several other friends. The retreat was part of the final leg of our Jesuit training. He has a huge laugh, is enormously witty, and is seemingly able to locate humor in almost everything in life. If the motto of the Jesuits is "Finding God in all things," Andy's motto might be "Finding humor in all things." And like many joyful souls, he laughed hardest at someone else's jokes, with a wide-open, belly-shaking laugh that never failed to lift me out of whatever spiritual doldrums I was navigating.

Andy had just gone through a rough patch; a few months earlier he had buried his mother, who had been ill for many years. Yet his good humor was undimmed. Recently, I was reading through my journal from the retreat and frequently found entries that read, "Andy made me laugh," or, "It's great having Andy around." I found myself thinking, then as now, "Why can't life be more like this?" Andy was not ignoring the pain or suffering in life; he was not a person untouched by trouble or sadness, but he was not letting those realities take away his joie de vivre.

All these experiences led me to ask: "Why can't contemporary faith be more like this?" We need, I would suggest, to recover the notion that joy, humor, and laughter do not lie outside the believing life, but are at the heart of it. They *are* the heart of that life.

Over the next few chapters I'm going to make a serious argument for joy, humor, and laughter as part of a healthy spiritual life. This sounds paradoxical, and perhaps it is in a way. But joy, humor, and laughter are important spiritual matters.

Between Heaven and Mirth is one person's encouragement to

consider faith as something that leads to joy.* And it is an invitation, a challenge even, to rethink the importance of humor and laughter in the life of believers. It is something of a bridge between scholarly takes on those topics and a living spirituality. That is, it approaches those topics primarily from a spiritual vantage point and will speak to readers interested in incorporating a lighthearted approach not simply into life, but into the spiritual life in particular. Along the way, I'll share with you insights from my own life, add to them what I've learned in my discussions with scholars, and mix in the most helpful ideas from some classic works on joy, humor, and laughter.

One caveat. Needless to say, I know more about my own tradition, Christianity—and more specifically Catholicism—than I do about other religious traditions. But I will draw on the wisdom of the Jewish, Buddhist, and Islamic traditions frequently as a way of showing how non-Christians view those themes.

Like the topic itself, the book is meant to be mirthful in itself, a *jeu d'esprit* as the French say, a lighthearted conversation with plenty of asides, digressions, and sidebars. The idea that a book on joy, humor, and laughter should be humorless is laughable. The book is divided into nine chapters and a brief conclusion. The first chapter is

---

* Here's what *Between Heaven and Mirth* is not. It is not meant to be overly scholarly, though I will draw on the work of many scholars, particularly when looking at Scripture. Nor is it meant to be an exhaustive treatment of joy, humor, and laughter throughout history. There are rafts of books on such topics—for example, on the Aristotelian notion of comedy, the use of satire in Western literature, the history of "jesters" in the courts of Europe, the place of "comic heroes" in the theater, the physiological reasons for laughing, and so on. Nor will this book be a complete treatment of those themes—joy, humor, and laughter—from a spiritual or religious point of view. The themes of religious humor and laughter have spawned several fine scholarly studies, many of which I will draw from. Moreover, the theme of joy, particularly from a Jewish or Christian vantage point, has spawned hundreds of academic treatments.

an overview of our topic: why joy, humor, and laughter need to be recovered in the spiritual life. The second looks at how and why those virtues have been downplayed in religious circles throughout history. The third examines how the great spiritual masters of every tradition, particularly the saints, used humor in their lives. The fourth offers specific reasons for joy, humor, and laughter in the spiritual life in general. The fifth maintains that joy is not simply something that is "found," but is an outgrowth of vocation, service, and love. The sixth takes aim at the place of joy in institutional religion. The seventh looks at how to find joy if you don't feel especially joyful, or even happy. The eighth shows how you can recover those gifts in your own personal spiritual life, and the ninth chapter looks more specifically at how your own private prayer can encompass joy and, sometimes, laughter.

In between the chapters are reflections on three specific selections from the Old and New Testaments, highlighting how these individual passages demonstrate the value of joy. With those three passages, we'll go a little deeper, to try to understand why such varied people as the writer of the Psalms, St. Luke, and St. Paul thought it important to talk about joy.

There's a tenth part too—jokes. There are plenty of jokes sprinkled throughout the book. Why? By the end of the book, I hope you'll agree that a better question is: Why not?

Chapter One

The Most Infallible Sign

Joy and the Spiritual Life

Many of my favorite jokes are about Catholics, priests, and Jesuits. The Jesuits, by the way, are a Catholic religious order for men (a group of men who take vows of poverty, chastity, and obedience and live in community) founded in 1540 by St. Ignatius Loyola, a Spanish soldier turned priest.

It's easy for me to tell jokes about Catholics, priests, and Jesuits, since I'm all three. And a self-deprecating joke may be the healthiest brand of humor, since the only target is yourself. The standard Jesuit joke plays on the stereotype that we're (a) overly practical, (b) overly worldly, or (c) not as concerned with spiritual matters as we should be. Let me share with you one of my favorites. (Don't worry if you're not Catholic or you've never met a Jesuit in your life. As with most good jokes, you can easily change the details or particulars to suit your own comic purposes.)

There's a barber in a small town. One day he's sitting in his shop, and a man walks in wearing a pair of sandals and a long brown robe with a hood. The man, very thin and quite ascetic looking, sports a short beard. He sits down in the barber's chair.

"Excuse me," says the barber. "I was wondering, why are you dressed like that?"

"Well," says the man, "I'm a Franciscan friar. I'm here to help my brother Franciscans start a soup kitchen."

The barber says, "Oh, I love the Franciscans! I love the story of St. Francis of Assisi, who loved the animals so much. And I love the work you do for the poor, for peace, and for the environment. The Franciscans are wonderful. This haircut is free."

And the Franciscan says, "Oh no, no, no. We live simply, and we take a vow of poverty, but I do have enough money for a haircut. Please let me pay you."

"Oh no," says the barber. "I insist. This haircut is free!" So the Franciscan gets his haircut, thanks the barber, gives him a blessing, and leaves.

The next day the barber comes to his shop and finds a surprise waiting for him. On the doorstep is a big wicker basket filled with beautiful wildflowers along with a thank-you note from the Franciscan.

That same day another man walks into the barber's shop wearing a long white robe and a leather belt tied around his waist. When he sits down in the chair, the barber asks, "Excuse me, but why are you dressed like that?"

And the man says, "Well, I'm a Trappist monk. I'm in town to visit a doctor, and I thought I would come in for a haircut."

And the barber says, "Oh I love the Trappists! I admire the way your lives are so contemplative and how you all pray for the rest of the world. This haircut is free."

The Trappist monk says, "Oh no. Even though we live simply, I have money for a haircut. Please let me pay you."

"Oh no," says the barber. "This haircut is free!" So the Trappist gets his haircut, thanks him, gives him a blessing, and leaves.

The next day the barber comes to his shop, and on his doorstep there is a surprise awaiting him: a big basket filled with delicious homemade cheeses and jams from the Trappist monastery along with a thank-you note from the monk.

That same day another man walks into the barber shop wearing

The Silent Monk

A man enters a strict monastery. On his first day the abbot says, "You'll be able to speak only two words every five years. Do you understand?" The novice nods and goes away.

Five years later the abbot calls him into his office. "Brother," he says, "You've done well these last five years. What would you like to say?"

And the monk says, "Food cold!"

"Oh, I'm sorry," says the abbot. "We'll fix that immediately."

Five years later the monk returns to the abbot.

"Welcome, Brother," says the abbot. "What would you like to tell me after ten years?"

And the monk says, "Bed hard!"

And the abbot says, "Oh, I'm so sorry. We'll fix that right away."

Then after another five years the two meet. The abbot says, "Well, Brother you've been here fifteen years. What two words would you like to say?"

"I'm leaving," he says.

And the abbot says, "Well, I'm not surprised. You've done nothing but complain since you got here!"

a black suit and a clerical collar. After he sits down, the barber says, "Excuse me, but why are you dressed like that?"

And the man says, "I'm a Jesuit priest. I'm in town for a theology conference."

And the barber says, "Oh, I love the Jesuits! My son went to a Jesuit high school, and my daughter went to a Jesuit college. I've even been to the retreat house that the Jesuits run in town. This haircut is free."

And the Jesuit says, "Oh no. I take a vow of poverty, but I have enough money for a haircut."

The barber says, "Oh no. This haircut is free!" After the haircut, the Jesuit thanks him, gives him a blessing, and goes on his way.

The next day the barber comes to his shop, and on his doorstep there is a surprise waiting for him: *ten more Jesuits.*

Now, if I recounted a second joke or a third joke (e.g., see p. 14), you might wonder when I was going to get to the point. But, in a way, jokes *are* the point of this chapter, which is that joy, humor, and laughter are underappreciated values in the spiritual life and are desperately needed not only in our own personal spiritual lives, but in the life of organized religion.

Joy, to begin with, is what we'll experience when we are welcomed into heaven. We may even laugh for joy when we meet God. Joy, a characteristic of those close to God, is a sign of not only a confidence in God, but also, as we will see in the Jewish and Christian Scriptures, gratitude for God's blessings. As the Jesuit priest Pierre Teilhard de Chardin said, "Joy is the most infallible sign of the presence of God."*

Humor is also an essential but neglected requirement of spirituality. Most of the saints, for example, had a terrific sense of humor and could easily laugh at themselves.

Finally, *laughter* is essential even in the most "spiritual" or "religious" of places. My friend Bill, a priest who works in a small parish in New Mexico, told me a story about attending his first

* Although this quote is most often ascribed to Pierre Teilhard de Chardin, the Jesuit paleontologist (the elderly priest in the movie *The Exorcist* is based on him, more or less), others attribute it to the French writer Léon Bloy. The Protestant theologian Karl Barth also had a variation of the phrase: "Laughter is the closest thing to God's grace." I've tried in vain for years to track down the original author of the notion that joy is the surest sign of God's presence. So if anyone asks you who said it, just say it was me.

silent retreat—during which you pray for several days and meet daily with a "spiritual director," with whom you discuss your prayer.*

Every day Bill quietly prayed in his small room at the retreat house, with the curtains drawn, growing ever more morose in the gloom. "That was what I thought prayer was all about," he told me.

Three days into his retreat, the retreat director came to his room and said, "Bill, I haven't heard you laugh since you arrived. And I'll wager that the devil hates laughter more than anything else. Get outside and enjoy the sunshine!"

Joy, humor, and laughter are spiritual gifts that we ignore at our peril.

Before continuing our conversation about joy, humor, and laughter in the spiritual life, let's define our terms. First, we'll look at the more common, or secular, definitions of the three words, and then we'll look at them from a religious viewpoint.

In a secular context, joy is generally understood as a kind of happiness. My old *Merriam-Webster's Dictionary* uses words like "delight" and "bliss" as definitions. Popularly understood, joy is a particular type of happiness, an intensified or long-lasting delight. In this understanding, it is something that everyone would naturally desire. Joy seems to be a relatively clear term in the secular mind.

Humor, on the other hand, is a quality or attribute, rather than an emotion. "That quality which appeals to a sense of the ludicrous or absurdly incongruous," says *Webster's*. Humor, wit, or a sense of the comic is something that one may have or develop, lack or learn.

* A spiritual director helps you in your relationship with God. This differs from pastoral counseling (which is focused on problem solving) or psychological counseling (which looks at the psychic underpinnings of our problems and struggles) and concentrates exclusively on helping you see more clearly God's activity in your prayer and daily life.

It also may inhere in a certain situation. A person can be said to be humorous—but so can a book, a movie, a play, a comment, or even a facial expression or physical gesture. And humor can be characterized as bad (racial, sexual, and ethnic humor that wounds; jokes that mock the underdog; name-calling, etc.) or good (self-deprecatory humor, humor that encourages, jokes that make everyone laugh and have no "victim").

Sigmund Freud believed that some comic impulses—more specifically, jokes—stem from the unconscious, from the psychological level that exists below our rational faculties. The French philosopher Henri Bergson in his essay "Laughter" notes: "Comic absurdity is of the same nature as that of dreams."*[2]

That makes sense. Sometimes it's hard to know precisely *why* something is humorous, why something seems funny, why we laugh. It seems almost primal, unconscious, bubbling up from within.

The jokester or the fool is also the one who often seems to have realized the truth. How many times have we listened to a comedian, seen a funny movie, or simply heard a clever joke and said to ourselves, "Yes, that's *exactly* the way it is. That's so *true*!" Something funny is often something true.

For instance, a friend recently told me the joke about a church that has a terrible problem with bats, which swoop over the people's heads during services. When the bats first settled in the rafters, the pastor bought a cat, which he let sleep in the church at night. But the bats remained. The next pastor retained the services of a professional exterminator, who, at great expense, fumigated the entire building. To no avail; the bats would not be moved. Finally, a new pastor was installed, and in a few weeks the bats were gone. The parishioners were delighted. On Sunday one of the congregants asked the new pastor how he had gotten rid of them. "Oh, it was easy," he said. "I baptized

* *"L'absurdité comique est de même nature que celle des rêves."*

and confirmed all of them, and I knew I'd never see them again."*

Laughter, finally, is a thing or an act. The act of laughing comes in response to something humorous or, as above, "absurdly incongruous." But it is also a natural expression of joy, unconcerned with something as complicated as absurd incongruity. Babies laugh out of sheer delight at seeing a mother's face. Laughing is a deeply human activity.†

Unlike joy—but like humor—laughter can be positive or negative. Someone laughing at your joke can make your day. Someone laughing at *you* can ruin it. And unlike humor, which is debatable (how many times have you discussed whether or not something was funny, silly, unfunny, offensive, or confusing?), laughter is plain. It's obvious when people laugh. *Why* they laugh is less obvious.

The three—joy, humor, and laughter—are also interrelated. It's hard to explain one without automatically thinking of one of the others. You might laugh out of joy. (Imagine hearing that you have earned a promotion, or you are expecting a child, or that you have won the lottery.) Sustained laughter leads to a feeling of joy. (Think of being in a roomful of friends and laughing uproariously at an old story from your youth. It may trigger an authentic feeling of joy.)

---

* Don't get it? Most churches lament the fact that when children raised in the church (i.e., who were baptized and confirmed) become young adults for whom church attendance is optional, they are often never heard from again. Don't worry if you didn't get this one. The rest of the jokes in the book are more easily "gotten."

† In 1862, the French neurologist Guillaume Duchenne de Boulogne concluded that the kind of involuntary facial expressions that are "only put in play by the sweet emotions of the soul" contract the muscles around the eye in a way that what you might call "fake laughs" do not. Brain scans later showed scientists that "Duchenne laughter," as it is now known, stems from the same part of the brain that is responsible for flight-or-fight decisions, a particularly ancient part of the human brain. Even chimpanzees, as Charles Darwin observed, "laugh" in response to tickling or pratfalls. Laughter is an ancient, even primordial, trait.

Finding a spirit of joy in your life may help you become a more humorous person, someone capable of seeing things from a "funny" side. Seeing something from a humorous vantage point can spontaneously fill you with joy. (Imagine a friend making a funny comment about a tough situation in your life that helps you gain some needed perspective.)

So the secular understandings of joy, humor, and laughter are overlapping. What's more, they are highly subjective. When we turn to a religious understanding of joy, humor, and laughter, the definitions shift somewhat, for looking at anything from a spiritual point of view reveals lights and shadows that may have been hidden, or at least overlooked.

LET'S START WITH THE last in our trio of gifts, laughter. The most comprehensive recent treatment of the place of laughter in Western spirituality is Karl-Josef Kuschel's short book *Laughter: A Theological Essay*. At the beginning of his enjoyable study, Kuschel, professor of theology at the University of Tübingen in Germany, admits the "conceptual impossibility" of developing a theology of laughter, since there are so many varieties. Some are praiseworthy, others not. "There is joyful, comfortable, playful and contented laughter," he writes, "and there is mocking, malicious, desperate and cynical laughter."

Kuschel thus identifies the two main ways of looking at laughter from a spiritual vantage point. "Like their Master from Nazareth," Kuschel writes, "Christians have to take into account both laughing and being laughed at." Laughter can heal or hurt. And although he is speaking mainly from a Christian point of view, his template can profitably be applied to many mainstream spiritual and religious traditions.

In short, one school of spirituality condemns laughter; the other praises it. (The same holds true for humor.)

The condemnatory strain finds voice in the writings of the fourth-century theologian St. John Chrysostom, who suggested that true Christians should weep out of sorrow for their sins. Chrysostom explicitly states that he does not wish to ban mirth, but rather to remind the world that tears more effectively bind us to God than does laughter. This predilection against laughter finds echoes in the thought of other early Christian theologians, who saw *risibilitas* (in Latin, the human ability to laugh) as dangerous in another way—it stood in opposition to reason.

Perhaps the most well-known fictional treatment of this condemnatory strain comes in Umberto Eco's novel *The Name of the Rose* (later made into a movie starring Sean Connery and Christian Slater). In Eco's bestselling book, first published in 1980, a Franciscan friar—playfully named William of Baskerville—investigates a series of gruesome murders in a fourteenth-century monastery. In the course of his sleuthing, William encounters Jorge de Burgos, a blind librarian who fulminates over the presence of clever drawings and doodles that decorate the pages of some of the books housed in the monastery's renowned library. Such *risibilitas* appalls Jorge.

Surely, counters William of Baskerville, those comical decorations—"humans with horses' heads, and horses with human legs, fish with birds' wings and birds with fishtails"—should make one smile. They may even have "edifying ends," that is, uplifting purposes.

At first Jorge mocks William, but then warms to the task of arguing against laughter. "What is the aim of this nonsense?" Jesus, counters the old monk, did not have to use such foolish things to make his point. "Christ never laughed," he says later, quoting Chrysostom. Thus the theological objection: it is against the Christian ideal. "Laughter shakes the body," says Jorge, "distorts the features of the face, makes man similar to the monkey." Thus the philosophical objection: it is against reason.

Jorge's crusade eventually takes a darker turn. In his beloved library is the only remaining copy of the second volume of Aristotle's *Poetics,* a work on comedy. To ensure that no one will read this terrible work—spoiler alert!—Jorge poisons the pages, so that any monk who dares to pursue laughter and moistens his finger to turn the page will die.

My own theology of laughter, similar to what Kuschel calls his "jokological" approach, is at odds with that of Jorge de Burgos. As long as it remains firmly in that first category of "joyful" and does not transgress into "mocking," human laughter is a gift from God, a spontaneous expression of delight at the world. As we'll soon see, traditions of laughter find their way into some of the most important stories of the Old Testament. Laughter also has a long tradition among the saints and spiritual masters in many religious traditions as a necessary component of a healthy life. So place me solidly in the pro-*risibilitas* camp.

Most contemporary religious traditions, Christian and otherwise, disagree with Jorge's overheated condemnation of laughter. *The Catechism of the Catholic Church*—hardly a frivolous book—includes a line in a chapter on "popular piety" that might have surprised many of the early church fathers, not to mention Jorge. At the core of the faith of believers there is, says the *Catechism,* a "storehouse of values" that offers wisdom for the Christian life. Such wisdom "provides reasons for joy and humor even in the midst of a very hard life."[3]

Recently I asked Margaret Silf, a British author of many books on prayer, what she thought about the place of laughter in the spiritual life. Her enthusiastic letter showed that she fell squarely in the "praiseworthy" school. "Sometimes, for example, you have a choice between laughing and crying over your own stupidly spilled milk," she wrote. "I recommend the laughter route. The other way leads to self-pity, and no one will love that. Laughter can even work retrospectively: when things are solemn and serious, I can go back to ridiculous situations and laugh all over again, with the same therapeutic effects. Laughter can also turn a disaster into a farce," she said.

Then she recounted the story of two friends whose mutual friend had died. "They missed her terribly," said Silf. "They planted what they thought were daffodil bulbs on her grave and grieved all winter. In the spring they returned to the grave to pay their respects and discovered a wonderful crop of . . . onions! They laughed until they cried—and they are convinced their friend was right in there laughing with them."

Laughter has edifying ends—and not simply in the Jewish and Christian traditions. Sheik Jamal Rahman, a Muslim scholar and the author of *The Fragrance of Faith: The Enlightened Heart of Islam,* pointed me to several passages from the Qur'an and several Islamic sources that highlight the value of laughter, which finds its source in divinity. "It is God who causes your laughter and your tears," says the Qur'an.[4] In one collection of sayings relating to the Prophet Muhammad a witness states, "I indeed saw the Messenger of God laugh till his front teeth were exposed."[5] God himself laughs in one tradition: "So Allah will laugh and allow him [the righteous one] to enter Paradise."[6] And in the Sufi tradition, Rahman noted, not laughing means "our knowledge is limited, and we don't understand the nature of reality."

"When laughter surges from the depths of one's being, we are able to glimpse, even for an instant, things as they really are," Rahman told me. That's why he enjoys the popular "Mulla stories," folkloric and often humorous tales from the thirteenth-century Turkish Muslim author Mulla Nasruddin. "Something awakens in me," said Rahman.

When I asked Lawrence S. Cunningham, professor of theology at the University of Notre Dame, about the theology of laughter, he pointed to a little-known Catholic tradition, also mentioned in Kuschel's study. "Ever heard of the *risus paschalis*?" Cunningham asked. My Latin isn't very good, so he translated it: "Easter laugh."

"Evidently in Germany," he explained, "it was customary for the parish priest to tell jokes during Eastertide. The idea behind it was laughing at Satan, who had been discomfited by the Resurrection."* Still, the old monk Jorge in Eco's book raises an interesting theological question: Did Jesus laugh? We'll explore that in the next chapter.

What about humor? Stories about the use of good humor (and humorous stories) run through the Scriptures and writings of nearly every major religious tradition, and soon we'll examine tales of hu-

* Kuschel dates this from around the early sixteenth century.

morous characters, sayings, and events in the Old and New Testaments. The Christian saints and spiritual masters of other traditions were frequently humorous in both their words and deeds and used wit to convey important teachings to their followers.

But is there a "spiritual" way to understand it? Kuschel's twofold approach to laughter is helpful when we look at humor from a spiritual vantage point. There is humor that builds up and humor that tears down, a humor that exposes cant and hypocrisy and a humor that belittles the defenseless and marginalized. Good humor and bad humor. Of course most secular observers would agree with this—there is a morality to humor. But religious observers see these two sides of humor slightly differently, for they see the two in the light of God's desires for humanity. "Good" or "bad" depends not only on a moral sense, but on how the humor deepens or cheapens the relationship with God.

Humor is a prelude to faith, and laughter is the beginning of prayer.
—Reinhold Niebuhr

The theological approach to humor—condemnatory or praiseworthy—depends, as with laughter, on its intention. The Roman soldiers mocking Jesus by robing him in a purple garment, pressing upon his head a crown of thorns, and placing a reed in his hand were engaging in a malicious humor, mocking him as a spurious king: "Hail, King of the Jews!"[7] (On the other hand, the Gospel writers use this episode to their benefit, and the soldiers' terrible humor makes an ironic theological point. Jesus truly is a king, though the soldiers do not know this. The joke is on them.)

On the opposite end is Jesus's own use of humor. Many of his parables, as we'll see, were most likely not only clever, but overtly funny. His barbed comments to Roman officials, some Jewish religious leaders, the wealthy, and the complacent often seem designed not only to silence the higher-ups, but to provoke some smiles among his listeners. It is usually gentle, but nonetheless effective.

So there is good laughter and bad laughter, good humor and bad humor. Once again, even secular commentators would agree. In general, the secular and religious approaches to humor and laughter differ little.

And now for something completely religious—for a spiritual understanding of joy is quite different from the secular definition.

When I started to study joy, I was overwhelmed. It is an immense field of scholarly research. The theme of joy runs throughout almost all the major religious and spiritual traditions. In the Old Testament, the people of Israel express their joy to God for having delivered them from slavery. In the Gospels, Jesus often uses that very word as a way of expressing a goal of discipleship. Later, St. Paul encourages the early Christians to "rejoice always." Joy is one of the traditional "fruits of the Holy Spirit," that is, gifts from God given to build us up.* Even if many religions don't seem particularly joyful, the religious literature on the topic is vast.

Many Christian saints spoke at length on joy, including St. Thomas Aquinas, the thirteenth-century theologian who carefully distinguishes between different kinds of joy and happiness. The great medieval scholar speaks of *delectatio* ("delight") over sensory things, but he reserves the term *gaudium* ("joy") for the attainment of an object that one regards as good for oneself or another. Later Thomas connects joy with love, "either through the presence of the thing loved, or because of the proper good of the thing loved," wherein one rejoices over the good fortune of another.[8] The highest joy, says Thomas, is seeing God "face to face," since one has attained all that one's heart can desire.

St. Thomas's writings helped me to perceive more clearly the

---

* The "fruits of the Holy Spirit" (Gal. 5:22–23) are love, joy, peace, patience, kindness, generosity, faithfulness, gentleness, and self-control.

difference between a religious understanding of joy and a secular one. The more I thought about Thomas's distinctions and researched the question of joy, the clearer the answer became. In popular terminology joy is happiness. For the religious person joy is *happiness in God.*

Joy is not simply a fleeting feeling or an evanescent emotion; it is a deep-seated result of one's connection to God. Although the more secular definition of joy may sometimes describe one's emotional response to an object or event, wonderful though it may be (a new job, for example), religious joy is always about a relationship. Joy has an object and that object is God.

Contemporary Christian theologians often make this point. Donald Saliers's book *The Soul in Paraphrase: Prayer and the Religious Affections* expands on this theme. Saliers, a professor of theology and worship at Emory University, notes that joy is a fundamental disposition toward God. What characterizes Christian joy in contrast to happiness, he says, lies in its ability to exist even in the midst of suffering, because joy has less to do with emotion and more to do with belief. It does not ignore pain in the world, in another's life, or in one's own life. (More about holding on to joy in tough times later in the book.) Rather, it goes deeper, seeing confidence in God—and for Christians, in Jesus Christ—as the reason for joy and a constant source of joy.

Pope Paul VI, in an extraordinary (and extraordinarily forgotten) papal letter called *Gaudete in Domino* ("On Christian Joy"), touches on this distinction.* Why, in a culture of plenty in the West, he wonders, where there is so much to satisfy us—wealth, clean water and readily available food, medical achievements, technological ad-

* Giovanni Battista Montini served as Pope Paul VI from 1963 to 1978. His letter (or in Vaticanese his "apostolic exhortation") *Gaudete in Domino,* which is literally translated "Rejoice in God," was published in 1975. This beautiful meditation is especially surprising from a man who was seen as somewhat dour in public. In his private life, however, he was a warm and gracious man. "He was amazing one-on-one," a friend told me recently. "In terms of people, that is, not basketball."

vances—is there so little joy? It is, says Paul, because we are missing what joy really is. "This paradox and this difficulty in attaining joy seem to us particularly acute today," Paul writes. "This is the reason for our message. Technological society has succeeded in multiplying the opportunities for pleasure, but it has great difficulty in generating joy, for joy comes from another source. It is spiritual."

For the purposes of our discussion, then, what can we say about joy, humor, and laughter from the secular and the religious standpoints?

First, laughter and humor are more or less defined the same way whether you're religious or not. Both secular and religious observers know that there can be good laughter and bad laughter, good humor and bad humor. (Religious people, however, see the act of choosing between good and bad as part of a life lived in relationship with God.) When it comes to joy, however, the secular mind sees it as an intense form of happiness or delight. The religious mind sees it as intimately connected to belief in God, grounded in faith even in tough times, and nourished by the relationship with the divine. Joy is happiness in God.

Here is one example of what leads me to believe that many modern believers often fail to link spirituality with anything joyful or even lighthearted.

For the past twelve years, I've worked for a Catholic magazine called *America,* which we often call the "National Catholic Weekly." (A few years ago, one of our detractors wrote saying that the magazine was so awful we should spell that last word "W-e-a-k-l-y.") One of the magazine's regular features is called "Faith in Focus."

"Faith in Focus" is reserved mainly for stories about a writer's personal spiritual life. Each week we get dozens of articles submitted for that section of the magazine. And guess what the most common topics for submissions are. Sickness, suffering, and death. How my illness led me to God. How losing a job led me to God. How my pain led me to God.

Now you might say, "Suffering is a way to God." And often that's true. We can sometimes experience God more intensely during times of suffering, since we are more vulnerable and, therefore, perhaps more open to God's help. With our defenses down, God can often more easily enter into our lives. Sometimes suffering can be a window into experiencing God in a new way.

But during the twelve years I've worked at the magazine, I've rarely seen a funny or even mildly humorous submission for that section. Lately the editors have even agreed to guard against running too many depressing articles in that section. Just recently we accepted an article called "A Journey to Death," about the writer's mother's final illness. (We changed the title to something less morbid, since we had published articles about illness in three consecutive issues.) This is just one indication that, at least in American Catholic culture, suffering is linked to spirituality far more often than joy is.

Joy SEEMS TO HAVE a disreputable reputation in some religious circles. And that's odd, not only because joy is a necessary component for a healthy emotional life, but also because it has a distinguished history among the spiritual masters and saints as an essential element for spiritual health. "Joy is not incidental to spiritual quest. It is vital," wrote the Hasidic Rebbe Nachman of Breslov in the eighteenth century.

Kathleen Norris, one of the leading Christian spiritual writers in the United States and the author of *The Cloister Walk* and *Acedia and Me,* recently spoke with me about her appreciation of joy in her spiritual life. "Joy has always been an important part of my life, but it wasn't until I became a Benedictine oblate [an associate member of a monastery] that I appreciated its place in my spiritual life," she said.

"I was muttering to one of the monks about my lack of spiritual discipline and my haphazard prayer life, when he said to me, 'I don't worry about you at all. You have joy, and that is one of the traditional fruits of the Holy Spirit.' This was news to me, and it cheered me immensely, reminding me that even when I wasn't 'doing' the stuff I felt I should be doing, the Spirit was working in me nonetheless."

JOY IS AN IMPORTANT component in many Eastern religious traditions as well, according to a Jesuit scholar and Harvard professor. Francis X. Clooney, professor of comparative theology and director of Harvard's Center for the Study of World Religions, told me that joy is "of great significance in Hindu religious sensitivity." He continued, "The higher form of joy in Hinduism is often called 'bliss,' or *ananda,* and this is even an essential attribute of the divine reality. And of course, one reads of the smile of Shiva and the smile of the Buddha, the Goddess's laughter, and Krishna's pleasure in the dance."

But you need not be a scholar of religion to see that anyone truly in touch with God is joyful. Think of the holy people in your life—and not just the "professional" religious people like priests, ministers, and rabbis. Think of a holy person in your family, a deeply spiritual friend, or a religious colleague at work. Think of people whose lives fully embody their religious faith, who are close to God. Aren't they full of joy?

Joy is the noblest human act.

—ST. THOMAS AQUINAS

Or think of the more well-known figures in the religious world who evince joy. Think of how often you see pictures of Mother Teresa or the Reverend Billy Graham smiling. Think of how easy it is to imagine someone like St. Francis of Assisi smiling. It's almost impossible to imagine St. Francis *not* smiling! From outside the Christian tradition, think of how often you see the Dalai Lama not simply smiling, but laughing aloud.

In his book *The Jew in the Lotus,* for example, about a Jewish man's exploration of Buddhism, the author, Rodger Kamenetz, recounts his very first meeting with the Dalai Lama in Dharamsala, India, in 1990. "My turn came," he writes. "The Dalai Lama smiled, radiant, yes, beaming, so that I couldn't help but smile myself." Kamenetz goes on to describe the innate appeal of this joyful man. Indeed, a great deal of the Dalai Lama's writings and teachings is given over to questions of joy and happiness, which flow, he teaches, from our actions. And his public teachings are almost always punctuated with laughter. A profile of the Dalai Lama in the *New Yorker* spoke of his making light of concerns about his health and the reporter described the great man "erupting in laughter."

Why are we naturally drawn to joyful people? One reason, I believe, is that joy is a sign of God's presence, which is naturally attractive to us. God's joy speaks to the joy that dwells sometimes hidden in our hearts. "Deep calls to deep," as Psalm 42 says.[9] Or, as St. Augustine wrote, "Our hearts are restless until they rest in you, O Lord." Augustine, a fourth-century North African theologian, understood something fundamental about human beings: we naturally desire God, the source of all joy. We are drawn to joy because we are drawn to God.

It's difficult to measure to what extent joy and laughter have been denigrated, downplayed, or deemed inappropriate throughout religious history, or how this setting aside of lightheartedness may have occurred. Both are hard to pinpoint. But it's not hard to see the *effects* of this downplaying, because you've probably met people who seem to think that being religious means being deadly serious all the time.

If you're Catholic, you may know priests who make you wonder how they can "celebrate" (the official term) the Mass when they never crack a smile. If you're a member of another Christian denomination, you may know pastors, ministers, or elders who exemplify the "frozen chosen."

At one church I attended, always seated in the front pew were two middle-aged laywomen who were sisters. They arrived early every Sunday, never greeted anyone, sat in precisely the same spot, and stared dead ahead at the altar during Mass. When it came time for the Sign of Peace, the moment when everyone shakes hands as a sign of Christian fellowship, the two sisters unsmilingly shook one another's hand, and they never, ever turned around to greet anyone else. They seemed deadly serious about their faith.

And when you're deadly serious, you're seriously dead. A better goal for believers is to be joyfully alive. That seems obvious, doesn't it?

But if joy is an obvious outgrowth of a life-giving faith, why does it seem absent from so many religious settings? Why do church services seem so devoid of humor? Why are religious people so often (fairly) characterized as gloomy? In short, when, why, and how were joy, humor, and laughter removed from religion? The next chapter will investigate how that unhappy turn of events may have happened.

Chapter Two

Why So Gloomy?

A Brief but 100 Percent Accurate Historical Examination of Religious Seriousness

There are several theories about why humor may not be valued as it should be in religious circles. And the reasons for this may have started early on. Let's take the New Testament as an example. And let's look first at the protagonist of the New Testament, Jesus of Nazareth. The way Jesus's humor—or lack of it—was portrayed in the Bible would inevitably influence the way later Christians would look at levity.

First of all, it's worth thinking about the extent to which the Gospel writers were interested in presenting Jesus as an overtly humorous person. Although the Gospels clearly show Jesus as clever and articulate, especially when it comes to his parables, there are a few moments in the New Testament that strike modern-day readers as laugh-out-loud funny. Why is this?

Recently I asked some distinguished New Testament scholars about Jesus and humor. Wouldn't it make sense that, if the evangelists (the men who wrote the Gospels) wanted to portray Jesus as an appealing figure, they would highlight his sense of humor? The evangelists hoped to attract people to the figure of Jesus through the narrative of the Gospels. And humor is something that most people find appealing, both today and in antiquity.

Moreover, according to Daniel Polish, a rabbi in the Reform

Jewish tradition and author of *Bringing the Psalms to Life,* anyone writing around the time of Jesus would have found plenty of humorous material in the Old Testament as well as in the Mishnah and the Talmud.* "There are parts of the Hebrew Scriptures that are intentionally funny," Rabbi Polish told me in a recent conversation.

So why is there so little humor from Jesus of Nazareth in the Gospels?

I put that question to Professor Amy-Jill Levine, a New Testament scholar at Vanderbilt University and the author of *The Misunderstood Jew.* Her book looks at the Jewish background of Jesus and the ways that the church has often misunderstood that particular aspect of his life. She argues that Christian preachers often misrepresent Jesus's words and deeds, because they fail to understand the Jewish context in which he lived.

When I asked Professor Levine about humor in the New Testament, she pointed out that one difficulty with the topic is that what was seen as funny to those living during Jesus's time may not seem funny to us at all. For someone in first-century Palestine, the setup, or premise, was probably more enjoyable. "The parables were amusing," she told me in an interview, "in their exaggeration or hyperbole. For example, the idea that a mustard seed would have sprouted into a big bush that birds would build their nests in would have been humorous." Parts of the parables, therefore, were not simply clever—but actually *funny* to a first-century audience.

Indeed, the very incongruity of the parables—the topsy-turvy, seemingly absurd nature of their message (the poor are rich; the rich are poor; the blind see; the sighted are blind)—is the stuff of comedy. The absurdity is even richer when listeners realize that Jesus's insights are, in fact, true. But we often overlook that aspect of the Gospels.

---

* The Mishnah, according to *The HarperCollins Dictionary of Religion,* is "a six-part rabbinic code of descriptive rules." The Talmud is a "compilation of clarifications and expansions of statements in the Mishnah."

"Why do we sit so solemnly through all the stories about trying to take the splinter out of someone's eye when you have a plank in your own or about camels going through the eyes of needles?" asked Margaret Silf, when I mentioned this phenomenon. "So many ridiculously exaggerated characters and situations that no one could forget! Can't you see the tongue in Jesus's cheek? Or even the cheek in Jesus's tongue?"

In his book *Laughing with God: Humor, Culture, and Transformation,* Gerald Arbuckle, a Catholic priest, agrees. In first-century Palestine, he suggests, people would have most likely *laughed* at many of Jesus's intentionally ridiculous illustrations, for example, the idea that someone would have lit a lamp and put it under a basket, or that a person would have built a house on sand, or that a father would give a child stones instead of bread. As Levine and Arbuckle suggest, we may be missing much of the humor that Jesus intended and his audience understood in his parables.

The Reverend Daniel J. Harrington, a Jesuit priest, professor of New Testament at Boston College, and the author of many books on the Gospels, is a leading expert on the New Testament. He echoed the insights of Levine and Arbuckle. "Humor is very culture-bound," Father Harrington told me. "The Gospels have a lot of controversy stories and honor-shame situations. I suspect that the early readers found these stories hilarious, whereas we in a very different social setting miss the point entirely." Let's repeat that: hilarious.

Professor Levine noted that there was no way of knowing for certain whether Jesus's humor—or even his jokes—might have been expunged from the Gospels by the early church. But she also pointed out that in many of the noncanonical Gospels, that is, the Gospels not officially accepted by the early church, there *are* several instances in which Jesus laughs. And, Levine said, the early church fathers (that is, the major Christian theologians in the early centuries) were, in general, more focused on combating heresy, which was seen as no laughing matter. Thus, these early theologians would probably have seen the genre of humor as inappropriate for their times.

Another reason that humor may have been downplayed in early Christian circles had to do with the Greek culture into which the Gospels were first introduced. When the Gospel writers were writing and editing the four Gospels, they were concerned not only with telling the story of Jesus as clearly as possible, but also with trying to present the story in a way that would appeal to the men and women of their time and culture.

The dominant influence during the time of Jesus was Hellenistic, or Greek, culture. Accordingly, the final versions of all four Gospels were written in what was known as *koine,* or common, Greek, the everyday language of the region. In that culture, someone like Jesus would have been presented as a "wisdom teacher," according to Father Harrington, rather than an overtly humorous person, though there are instances of humor in the Greek philosophers.

"By and large, in the biographies of the time, wit was not focused on," said Harold Attridge, New Testament scholar and dean of Yale Divinity School, who specializes in the study of Hellenistic Judaism and the early church. "Rather," he told me, "writers emphasized the person's virtues and accomplishments. The evangelists might be conforming more to the norms of biographies of the time."

So perhaps some of Jesus's natural humor was tamped down by the Gospel writers to conform to the standards of the day. But the unintentional result is that today we more easily associate Jesus with seriousness rather than levity.* Father Harrington told me an amusing (and true) story that illustrates how even those who know a great deal about the New Testament can unwittingly fall into this trap.

Once, he said, a religion journal was preparing a review of a book about the "Comic Christ." The journal's copy editor figured that this title *must* have been a mistake. How could Jesus be comic? So the

---

* A wildly popular and highly influential fourteenth-century text, *Vita Christi* (Life of Christ), by Ludolph of Saxony, quoted approvingly a supposed eyewitness description of Jesus of Nazareth. (That source was later revealed as a forgery.) "He sometimes weeps," it reported, "but never laughs."

editor changed the title to "*Cosmic* Christ" instead. Like that confused copy editor, many of us have never admitted the possibility of the joyful Jesus, the smiling Savior, or the comic Christ.

The tamping down of humor may have continued after the Gospels were written, during the first few centuries of Christianity. Hugo Rahner, a German Jesuit theologian (like his more famous brother, Karl), wrote a wonderful little book in 1967 called *Man at Play,* which traces the notion of playfulness throughout Greek, Roman, and early Christian thought. His work further underlines why early church leaders would have moved away from humor.

Father Rahner begins his analysis with the Greeks. Aristotle, he notes, encouraged people to balance humor and seriousness. But many early Christian writers favored a far more serious approach to life, since, as Professor Levine observed, they were concerned with facing the dangers of the world and the evils of Satan. St. Paul, for example, writes in his Letter to the Ephesians that we must avoid any talk that is "silly."[10] In the third century, St. Clement of Alexandria warns against "humorous and unbecoming words." Around the same time, St. Ambrose says that "joking should be avoided even in small talk." St. Basil says that Christians "ought not to laugh nor even to suffer laugh makers."

However, St. Augustine, a student of Ambrose, recommends *some* joking from time to time. Later on, in the thirteenth century, St. Thomas Aquinas recommends play in his writings, saying that there is a virtue in playfulness, since it leads to relaxation. Throughout his book, Rahner frequently points out the need for lightheartedness in life, and in the church in particular. In his final chapter he writes, "Not everything in our civilization is in the hands of the devil, and thundering from the pulpit is not always in place."

Writing around the same time as Rahner was the wonderfully named Elton Trueblood, who published a marvelous book entitled *The Humor of Christ.* Trueblood, a Quaker theologian, was a chaplain at Harvard and Stanford universities and the author of more than thirty books before his death in 1994. He offers a slightly different analysis of why we might fail to see humor in the New Testament and why the church might have downplayed humor.

First, says Trueblood, we are overly familiar with the stories, and so we often overlook their inherent humor. We've simply heard the stories too many times, and they become stale, like overly repeated jokes. "The words seem to us like old coins," he writes, "in which the edges have been worn smooth and the engravings have become almost indistinguishable." Trueblood recounts the tale of his four-year-old son, who, upon hearing the Gospel story about seeing the speck of dust in your neighbor's eye and ignoring the log in your own,[11] laughed uproariously. The young boy readily saw the humor missed by those who have heard the story dozens of times.

Or perhaps we simply "know" the punch line in a different way. That is, we already understand the story of the "speck of dust" in the sense that we already know the moral. Jesus is saying, in essence, stop looking at your neighbor's shortcomings; you've got your own to attend to. But the comedic "hook" that Jesus was using to get our attention, the vehicle for his message, has ceased to be of interest to us, since we move directly to the deeper meaning. The need for his humor has, it would seem, disappeared, and so it may therefore seem irrelevant. But for those listening to this itinerant preacher for the first time, the joke would have stood out.

Think too of the way that some of the disciples are presented in the Gospels and how the early Christian community, in reading these texts, might have seen these distinctive characters. St. Peter, for example, is often portrayed in ways that can easily be seen as comic.

To begin with, like many of the disciples, Peter repeatedly misunderstands Jesus's message, which leads to some arguably comic moments, even in the most serious of situations. At the Last Supper, when Jesus washes the feet of the disciples as a symbol of the way in which his followers must treat one another (in humble service), Peter balks. "You will never wash my feet," he exclaims. Jesus replies that if he cannot bear to have his feet washed, then he will have no place in his ministry.

A somewhat uncomprehending Peter shouts, "Lord, not my feet only but also my hands and my head!"[12] You can imagine Jesus smiling inwardly at Peter's bluster and thinking, "Well, that's not *exactly* what I meant."

Peter is often presented as bursting with enthusiasm, if not always with a sense of discretion. That rashness—which is by turns charming, touching, and sometimes funny—leads him earlier in the Gospels to ask Jesus to command him to walk on water, after he sees Jesus doing the same on the Sea of Galilee: "Lord, if it is you, command me to come to you on the water." Jesus does just that. So Peter enthusiastically jumps out of the boat (perhaps to the astonishment of the rest of the disciples aboard), finds that he can in fact walk on water, and then promptly sinks. "Lord, save me!" he cries. Jesus then reaches out his hand to save his impetuous friend.[13]

Jesus clearly cherished Peter's friendship and designated him as the "rock" upon which he would build his church.[14] But some scholars say that this famous name has another hidden meaning. Traditionally, Jesus renames Simon as Peter (in Aramaic, *cephas,* or "stone"; in Latin, *petrus*) to signify his solidity, his permanence. But the appellation, Father Harrington suggested, could also indicate a kind of angularity or sharpness in his personality, in other words, a playful nickname—Rocky.* But once again, the comic element in the story of Peter's renaming, so familiar to Christians, is often overlooked.

THIS IS THE CASE for the Old Testament as well. As Rabbi Polish suggested, there are parts of the Hebrew Bible that are "intentionally

*Jesus also bestows the nickname "Boanerges" on two other disciples, James and John, both sons of Zebedee (Mark 3:17). The Aramaic name, which means "Sons of Thunder," seems to indicate their tendency toward a violent temper. The use of nicknames may reveal a kind of playfulness on Jesus's part.

funny." In *Laughing with God,* Gerald Arbuckle points out many Old Testament stories that would have seemed naturally humorous to their original audiences. Take Noah, who is told to build a colossal boat far from the water. Better yet, take Balaam, a non-Israelite prophet with a gift for divination who encounters an angel of the Lord, but fails to recognize him. Instead his donkey, who is miraculously given the power to speak, recognizes the angel. (The talking donkey also takes the opportunity to rebuke Balaam for his mistreatment: "What have I done to you, that you have struck me these three times?")[15] Rabbi Polish believes the implicit question in this story is, to make the point in vernacular English, "Who's the jackass here?"

The lives of the great Hebrew prophets also included many "comic actions," as Arbuckle points out. Jonah conceals himself under shrubbery, Isaiah runs around naked for three years, and Jeremiah places a yoke about his neck. Part of the story of Jacob, who cleverly tricks his brother, Esau, out of his father's inheritance, could also be seen as humorous.* These comedic stories would most likely have amused the people of the time. (Later we'll look at the story of Abraham and Sarah, from the Book of Genesis, where laughter is an explicit part of the saga of the people of Israel.)

The Reverend Richard J. Clifford, S.J., professor of Old Testament at Boston College's School of Theology and Ministry, suggested a purpose beyond amusement, a serious reason for the humor. Such stories would have also made listeners smile about the universality of human nature. Father Clifford pointed to several of the proverbs and many of the stories in the Old Testament—for instance, the story of Jacob tricking his father on his deathbed—as examples of "folk humor" that served a specific purpose. "It makes the great figures of the Old Testament more human," said Clifford. "It reduces them to

* Jacob cheats his brother, Esau, out of their father's blessing by pretending that he is the elder brother. Esau is described as a "hairy man," and so when Jacob presents himself at his father's deathbed, he wears an animal skin on his hands and neck (Gen. 27:1–40).

a human scale in case you imagined that they were so majestic they had nothing to do with you."

Let's look at the first Old Testament example mentioned, the frankly incredible and darkly comic tale contained in the Book of Jonah. If you ask most people—most believers even—what they remember about poor old Jonah, they'll tell you one thing: he was swallowed by a whale. So far, so good. But that short but well-told story (one of the easiest of all the books of the Bible to read) is an "intentionally funny" tale, as Rabbi Polish would say, whose prophetic protagonist is certainly reduced to "human scale," as Father Clifford would say. It deftly employs irony, satire, and outright comedy to make some important points.

To begin with, Jonah is an unlikely prophet, indeed a recalcitrant one. In the first lines of the story, he is asked by God to go to Nineveh, the capital of Assyria. But since the Assyrian Empire is the great enemy of Israel, Jonah decides, in essence, to say no to God. Already the comedy is apparent. God could not have been clearer in his call to Jonah: "Go at once to Nineveh, that great city, and cry out against it; for their wickedness has come up before me." And Jonah couldn't be any clearer in his opposition to God. In order to avoid his prophetic mission he boards a ship bound for Tarshish, in the opposite direction from Nineveh. (More comedy: Nineveh would be reached by *land*. Taking a ship is a clear sign of Jonah's response to God: "No!")

Once aboard the ship (which Jonah assumes will somehow hide him from the all-seeing God, who found him in the first place), a great storm arises. The experienced mariners are terrified by the awful storm and jettison as much cargo as they can into the sea. Jonah, however, is happily below deck, snoozing away. (More ironic humor: the mariners are terrified; the landlubber is not.) Upon discovering Jonah, the captain orders him aboveboard, where the crew members are casting lots in order to determine who is responsible for the storm.

Not surprisingly for readers, the lot falls upon Jonah. The terrified mariners ask their strange passenger why he believes this terrible fate has befallen their ship. Somewhat proudly (particularly given his behavior until this point) he declares that he is a prophet of the Hebrew God, who has, he informs the crew, created the seas. Intuiting that Jonah must have acted in some way contrary to that powerful God, they shout, "What is this that you have done!" Good question, think readers. What *are* you doing, Jonah?

Desperate now, the mariners ask Jonah what they should do. (A ridiculous question since he's the fellow who brought this predicament upon them; on the other hand, it's *his* God, they probably reason, so maybe Jonah will know how to mollify him.) Jonah blandly advises them to toss him overboard, which they do, after trying in vain to row to shore. Then the sailors give thanks to the Lord God. (More ironic humor: they appear more devout than the prophet.)

Once Jonah is in the sea, the Lord "provides" a "large fish" (or "whale," depending on the translation) to swallow up Jonah. Thereupon the previously impious prophet immediately utters a long prayer of thanksgiving. God has rescued Jonah, even though he has done little to merit the salvation. After three days and three nights the large fish spits out Jonah on the dry land, clearly a comic moment for readers both then and now.

An exceedingly patient God then gives the poorly performing prophet *another* message. It is basically the same as the first one, which Jonah had ignored: "Get up, go to Nineveh, that great city [in case he forgot which city], and proclaim to it the message that I tell you." Grudgingly, Jonah journeys to Nineveh, where he simply spits out the message, much as the fish spat him out, with little ardor: "Forty days more, and Nineveh shall be overthrown!"

And then—surprise!—the words of Jonah, the lousy prophet, are astonishingly effective. The entire city virtually leaps into penitential action. Few prophets have had such success. When the Assyrian king hears the news of Jonah's prophecy, he promptly strips off his robe, covers himself in sackcloth and ashes, and orders all the Ninevites to don sackcloth as well—including the animals. (The image of the "sinful" Ninevite cows repenting for their bovine sins is wonderfully comic: "Forgive us, Lord! We have eaten too much grass! In this great city!") Seeing the repentance of all the living, God relents from his punishment. Nineveh is saved.

More humor: Jonah is furious! Apparently, he had preached the same message in his own country to no avail. Why do the Ninevites listen when his own people do not? Or perhaps Jonah is angry that God's terrible wrath did not come upon his enemies.

So Jonah does what any petulant prophet would do—he asks the Lord to kill him. "Please take my life from me," he says.

God says, bluntly, "Is it right for you to be angry?" Apparently, even the all-knowing God has a hard time understanding Jonah.

Now Jonah pouts. Or sulks, as one commentator suggested. Venturing east of the city, to a sunny spot, he constructs a "booth" (for shade) and waits to see what else will happen to the hated Ninevites. (At times, Jonah sounds like a sports fan whose team has lost the World Series; he *hates* the other city for its ridiculous good fortune.)

An incredibly patient God takes pity on his reluctant prophet by causing a little tree to "come up over Jonah" and provide some shade. Finally, *here* is something that pleases the prophet—not the fact that the Lord God had spoken to him directly; not the fact that he was given a divine mission to complete; and not the fact that his prophetic words were immediately acted upon. Jonah is content because he has some shade: "So Jonah was very happy."

Then God, readying to teach Jonah a lesson, sends a worm to destroy the plant, and then a "sultry east wind," and finally the sun, which beats down on Jonah's uncovered head. Furious once again, Jonah demands to die. (As one Bible commentary notes, "Jonah's reactions border on farce, as they have throughout the story."[16]) By this point, Jonah is focused solely on his own physical comfort. (Perhaps this is defensible for someone who spent three days inside a fish.) Still, Jonah is angry.

So God asks him, "Is it right for you to be angry about the bush?"

That patient question can be taken in many ways. Is it morally right, emotionally healthy, or spiritually wise to be angry about something so small, especially in light of what has happened to the Ninevites? Is this really what you should be concerned about? Yes, says Jonah, sounding more and more like a five-year-old.

Now God gets to the point: "You are concerned about the bush, for which you did not labor and which you did not grow; it came into being in a night and perished in a night. And should I not be concerned about Nineveh, that great city [as if I need to remind you], in which there are more than a hundred and twenty thousand persons who do not know their right hand from their left, and also many animals?"

In between chuckles, readers, then and now, have learned some valuable lessons from this story—lessons about the patience, forgiveness, gentleness, and wisdom of God. In laughing about the manifestly human Jonah, readers may have also learned something about themselves. The funny story raises serious questions for believers: When do I not listen to God's voice? When do I resist doing the right thing even though it couldn't be clearer?* Are my "enemies" better at listening to God than I am? And where do I fail to rejoice over what I see as God's compassion for those I feel don't "deserve" it? The Book of Jonah is filled with irony, comedy, and moments that are laugh-out-loud funny. Too often we overlook the way that humor can lead us to deep truths, even when it comes to well-known Bible stories.

So I commend enjoyment, for there is nothing better for people under the sun than to eat, and drink, and enjoy themselves, for this will go with them in their toil through the days of life that God gives them under the sun.

—ECCLESIASTES 8:15

---

* The Trappist monk Thomas Merton (1915–68) used this story as the title of his book *The Sign of Jonas* and noted that in his own life, as in Jonah's, God eventually took him where God wanted him to go, despite Merton's reluctance.

* * *

LAUGHTER AND HUMOR ARE not the only spiritual gifts overlooked by some readers of the Old Testament. Joy is as well. The Book of Psalms, for example, is filled with frequent expressions of joy in response to God's goodness. The psalms are sometimes divided into three groups: *lament psalms,* which are prayers calling on God for help; *wisdom psalms,* which are primarily didactic; and *praise psalms,* which sing of gratitude. And one natural expression of gratitude is joy.

Or plain old happiness. "Happy are those whose way is blameless," says Psalm 119. Believers should be so gleeful that we sing: "Make a joyful noise to the LORD, all the earth; break forth into joyous song and sing praises." Our prayers can and should reflect this joy, says the psalmist: "Worship the LORD with gladness." Joy—even laughter—runs like a bright thread through the communal songs of Israel. Psalm 126 begins with the moving lines: "When the LORD restored the fortunes of Zion, we were like those who dream. Then our mouth was filled with laughter, and our tongue with shouts of joy."[17]

In the Old Testament, joy can be a religious expression of gratitude, whether contained in a psalm composed by a single person or as part of the larger narrative of a whole people. The Book of Nehemiah, for example, tells the story of the eponymous cupbearer to Artaxerxes, the Persian king, around the fifth century BC. Nehemiah is distressed at the ruined condition of Jerusalem and asks the king for permission to restore the city and repopulate it with the Jewish people in exile. At the dedication of the wall that surrounds Jerusalem, Nehemiah depicts the profound gratitude of the people in vivid terms: "They offered great sacrifices that day and rejoiced, for God had made them rejoice with great joy; the women and children also rejoiced. The joy of Jerusalem was heard far away."[18] Joy is a traditional expression of the gratitude of the people of Israel, who at various times rejoiced, sang, and even laughed in praise of their God.

* * *

ARMED WITH A LITTLE more understanding of lightheartedness in the Old Testament, let's return to the Gospels. Another reason for the apparent downplaying of humor in the New Testament may lie in the enormous emphasis that the Gospels place on the Passion (the events leading up the crucifixion of Jesus). The writers of the four Gospels needed to portray clearly, and in great detail, the complicated events of the Passion for readers who most likely had a hard time understanding why Jesus had to suffer.

For Jesus's disciples as well as for the early Christians, the idea of a suffering God must have seemed almost unbelievable. The Gospels indicate a populace apparently convinced that the Messiah would come "in glory," that is, as a conquering king who would forcibly end the Roman occupation of Palestine. But the opposite happened: Jesus was arrested, tried, and executed by Rome. "Death on a cross," writes the Catholic theologian Gerald O'Collins, S.J., in *Christology*, "signified being cursed by God as one who had violated the covenant. . . . At the time of Jesus the popular messianic hopes did not include a suffering Messiah. To proclaim a crucified Messiah was incredible, even blasphemous talk."

Why, people must have wondered, was Jesus executed like a common criminal? What possible reason could there be for his not overturning the Roman authorities and booting them out of Palestine, as many had expected? In short, why did he need to suffer and die, especially in such a shameful way?

The evangelists needed to answer these critical questions for the early Christians. As a result, a great deal of their narratives focuses on the Passion. The Gospel of John, for instance, is traditionally divided into two parts: the Book of Signs, concentrating on the words and miracles of Jesus, and the Book of Glory, which focuses on his farewells, trial, crucifixion, death, and resurrection. In other words, an enormous section of the Gospel of John focuses almost exclusively on the *last few weeks* of Jesus's life. The Last Supper begins in chapter

13 and the burial of Jesus concludes at the end of chapter 19. The Gospels of Matthew, Mark, and Luke, often called the Synoptic Gospels (because they see the story similarly, or "with one eye"), likewise emphasize the sufferings of Jesus, again focusing on the last few weeks of the life of a man who walked the earth for thirty-three years.

This is not to minimize the immense importance of the Passion narratives in Christian theology, the significance of the Cross in Christian spirituality, or the value for Christians of meditating on Jesus's suffering and our own. However, those parts of the narrative may come to dominate the overall story of Jesus. After all, Jesus lived for some *thirty years* in Nazareth before he began his public ministry and, according to some accounts, carried on his ministry of preaching and healing for one to three years. This included activities that were most likely enjoyable: going to wedding parties, visiting towns in the surrounding areas, spending time with little children, passing the hours in conversation with his disciples, speaking about the promises of God's kingdom, and, by the way, healing the sick—which surely must have been occasions for joy.

Let's look at one distinctive feature of his ministry, what scholars call "table fellowship," that is, dining with friends. Jesus frequently called together his disciples, his followers, and often strangers to dine with him. It doesn't take too much imagination to picture these as joyful events—just think of enjoyable dinner parties and celebrations in your own life, full of laughter and good cheer, everyone delighting in one another's company. There is a reason that one enduring image of heaven is as a banquet. My friend Maureen O'Connell, an assistant professor of theology at Fordham University, told me, "At my house we often laugh ourselves sick around the dinner table. Isn't this the point of dinner parties?"

In first-century Palestine there would have been other reasons to be joyful at table (besides simply being with Jesus), for the itinerant carpenter often gathered together people who had been rejected by polite society. As Elisabeth Schüssler Fiorenza notes in her book *In Memory of Her*, Jesus exercised a "discipleship of equals," in which all were included. His detractors used this against him. Mark reports: "When the scribes of the Pharisees saw that he was eating with sinners and tax collectors, they said to his disciples, 'Why does he eat with tax collectors and sinners?' "[19] Think of how happy those on the fringes of society—tax collectors, prostitutes, "sinners"—would have been to be included in the community. The joy around the table was magnified by their gratitude.

Likewise, many of Jesus's parables include joyful moments. One of the most famous, the parable of the prodigal son, the story of a wayward young man returning home to seek forgiveness, includes his loving father preparing what one scholar calls a "feast of joy"[20] and even remonstrating with the elder brother, who refuses to share in his joy.

Much of Jesus's earthly life and ministry were about joy. But, as Elton Trueblood points out in *The Humor of Christ,* because of the need to explain the suffering of Jesus, the sad parts can overwhelm the happy parts.

Trueblood also notes a basic failure of our modern human imagination about Jesus. Simply because Jesus could weep does not mean that he did not laugh. Cal Samra in his book *The Joyful Christ* notes simply, "Jesus said and did a lot of things the Gospel writers didn't record." The Gospel of John admits this, saying explicitly, "Now Jesus did many other signs in the presence of his disciples, which are not written in this book."[21] In other words, the absence of many stories about Jesus joking or laughing is not proof that they did not occur. Most likely, Jesus laughed. To deny this is to turn Jesus into a wooden stick.

Samra, who edits a monthly newsletter on Christian joy, points to numerous passages in the Gospels that stress the joy of Christ and those who encountered him:

> At that same hour Jesus *rejoiced* in the Holy Spirit and said, "I thank you, Father . . ."
>
> The entire crowd was *rejoicing* at all the wonderful things that he was doing.

"You have pain now; but I will see you again, and your hearts will *rejoice,* and no one will take your *joy* from you."

"Ask and you will receive, so that *your joy* may be complete."

While in their *joy* they were disbelieving and still wondering . . .

The disciples *rejoiced* when they saw the Lord.[22]

If that's not enough, read St. Paul, whom many people associate with gloom, though he pointedly calls himself a "fool for Christ." His letters are filled with references to joy:

I am *overjoyed* in all our affliction.

For the kingdom of God is . . . righteousness and peace and *joy.*

Rejoice in hope.

Rejoice in the Lord always; again I will say, *Rejoice.*

The fruit of the Spirit is love, *joy,* peace, patience . . .[23]

These are just a few of the New Testament passages that speak of joy. But again, we may be so familiar with the stories and so accustomed to what Samra calls a "gloomy Messiah" that we miss, downplay, or ignore them.

We may even be misinterpreting the most basic of Jesus's teachings, the Beatitudes from the Sermon on the Mount.[24] The Beatitudes consist of a long list of "blesseds," each beginning with "Blessed are . . ." But the Greek word used in the text, *makarioi,* can be just as accurately translated "happy." Imagine how different the Beatitudes would sound if we heard Jesus saying, instead, "Happy are the poor in spirit. . . . Happy are the meek. . . . Happy are the merciful," and so on. Writing about the Sermon on the Mount in *Celebrating Joy,* the Catholic moral theologian Bernard Häring says, "The prevailing mood here is one of joy."

* * *

Another tantalizing historical explanation of the dearth of humor and playfulness in some religious circles is advanced by the author Barbara Ehrenreich, who often writes about social questions. Her widely praised book *Nickel and Dimed,* for example, saw her working at minimum-wage jobs, as the poor must do, to see if she could make ends meet. (She couldn't.) In 2007, she published *Dancing in the Streets: A History of Collective Joy.* Her thesis is that something bothered those in authority in Western culture about enthusiasm and collective joy, which is often seen as primitive or hedonistic. And she's speaking not simply about the Christian church, but other institutions as well.

In her book, Ehrenreich carefully leads readers through Greek, Roman, and western European history to show how high-spirited public gatherings—ecstatic religious rites, group dances, celebrations during Carnival—which express both communal and private joy, were suppressed by fearful authorities. In medieval times, for example, the traditions of Carnival (literally, "Good-bye to meat"), the festive period before Lent, encouraged the local populace to poke fun at civic and church leaders (sometimes by dressing up as the king or other authorities), thus posing an implicit threat to social order. She says:

> More striking, from a modern point of view, were the ritual activities aimed at dissolving the normal social boundaries of class and gender. There would very likely be ribald humor enacted by a man dressed up as a "king of fools" or "lord of misrule" and aimed at mocking real kings and other authorities. . . . No aspect of carnival has attracted more scholarly attention than the tradition of mocking the powerful, since these customs were in some sense "political," or at least suggestive of underlying discontent.

Ehrenreich suggests that what bothered the powers-that-be is that when their social inferiors assembled to enjoy themselves, asserting their camaraderie and friendship, they often ended up making fun of their rulers. Such gatherings could so alter the status quo that they might pose an actual threat, as they did during, say, the French Revolution. Joy can be subversive.

Conrad Hyers, a Presbyterian minister and professor of the history of religion, makes a similar point in his book *The Comic Vision and the Christian Faith.* "Because of the variety of illiberal forms of laughter," Hyers writes, "it has been easy for sensitive souls to see it as a dangerous and volatile gas that must be tightly bottled up."* Laughter can be rebellious.

For their part, church leaders, Ehrenreich believes, sometimes set aside the parts of Jesus's message that embrace what she calls a "sweet and spontaneous form of socialism" for something far duller, because spontaneity often threatens the status quo. Her description of early church services may surprise anyone accustomed to a boring Sunday morning. Much of Christian worship in the first and second centuries, she points out, remains largely unknown, but the "general scholarly" view is that church services may have been much noisier, livelier affairs than today.† One passage is worth quoting at length:

> They met in people's homes, where their central ritual was a shared meal that was no doubt washed down with Jesus's

* In an essay accompanying Henri Bergson's "Laughter," Wylie Sypher says something similar: "Comedy is a momentary and publicly useful resistance to authority and an escape from its pressures; and its mechanism is a free discharge of repressed psychic energy or resentment through laughter."

† In 1 Corinthians, St. Paul complains about people carousing and eating too quickly during the liturgy (which was probably closer to what we think of today as a full "meal"): "When you come together, it is not really to eat the Lord's supper. For when the time comes to eat, each of you goes ahead with your own supper, and one goes hungry and another becomes drunk. . . . Do you not have homes to eat and drink in?" (1 Cor. 11:20–22). So these were apparently not sedate affairs—perhaps more celebratory than gloomy.

> favorite beverage, wine. There is reason to think they sang too, and that the songs were sometimes accompanied by instrumental music. Justin Martyr, a gentile convert, . . . once wrote that children should sing together, "just as in the same way one enjoys songs and similar music in church." Very likely, Christians also danced; at least this is how the historian Louis Backman interpreted various statements of the second-century Church fathers. Clement of Alexandria, for example, instructed the faithful to "dance in a ring, together with the angels, around Him who is without beginning or end," suggesting that the Christian initiation rite included a ring-dance around the altar. At another point Clement wrote that in order to invoke the "zest and delight of the spirit," Christians "raise our heads and our hands to heaven and move our feet just at the end of the prayer—*pedes excitamus*."

The meaning of that Latin term? "Dancing."

Ehrenreich's insights remind us that humor and laughter can be subversive and therefore frightening to those in power. Think of late-night television satire, humorous political columnists or bloggers, or acerbic editorial cartoons—always a threat to authorities. Perhaps this was part of the reason for worried hierarchs to suppress it.

To sum up, a few reasons why humor might have been given a short shrift in Christian circles are: a contemporary lack of understanding of what was considered funny in biblical times, the prevailing norms of the Greco-Roman culture into which the Gospels were introduced, an overfamiliarity with the stories in the Old and New Testaments, an overemphasis on the Passion in the Christian narrative, a failure of the imagination, and the sociology of hierarchical institutions.

* * *

Although I can't speak for every religion, I can say that humor is not all that highly valued in the Catholic Church today, at least on an official level. Catholics might know a funny priest, a humorous pastor, a jokey nun, or a hilarious pastoral associate, but not many newly appointed bishops are described in Vatican press releases as funny or having a sense of humor.

For instance, when the Vatican press office or a local diocese announces the appointment of a new bishop, it typically furnishes a long list of his academic degrees and work experience; he earned his master's degree here, his doctorate here, and he worked in this diocese or that Vatican office. When was the last time the Vatican described an episcopal appointment as follows: "The new bishop has a terrific sense of humor"?

Whenever I pose that question to a Catholic audience, they invariably laugh. But why? Why does that sound odd to our ears?* Because humor, as Ehrenreich suggests, is seen almost as a strike against a church leader, when it should be seen as a requirement.

That's not to say that every bishop is humorless. Cardinal John O'Connor, the Catholic archbishop of New York in the 1980s and 1990s, was once at a fund-raising dinner. At the end of the meal, the master of ceremonies made his way to the microphone and plodded through a long list of all those who had helped with the dinner. Unfortunately, he had a poor memory and forgot everyone's name. Each time he forgot a name, he would pull out a little note card from his pocket to help him remember.

"I would like to thank our fund-raising chairman, um . . . [he pulled out his note card and glanced down] . . . Mr. Smith. And I

---

* On the other hand, one Catholic college, when asking its students to rate professors at year end, includes a question on the professor's sense of humor. One professor wrote me saying, "Perhaps this is a way of measuring a professor's ability to connect with students, and ensure against taking one's discipline too seriously, or not creating an environment in the classroom conducive to learning."

would like to thank our communications director . . . [he pulled out the card] . . . Mr. Jones. And I would like to thank our board chairman . . . [out came the card] . . . Ms. Johnson."

Finally, he said, "And now Cardinal O'Connor will come to the dais and give us his benediction."

The cardinal walked up to the podium and said, "Almighty God, we thank you for all the blessings you have bestowed on us. And we do this in the name of your Son, um . . . [and he slyly pulled out his own little note card and glanced down] . . . Jesus Christ."

What I see as the undervaluing of humor in church circles is even more surprising when we look carefully at the person of Jesus, whom the Gospels reveal as a man with a palpable sense of joy and even playfulness. You can catch glimpses of this in his interactions with the men, women, and children of his time as well as in many of the parables. "Jesus's parables are witty in their surprise and catching his listeners off guard," said Professor Attridge.

Indeed, it's hard to imagine a good storyteller who doesn't know the value of humor. Jesus probably knew that he had to "grab" his listeners. His stories were often sharp and provocative. After all, he was an itinerant preacher and so needed to attract his listeners quickly through a funny story, a clever parable, or a humorous aside. Also, the constant themes of his preaching—love your enemies and pray for those who persecute you; forgive someone seventy times seven times; the kingdom of God is at hand—were so ridiculous, so incongruous, that they may at first have seemed humorous to listeners.

His parables are the stuff of comedy—expectations are frustrated, the poor come out on top, and the rich are revealed as fools. Many parables also delight in the use of hyperbole. In one tale, often called the parable of the talents,[25] before beginning a long journey, a wealthy man calls together his servants and entrusts them with money for safekeeping. To one servant he gives five talents, to another two talents, and to a third one talent. After a time the rich man returns. The first servant, he discovers, has invested the money wisely and has made five more talents, which pleases his master. The second has made two talents over the two he had been given. The third, however, has not invested the money at all and merely returns the one talent. He is punished for his lack of industry. The parable is often used by preachers to illustrate the need to use our "talents" in life to the full; Jesus himself draws that serious lesson from the story.

But for the listeners of the day, there would have been a clear element of the absurd in the story, for a "talent" was the equivalent of a worker's daily wages for *fifteen years*. The idea of a wealthy man blithely handing over to one of his servants an extraordinary sum—seventy-five years of wages!—would have evoked a sense of the ridiculous in his hearers. Jesus was not above using a little comic exaggeration to make a point.

Besides the parables, there are other indications that Jesus of Nazareth was a joyful person. Children felt comfortable in his presence, which points to a pleasant, even cheerful disposition. At one point Jesus in the Gospels is castigated for not being as serious as John the Baptist. "John came neither eating nor drinking. . . . The Son of Man came eating and drinking," says Jesus, "and they say, 'Look, a glutton and a drunkard.'"[26] In other words, the Gospels record criticism of Jesus for being too high-spirited and joyful *in his own lifetime*. "Jesus and his disciples," says Father Clifford, "are criticized for living it up."

Even Jesus's response to that particular critique shows some humor. In his book *God Makes Me Laugh: A New Approach to Luke,* Joseph A. Grassi, a New Testament scholar, writes that Jesus "saw his own contrast to the Baptist and the Pharisees with a great sense of humor." Jesus's response to the criticism that his disciples don't fast is to offer an "absolutely ridiculous" question. "You cannot make wedding guests fast while the bridegroom is with them, can you?" he asks.[27] "In likening himself to a bridegroom," Grassi suggests, "Jesus was effectively saying that his approach changed the ordinary somber picture of religion . . . to the most joyous images of human life."

After his time on earth, however, some of this natural playfulness may have been downplayed by the Gospel writers. They may even have felt pressured by the mores of their day to present a more serious Jesus. "There were probably things that were compressed and shortened, and some of the humor may have been leeched out," says Clifford. "But I see Jesus as a witty fellow, someone who is serious without being grim. When the disciples argue among themselves, Jesus brings a little wit into the discussion."

Arbuckle suggests two forms of Jesus's wit—relaxing and prophetic. *Relaxing humor* puts people at their ease, as when he tells them a gentle parable to illustrate a difficult point. *Prophetic humor* challenges the status quo, as when he playfully mocks religious authorities who try to trap him with arcane questions.

Jesus also embraces others with a sense of humor. In the beginning of the Gospel of John comes the remarkable story of Nathaniel, who has been told by his friends that the Messiah is from Nazareth.[28]

Nathaniel responds, "Can anything good come out of Nazareth?"

This is a joke about how insignificant the city was. Nazareth was a backwater town where only a few families lived.

In any event, what does Jesus do? Does he castigate Nathaniel for mocking his hometown? You might expect the dour Jesus of popular imagination to say, "Make not fun of the small town of Nazareth!" or "You who condemn the small town will yourself be condemned!"

Jesus says nothing like that. Nathaniel's humor doesn't bother Jesus at all. In fact, it seems to delight him. "Here is truly an Israelite in whom there is no deceit!" says Jesus. In other words, here is someone I can trust. Nathaniel then becomes one of the apostles. Jesus's welcoming of Nathaniel into his circle is perhaps the clearest indication that he had a sense of humor. (Other than the other men he chose as apostles.) It also indicates that St. John, the writer of the Gospel, appreciated a humorous story enough to preserve it in his narrative.

When I imagine Jesus, it is not simply as a person who heals the sick, raises the dead, stills the storm, and preaches the good news. It's

The Disciple with a Sense of Humor

Here is the story of Nathaniel, from the Gospel of John:

> The next day Jesus decided to go to Galilee. He found Philip and said to him, "Follow me." Now Philip was from Bethsaida, the city of Andrew and Peter. Philip found Nathaniel and said to him, "We have found him about whom Moses in the law and also the prophets wrote, Jesus son of Joseph from Nazareth." Nathaniel said to him, "Can anything good come out of Nazareth?" Philip said to him, "Come and see." When Jesus saw Nathaniel coming toward him, he said of him, "Here is truly an Israelite in whom there is no deceit!"

also as a man of great goodwill and compassion, with a zest for life, someone unafraid of controversy, free to be who he knows himself to be, and brimming with generous good humor. Full of high spirits. Playful. Even fun.

Interestingly, in the past few decades two images of a joyful Jesus have enjoyed some popularity. The first is *The Laughing Christ,* by Willis Wheatley, a sketch that shows Jesus's head thrown back in open-mouthed laughter. The second is *The Risen Christ by the Sea,* a colorful portrait of Jesus wearing a broad smile and standing beside a fishing net, painted by Jack Jewell, a seascape artist, in the 1990s. These two paintings, among others, serve to counteract countless images of the gloomy Messiah. But both images are often mocked in sophisticated religious and academic circles. Admittedly, they are not "high art." (We're not talking about Michelangelo or Caravaggio here.) But I wonder if some eschew these portraits not for the quality of the artistry, but rather for their subject material. Is there something about a smiling Jesus that threatens our understanding of the man?

* * *

Let me be more provocative and suggest that thinking about Jesus *without* a sense of humor may be close to heresy.

One of the most difficult questions the early Christians were forced to confront was whether Jesus was divine or human. The traditional answer in Christian theology is that Jesus is "fully human and fully divine." But it took the church several centuries to arrive at that understanding. During the first few hundred years of the church, questions about the identity of Jesus occupied bishops, theologians, and laypersons, all of whom were struggling to understand just who this man—or who this God—was.

You can see the problem they faced. On the one hand, Jesus is manifestly human. That would have been abundantly clear to his followers, who had watched him eat, sleep, grow angry and impatient, and weep over the death of his friend Lazarus. And they watched him suffer physically and undergo an agonizing death on the cross. So he was clearly human.

On the other hand, Jesus performed astonishing miracles. He gave sight to the blind and hearing to the deaf; he cured the sick and raised the dead. There were also his "nature miracles," like stilling storms at sea. And his disciples (and others) attested to his resurrection from the dead. His miracles, in fact, are one of the most well-attested parts of the Gospels. The Reverend John Meier, a New Testament scholar at Notre Dame, in his work *A Marginal Jew* notes, "The statement that Jesus acted as and was viewed as an exorcist and healer during his public ministry has as much historical corroboration as almost any other statement we can make about the Jesus of history." Even Jesus's *detractors* allude to his miracles. The Pharisees, according to the Gospels, complain that Jesus healed someone on the Sabbath. So his followers must have thought at various points that he was God, or at least divine.

So then the question arose: Was he human or divine? In the early church (and this is a simplification of a devilishly complex history) two camps sprang up. On the one side were those who believed that Jesus only *appeared* to be human. Those groups are generally called Docetists, from the Greek word *dokein,* meaning "to appear." On the other were the Adoptionists, who believed that Jesus was simply a human being, not divine all, merely the "adopted" son of God.

In the end, the emperor Constantine, a convert to Christianity, grew increasingly annoyed with the disunity of the church, which threatened the unity of his empire. To settle the question of the "nature" of Jesus, Constantine convened the Council of Nicea in 325. There the assembled bishops ultimately settled on a theological middle ground: Jesus was not "made" by God; he was God, and he was of the same "substance" as God the Father. In other words, he was fully human and fully divine. Denying either attribute was seen to be heretical, outside the boundaries of Christian belief.

If Christians truly believe that Jesus was "fully human," they must also believe that he had a sense of humor, which is a constituent part of being "fully human."

Frankly, I think that more than a few contemporary Christians are still "closet Docetists." That is, although they buy into the idea of Jesus's humanity, they are still inclined to think of him as God simply pretending, or playacting, at being human. But if we accept the idea of him as a human being, we must accept *all* human attributes for him—laughing as well as suffering.

Can anyone doubt that part of humanity is having a sense of humor? As the English essayist William Hazlitt writes, "Man is the only animal that laughs and weeps; for he is the only animal that perceives the difference between what things are and what things might have been." Although some anthropologists and biologists who study the behavior of higher primates might quibble with Hazlitt—chimpanzees, for example, seem to "laugh" and enjoy playing with one another—few people would argue with the proposition that a sense of humor is a necessary part of being a fully alive, emotionally mature, psychologically healthy human being.

To put it another way: What kind of a person has zero sense of humor? That's a robot, not a person. I asked Eileen Russell, a clinical psychologist based in New York who specializes in the role of resilience in the emotional life, how she would describe the psychological makeup of a person without a sense of humor. Russell is the author of *Recovering Resilience: Transformative Therapy at Work*. She said, "A person without a sense of humor would be having significant social problems. He would most likely have difficulty making social connections, because he wouldn't be able to read signals from other people and would be missing cues. He would have difficulty in social relations."

That sounds like the opposite of what we know about Jesus from the Gospels. Yet that's the kind of one-sided image that many Christians have of Jesus. It shows up both in books and sermons and in artwork. And it has an effect on the way Christians live their lives.

"I imagine Jesus as a psychologically healthy person, and so he must have laughed," said Russell, a practicing Catholic. "He had many friends, and friends are bonded in groups through sharing not only depth, but lightness."

If Jesus was fully human, then he had a fully developed sense of humor. That should be clear enough from the Gospels. He told clever stories, made funny asides, and welcomed apostles who had a sense of humor. Indeed, his sense of humor may be one largely unexamined reason for his ability to draw so many disciples around him with ease. Denying his humor, for whatever reason, denies his humanity.

In my own mind, Jesus must have been a clever, witty, and even funny man. His humor nearly leaps off the page in some of his highly original parables, in his zippy asides to the Roman authorities, in his tart replies to the scribes and the Pharisees, and even in his off-the-cuff remarks. If we look at his human side, it's hard to imagine someone being able to put up with the often spectacularly obtuse disciples without a sense of humor. If we look at his divine side, it's hard to imagine God not smiling at some of the absurdities of the world.

So let us set aside the notion that Jesus was a humorless, grim-faced, dour, unsmiling prude. Let's begin to recover his humor and, in the process, his full humanity.

* * *

OTHER RESIDUES OF GOSPEL mirth from the evangelists themselves—that is, from the way that Matthew, Mark, Luke, and John wrote and edited the Gospels—are waiting to be discovered by attentive readers. But again, we may be so familiar with these clues that we overlook them. The story of Zacchaeus in the Gospel of Luke,[29] a tax collector who climbs up into a sycamore tree to get a better look at Jesus, is a touching but also amusing story, as written by the evangelist. The wealthy Zacchaeus scurries up the sycamore tree because he is "short in stature" and can't see over the heads of those in the crowd.* In those days, Zacchaeus would probably have been wearing a loose-fitting robe or tunic, and so, as one Scripture scholar told me, *all* of Zacchaeus would have been visible to the crowd below, making the story of this undignified tax collector doubly funny.

Again, Jesus seems delighted. You can easily imagine Jesus smiling at the sight of the wealthy man perched in the tree. He says, "Zacchaeus, hurry and come down; for I must stay at your house today." After the tax collector promises to give away half his possessions and repay anyone he has defrauded four times over, Jesus says, "Today salvation has come to this house, because he too is a son of Abraham." It is a story with an important point.† It is also a humorous way of portraying the humanity of Zacchaeus.

Likewise, the story of Eutychus, in the Acts of the Apostles,[30] re-

---

* Zacchaeus's inability to see "on account of the crowd" is also an interesting commentary of our inability to encounter God if we blindly go along with what everyone else is thinking or doing.

† Stories from the Bible typically have multiple points. Here is a story about, among other things, the value of humility (Zacchaeus is not too proud to climb a tree and look ridiculous), Jesus's loving-kindness (notice that Jesus offers to stay at his home *before* Zacchaeus makes his offer of restitution), and repentance (salvation comes to Zacchaeus after his apology). Incidentally, there is an ancient sycamore tree today in Jericho said to be Zacchaeus's tree.

veals the writer's sense of play. Eutychus, a young disciple of St. Paul, is sitting on the ledge of a window in a room in which St. Paul is talking and talking and talking until midnight. Eutychus falls asleep during the long discourse, tumbles out the window, drops several stories to the ground, and is presumed dead, until Paul heads downstairs, finds out that he's not dead, revives him, and then goes back upstairs and continues talking until dawn. It's a lighthearted way to illustrate Paul's long-windedness.

It's easy to see the stories of both Zacchaeus and Eutychus as funny. But Gerald Arbuckle suggests that a more subtle "divine humor" may be at work as well in other familiar New Testament stories.

Take the story in the Gospel of Luke in which, after Jesus's crucifixion, two disciples are en route to a town called Emmaus.[31] Dejected after what has happened, they run into the resurrected Christ, though they utterly fail to recognize him. When Jesus asks what the two are discussing, they say, in words that can be read as either surprise or sarcasm, "Are you the only stranger in Jerusalem who does not know the things that have taken place?" This is a lightly comic scene because, as Arbuckle notes, Jesus is the *only* one who understands what has been taking place. And in the English translation the disciples who "miss" (grieve the loss of) Jesus are "missing" (not seeing) Jesus, who is standing right in front of them.

Father Harrington pointed me to the story of the Gerasene demoniac as another example of the humor that readers might overlook. In that recounting of an exorcism, which is included in the Gospels of Matthew, Mark, and Luke,[32] Jesus asks the name of the unclean spirit in a possessed man. "My name is Legion," says the man in response to Jesus's request, "for we are many." The demons beg Jesus to send them into the pigs that were grazing nearby, which he does. The herd of pigs "numbering about two thousand, rushed down the steep bank into the sea, and were drowned in the sea." Not surprisingly, the swineherds are furious, and then *they* beg Jesus to leave their neighborhood.

It is a story familiar to modern-day Christians. But like many of the Gospel stories, perhaps too familiar. "For us, a pig is a pig," Harrington told me. For the Jews, however, a pig was unclean, nonkosher, so there was no great loss in their demise. Other listeners would have quickly picked up on the reference to "legion," which may have been Jesus's way of mocking the Roman legions. "The Romans are cast as pigs," said Harrington. "So the story works on both levels."

Humor is hardly absent from the Bible. As with most things in life, you just have to know where to look in order to find it.

A Study in Joy: Psalm 65

So far, I've offered a few brief examples of how the theme of joy runs through the Old and the New Testaments. In between the next few chapters, I'll look at three individual passages more carefully—one from the Old Testament, two from the New—with an eye toward uncovering the joy that underlies selected stories. They will show that in the Bible joy is not about simply telling jokes; there is a deeper level involved.

Many passages from the Bible lend themselves to what you might call a "joyful exegesis," that is, a "breaking open" of the text that reveals joy as a theme. If we read attentively, these familiar passages can speak to us in new ways. Let's look first at one of my favorite passages from the Psalms by way of an unusual source.

One of my favorite sources of laughter is the 1975 film *Monty Python and the Holy Grail.* Briefly put, the British comedy is based on the story of King Arthur and his quest for the Holy Grail, the cup that Jesus used at the Last Supper. Like all the Python movies, *Holy Grail* is a mashup of surprising scholarship (it hews closely to the legend of Arthur) and sublime silliness (it features a "killer rabbit"). It may be the funniest movie ever made.*

* I'll go farther: it *is* the funniest movie ever made. My top ten would be: (1) *Monty Python and the Holy Grail,* (2) *Animal House,* (3) *Airplane!,* (4) *Withnail & I,* (5) *Tootsie,* (6) *The Producers,* (7) *Some Like It Hot,* (8) *Ghostbusters,* (9) *Bringing Up Baby,* and (10) *It's a Gift.*

At one point Arthur and the knights of the Round Table are visited by a dazzling vision of God, who appears in the heavens framed by fluffy white clouds and wearing a bejeweled crown.

"Arthur, Arthur, King of the Britons!" he thunders. When King Arthur bows down, God reacts in an unexpected manner.

"Oh, don't *grovel*!" says God. "If there's one thing I can't stand it's people groveling!" Apparently, God doesn't like people apologizing either. "Every time I try to talk to someone it's 'Sorry this' and 'Forgive me that' and 'I'm not worthy.'"

In response, King Arthur adopts a reverent pose.

"What are you doing now?" shouts God.

"I'm averting my eyes, O Lord," says Arthur.

"Well, *don't*!" says God. "It's like those miserable psalms. They're so *depressing*!"

Yes, those miserable psalms. So depressing. That's a popular conception of the psalms: always lamenting some woe that has befallen the people of Israel, mourning over the sad days, repenting of sinfulness, and weeping "by the rivers of Babylon." There is, in fact, an entire category of psalms called the "psalms of lament."

There are, however, several other categories of psalms. Scholarly commentaries note a wide variety of typologies: "royal psalms," in which the king speaks; "wisdom psalms," which are connected with wisdom literature from the Old Testament and offer advice and counsel; "liturgical psalms," which played a role in ancient worship services; and "historical psalms," which recount narratives of the people of Israel.

But there is another important category called "praise psalms." One Bible commentary lists three parts to a psalm of praise: an introduction that sets a "tone of praise"; the body of the text, in which the reasons for praising God are listed; and a conclusion that often includes a "wish or blessing."[33]

Central in most praise psalms is joy. Indeed, finding joy in the psalms is not hard at all; the very first word in the very first psalm is "happy." "Happy are those who do not follow the advice of the wicked," says Psalm 1, "but their delight is in the law of the Lord." You don't have to look hard in the psalms for joy, happiness, and delight, which flow naturally from gratitude to God.

One obvious example of this is the relatively straightforward Psalm 65, which most scholars identify as a psalm of thanksgiving for an abundant harvest (or, say a few scholars, a prayer for rain). Let's look at this psalm in greater detail, as a way of revealing its joyful undertones.

Psalm 65 praises God for three things. First, for making Zion a place for the holy people, where their sins are forgiven. Second, for overcoming the primordial waters (water was a terrifying thing for ancient peoples, connected as it was to floods and drownings) that had covered the earth and made it an inhospitable place for people. Third, for the abundance of those same waters, which make the plants grow and the earth bear fruit.

In that final part the psalmist includes some of the most vivid imagery in the Old Testament. God visits the land with water and enriches it, "softening it with showers, and blessing its growth," so that people may enjoy its harvest of grain and fruit. In response to this wonder, the earth itself exults in joy: "The pastures of the wilderness overflow, the hills gird themselves with joy, the meadows clothe themselves with flocks, the valleys deck themselves with grain, they shout and sing together for joy."

Why do the hills "gird themselves with joy"? One possible answer is that the earth puts on a mantle of happiness in response to the Lord's blessing. In the Anchor Bible series commentary *Psalms II: 51–100,* Mitchell Dahood, S.J., a Catholic Scripture scholar, translates that same line as follows: "Visit the earth, make her skip with mirth." The visitation of God leads to joy.* This is why the hills gird themselves in joy and the valleys sing—in praise of God's blessing, of God's visitation.

---

* We will see the same reaction to a visit by God in the stories of the Annunciation and the Visitation (Luke 1:26–56), which we will consider in another *Study in Joy.*

Is there a more joyful passage in the psalms? The earth cannot contain its joy over the wonders of the God who created it. It is hard to read this without feeling a little of the happiness that the psalmist must have felt when he wrote it, around the time of King David.

Preceding those beautiful lines is this one: "You make the gateways of the morning and the evening shout for joy." Dahood offers a more playful translation: "Make the twinkling stars of dawn and dusk shout for joy!" Dahood notes that in ancient times the stars were thought of as the source of rain. Thus, the exaltation of the stars sends forth showers on Israel. It is strange, and strangely wonderful, to think of the earth and the heavens shouting for joy and in their joy nourishing humanity.

Now, you may live nowhere near a meadow, a valley, or a pasture. (When I look out my window in New York, for example, I don't see any meadows, valleys, or pastures. I can't even see any trees or grass, just the brick wall of a neighboring building.) But I'll bet you know something of the feeling that the psalm describes. That is, it may not be all that strange for the psalmist to imagine the earth having human feelings. How else could the psalmist speak not only of what he was seeing around him (the glorious vision of the earth's richness), but also what he felt inside of him (gratitude)?

When you're happy, you sometimes feel that you might burst out—in song, in praise, in thanksgiving. You feel covered in delight. You "gird yourself with joy." And when a "happiness-inducing" event occurs in your life, the world around you seems changed, transformed. Things around you look different. The *earth itself* feels happier.

Earth laughs in flowers.

—Ralph Waldo Emerson

A few years ago, I found myself on an eight-day retreat in Gloucester, Massachusetts. The Jesuit retreat house is located right on the Atlantic Ocean and is also only a few hundred yards away from a freshwater pond. It is one of the most beautiful spots you could imagine. The place teems with wildlife among all manner of trees and flowers.

For several days I was praying about a difficult problem in my life. Suddenly I had a wonderful insight that cleared everything up. This I ascribed to the working of grace. After I spoke about it with my spiritual director, I walked out of the house to get a little fresh air. When I did, I noticed that things seemed to look different. On that cold and clear New England winter's day, the air seemed fresher, the sky bluer, and the snow whiter than they had been just a few hours earlier. The earth seemed, well, happier.

In reality there was no physical change in my surroundings. The weather hadn't altered at all. (I had been outside not long before my meeting.) Nor had someone scrubbed the sky or bleached the snow. Rather, I was able to notice the beauty around me more easily. My happiness enabled me to focus less on myself and more on the world around me. My surroundings seemed girded with joy. Perhaps the writer of Psalm 65 once had a similar experience.

Sometimes the earth even seems to share its joy with us. Now I realize that I am, like the psalmist, anthropomorphizing the earth, but so be it. There are few things that cheer me up as much as seeing the countryside, perhaps because of my citified life. When I am out of doors or even catch sight of trees or flowers from the window of a car or train, I am filled with a particular sort of joy. Sometimes I wonder if we are "hardwired" to respond to the sight of nature. Seeing a flowering field or autumn leaves or the winter sky has an immediate calming effect on me. And a "joying" one too.

By ascribing the human experience of joy to the earth, the psalmist may be describing several experiences at once. First, his gratitude for the abundance of the land. Second, his idea of the gratitude that the earth, a divine creation, must have for God. Third, his gratitude for the blessings of his own life. So along with him, and the land, we "shout and sing together for joy."

Like Psalm 65, the psalms of praise, which have nourished believers for thousands of years, are filled with joy, delight, and gratitude. In the end, many of the psalms aren't so depressing after all. Maybe Monty Python's God didn't know his Bible as well as he should have.

Psalm 65: 9–13

You visit the earth and water it,
you greatly enrich it;
the river of God is full of water;
you provide the people with grain,
for so you have prepared it.
You water its furrows abundantly,
settling its ridges,
softening it with showers,
and blessing its growth.
You crown the year with your bounty;
your wagon tracks overflow with richness.
The pastures of the wilderness overflow,
the hills gird themselves with joy,
the meadows clothe themselves with flocks,
the valleys deck themselves with grain,
they shout and sing together for joy.

Chapter Three

Joy Is a Gift from God

Humor and the Saints

Although some believers are deadly serious, many saints were not. Most of the saints were men and women whom others wanted to be around. (Otherwise how else would they have founded all those religious orders?) And, in general, we want to be around people with a sense of humor. Joy, humor, and laughter are constant threads through the lives of many saints, disproving the stereotype of the dour, depressed, grumpy saint.

Traditionally, Christians relate to the saints in two ways: as patron and companion. The patron model may be the one with which most people are familiar today. Christians, especially Catholics, ask for the saint's help, for his or her prayers in heaven, in the same way that you would ask for a friend's prayers here on earth. Many Catholics regularly ask for a saint's prayers, also called "intercession."*

But the model more prevalent in the early church, and the model that has been of greatest influence in my own life, is the saint as companion.[34] The saint is seen as a fellow traveler along the way to God;

* There are serious reasons to pray for a saint's intercession: suffering, illness, despair. But there are also lighthearted prayers for smaller needs. When looking for a parking space, a friend of mine uses a prayer to St. Frances Xavier Cabrini (Mother Cabrini), who worked with Italian immigrants in New York City in the early 1900s. Apparently her time in New York makes her sympathetic to anyone searching for a parking space. The prayer goes: "Mother Cabrini, Mother Cabrini, please find a spot for my little machine-y."

the saint provides us with a model of Christian life, and we are helped by following his or her example. In other words, the saints serve as our models. So we can look to the saints as examples of those who not only led joyful, laughter-filled lives, but often worked against the kind of deadly seriousness that infects religion.

St. Teresa of Ávila, the sixteenth-century Carmelite nun and reformer, herself spoke out against that kind of deadly serious Catholicism. "A sad nun is a bad nun," she said. "I am more afraid of one unhappy sister than a crowd of evil spirits. . . . What would happen if we hid what little sense of humor we had? Let each of us humbly use this to cheer others." Here is a woman whom the Catholic Church has designated as a Doctor of the Church, an eminent teacher of the faith, recommending a sense of humor.

Humor suffuses the writings of St. Teresa, an intelligent, capable, and strong-willed woman. Indeed, the first line of her autobiography is famously lighthearted. She begins, "Having virtuous and God-fearing parents would have been enough for me to be good if I were not so wicked." Later on, after a lengthy description about the nature of prayer, Teresa writes, "It seems to me I have explained this matter, but perhaps I've made it clear only to myself." It is a charmingly self-deprecating remark, which instantly evokes readers' sympathy and friendship. And throughout her writings she regularly addresses God in the most familiar, even playful terms.[35] One of her most famous lines, though probably apocryphal, is also apposite: "From somber devotions and sour-faced saints, good Lord, deliver us."*

---

* This quotation of Teresa's is one of the most well-known of the saint's and is found in many popular books on her spirituality, not to mention all over the Internet. And it is certainly in keeping with her zestful approach to the spiritual life. There's only one problem—it seems to appear nowhere in her writings. Kieran Kavanaugh, a Catholic scholar, a translator of her works, and a member of the men's branch of the Carmelites (Teresa's order), told me that he could not find it in any of her writings, though he pointed me to other places where she speaks about joy and lightheartedness in the spiritual life. "That doesn't mean that she didn't say it," he told me, "only that it's not written down." In any event, it's a great little prayer.

The happiness of the saints flows from their closeness to God and from the perspective on life that their faith brought them. Typically, they have also lived out their heartfelt desire to follow God, and so they find joy. "Please don't say that some great sorrow drove me into the convent," said St. Katharine Drexel, a twentieth-century Philadelphia heiress who gave away a fortune to start a religious order that would serve blacks and Native Americans. "That's nonsense. I am, and have always been, one of the happiest women in the world."

When I first began reading the lives of the saints, nothing surprised me more than the frequent stories of their lightheartedness, playfulness, or sheer sense of joy. Open up almost any contemporary life of a saint and you will find not a gloomy, depressive character, but someone blessed with a zestful spirit. Even those saints traditionally thought to have been overly pious are often revealed to have had a surprising joie de vivre.

St. Ignatius Loyola, often described as an austere ascetic, used to cheer up sad Jesuits by spontaneously performing dances from the Basque country in Spain, his homeland. St. Bernadette Soubirous, the famous nineteenth-century visionary (whose visions of the Virgin Mary in the French town of Lourdes inspired the book and the movie *The Song of Bernadette*), is typically portrayed in both statuary and portraiture as grim-faced. Perhaps because of the conventions of her time, even photographs show her as an unsmiling prude. But biographies of the former shepherdess reveal a charming, down-to-earth woman with a delightful sense of humor. Toward the end of her life, suffering from a fatal illness, she took to embroidery, favoring heart-shaped patterns. One day, she joked with one of the sisters in her convent, "If anyone tells you I don't have a heart, tell them I make them all day!"

Humor seems almost a prerequisite for sanctity. The saints knew to take the long view of things, were quick to laugh at life's absurdities (and at themselves), and always placed their trust in God. They were also, for the most part, remarkably self-aware men and women who had often faced severe difficulties in life, undergone a dramatic conversion (which gave them a realistic sense of their own flaws and foibles), and came into contact with people who themselves were facing great suffering. Thus the saints had a clear-eyed outlook on life, which meant that they took the serious things seriously and the not-so-serious things not so seriously. Overall, their healthy perspective led to a healthy sense of humor.

Un saint triste est un triste saint.
("A sad saint is a sad sort of saint.")
—St. Francis de Sales

So why does the popular imagination overwhelmingly think of the saints as grumpy, or at least overly serious? Well, if all traces of humor have been removed from our understanding of Jesus's personality, and if the Christian tradition has had a good deal of its natural humor leeched out, and if "real" religion is supposed to be serious, then the saints, the models par excellence of Christian life, are, not surprisingly, portrayed as the most serious Christians of all. In short, if religion is supposed to be gloomy, then the saints must be depicted as the gloomiest of all men and women.

Take a look at the many marble, stained-glass, and mosaic portrayals of saints, and see if you can find any who look cheerful. Typically, they appear with their hands folded, eyes downcast, and a morose look on their faces. Or they are pictured gazing piously heavenward, far removed from the vanities of this world. In my years of perusing the statues of saints in churches across the world, I have seen none smiling. Mary and the angels may smile occasionally,* but never the saints.

This is not simply an aesthetic fault, but a theological one, with serious implications for Christians. The images of dour-looking

* The charming "Smiling Angel" on the façade of Reims Cathedral, in France, is a notable example.

saints that predominate in churches influence the way we understand the saints, the way we understand holiness, and, therefore, the way we understand God.

Another reason we may have historically downplayed holy humor is that we may wish the saints, consciously or unconsciously, to be other than ourselves. It is tempting for us to distance the saints and the spiritual masters of any tradition from our own lives, because this, in a sense, lets us off the hook. It's easier that way. If we imagine them as essentially different from us, then their lives make little claim on our own. Labeling the saints as "other"—imagining them as always being gifted with fruitful prayer, never having any doubts about God's existence, or, in this case, always remaining deadly serious—means that their lives remain largely irrelevant to our own. Their examples of charity and service cease to be relevant to us, and therefore we can look at them as nothing more than spiritual oddities. In a way, it's a dehumanization of the saints.

But a close reading of the lives of the saints shows us that they were like us in every way—even in their sense of humor and playfulness. In fact, because of their great holiness, their perspective on life, their faith in God, and their appreciation of the absurdities in life, some of them are famously witty.

Just look at the historical record. Stories about the overt humor of the saints reach as far back as the early Roman martyrs—that is, from the very earliest days of the church. In the third century, St. Lawrence, who was burned to death on a grill over hot coals, called out to his executioners (in perfectly conjugated Latin, no less), "This side is done. Turn me over and have a bite."* In the fourth century, St. Augustine of Hippo puckishly prayed, "Lord, give me chastity, but not yet." (Yes, that's the same Augustine who was suspicious of humor. Fortunately, his most famous joke shows that he wasn't always suspicious.)

* "*Assum est, inquit, versa et manduca.*"

Besides their sense of humor, the saints often followed in a long tradition of being a "fool for Christ," as St. Paul wrote.[36] Paul and the early Christians would have been thought of as "fools" for doing things that would seem "foolish" to anyone who does not believe in the "folly" of what Jesus preached: forgiving your enemies, praying for your persecutors, and the like. This is part of the appeal of the Christian message—its otherworldly, ridiculous, and indeed foolish way of approaching life.

Radical faith is seen as foolish in more contemporary times as well. The nineteenth-century Belgian priest Damien de Veuster volunteered to work with those suffering from "leprosy" (known today as Hansen's disease) on the island of Molokai. Damien knew well that close contact with the disease would mean that he was bound to contract it, which he did, over the course of his sixteen years on Molokai. Ultimately, his care for the sick on Molokai, where he was beloved, led to his death. Surely his selfless ministry would have seemed foolish to many. For his foolishness he was canonized by the Catholic Church in 2009 and is now known as St. Damien of Molokai.

A more recent example is Dorothy Day, the founder of the Catholic Worker movement, who died in 1980. During her lifetime, Dorothy, as her followers called her, along with the French peasant-philosopher Peter Maurin, founded dozens of "houses of hospitality" for the poor in the inner city, protested against war, and lived a life of simplicity in communion with the homeless and dispossessed. Her efforts on behalf of the poor and on behalf of peace were seen by many mainstream Catholics as naive at best. At one point the powerful archbishop of New York, Francis Cardinal Spellman, tried unsuccessfully to get Dorothy to drop the word "Catholic" from *The Catholic Worker,* the newspaper that the group published. She too was a "fool for Christ."

Jesus was seen as crazy in his day—and not just his message, but the man. Imagine how a shabbily dressed, itinerant preacher from a tiny backwater town in Galilee must have appeared to those who first met him. We may be so accustomed to thinking of the

Messiah, the exalted Son of God, the Risen Christ in glory, that we often forget the impression that this thirty-something carpenter must have given. But if we do forget, the Gospels remind us in the starkest ways. In the Gospel of Mark Jesus's own family recoils from his early preaching and miracle working: "When his family heard it, they went out to restrain him, for people were saying, 'He has gone out of his mind.'"[37] Both he and his message seemed ridiculous to many in his day.

Even more ridiculous is the fact that Jesus was right. This is the beginning of the tradition in Christian theology of the fool as the one who sees, as the only one who knows the truth. Here is the intersection between the comic and the true.

This notion of the "fool for Christ" or the "holy fool" runs through the lives of many of the most well-known saints, of whom St. Francis of Assisi is the most notable example. During his life in the thirteenth century, Francis engaged in what would be seen today as "crazy" actions. (In his time Francis was called *pazzo,* the Italian word for "crazy.")

Immediately after his conversion, for example, in his youthful quest to divest himself of his worldly goods and sever all ties to his wealthy father, Francis stripped naked in Assisi's town square. When his brother Franciscans built themselves a house that Francis considered not in keeping with their simple lifestyle, the saint-to-be clambered to the rooftop and began pulling it apart, most likely to the horror of onlookers. When he preached in the nude, the townspeople in Assisi first laughed at him and then were won over by his words. Loving all of creation, even the lowliest of creatures, Francis is said to have preached to the animals (and at one point scolded a group of swallows for chirping too loudly during the Mass).

Those last two stories come from *The Little Flowers of St. Francis of Assisi,*[38] a series of tales about the saint, some based in fact, some legendary, and some clearly fictional, which nonetheless communicate prophetic humor.

All Those Birds Began to Open Their Beaks

Here is the story of the holy fool Francis of Assisi, preaching to the birds, from *The Little Flowers of St. Francis of Assisi:*

Now the preaching of St. Francis was after this manner: "My sisters the birds, you are much obliged to God your Creator, and always and in every place you ought to praise Him, because He has given you liberty to fly wherever you will and has clothed you with twofold and threefold raiment. Moreover, He preserved your seed in Noah's Ark that your race might not be destroyed. Again, you are obliged to Him for the element of the air which He has appointed for you. Furthermore, you sow not, neither do you reap, yet God feeds you and gives you rivers and fountains from which to drink. He gives you mountains and valleys for your refuge, and high trees in which to build your nests. And, since you know neither how to sew or to spin, God clothes you and your little ones; so, clearly your Creator loves you, seeing that He gives you so many benefits. Guard yourselves, therefore, you sisters the birds, from the sin of ingratitude and be ever mindful to give praise to God."

As St. Francis spoke these words to them, all those birds began to open their beaks, and to stretch out their necks, and to open their wings, and reverently to bow their heads to the ground, and to show by their motions and by their songs that the holy father had given them very great delight. St. Francis rejoiced with them and was glad and marveled much at so great a multitude of birds and at their most beautiful diversity, and at their attentiveness and fearlessness, for which he devoutly praised the Creator in them.

Another fanciful story in *The Little Flowers* concerns one of St. Francis's brother Franciscans, St. Anthony of Padua, who preaches to the people of Rimini. But they, "hard of heart and obstinate," refuse to listen to him. So Anthony decides to take his message elsewhere—he preaches to the fish. "Hear the word of God, you fishes of the sea and of the river," Anthony says. The fish, we are told, prove quite attentive:

> When he had said this, there came to him on the river bank so vast a multitude of fishes—big, little, and of middling size—that never in the sea or in that river had there been seen so many. All of them held their heads out of the water and gazed attentively on the face of St. Anthony, remaining there in great peace and gentleness and order. In the front rank and nearest to the shore were the tiny little fish; behind them were the moderately large fish; and farther out, where the water was deeper, were the biggest fish.

The fish communicate their approval of Anthony's words by nodding their fishy heads. Not surprisingly, the amazed townspeople begin to listen to Anthony. Clearly this is a legendary story, as are many of the stories about St. Francis. But it effectively communicates some of the sweet and gentle humor of St. Francis and his followers.

One of the most enjoyable tales in the Franciscan annals concern the lovable Brother Juniper, whose lavish generosity constantly exasperated his Franciscan brothers. Juniper, one of the early companions of Francis, thought nothing of giving everything away to the poor, and so his brothers were forced to forbid him from giving away his tunic to any beggar he encountered. Once, encountering a poor man, Juniper slyly told him that although he was forbidden to give him his cloak, there was nothing to say that the man couldn't *take* it from him.

On another occasion, the guileless Franciscan was caring for a sick man who professed a craving for a special delicacy: pig's feet. In response to the man's need, Juniper went into a nearby field, spied a pig, cut a foot off of the unfortunate animal, cooked it up, and served it to the man. The pig's owner, predictably furious, berated Juniper's superior and called the Franciscans thieves.

Genuinely surprised that someone should be upset by his act of charity, Juniper promptly returned to the man and told him the reasons behind his actions. The irate farmer called him, according to one translation, "a fantastical fool." Juniper simply repeated the story with greater passion, wondering all the while how someone could misunderstand his intentions. Taken with Juniper's sincerity and charity, the man had a change of heart. Ultimately, he gave the Franciscans the rest of the pig. Upon hearing the story of this "holy fool," St. Francis exclaimed to his companions, "Would that I had a whole forest of Junipers!"

Some saints were known specifically for their rich sense of humor. St. Philip Neri, a sixteenth-century Italian priest, for example, was called the "Humorous Saint." Over his door he posted a small sign that read, "The House of Christian Mirth." En route to a ceremony in his honor, he once shaved off half his beard as a way of poking fun at himself. "Christian joy is a gift from God, flowing from a good conscience," he said. One biography suggests that much of Neri's humor was a way of keeping him humble, as he engaged in what could only be called acts of public silliness, like wearing a cushion on his head like a turban or wearing a foxtail coat in the middle of the summer.[39] Here is how Robert Ellsberg describes the lighthearted Philip Neri in his book *All Saints:*

> He was widely revered as a saint, and like all saints Neri disdained such acclaim, but he had his own way of coping with it. He liked to dress in comical outfits, assume outlandish disguises, go about with only one side of his face shaved, or

> indulge in elaborate practical jokes. This was part of a deliberate campaign to keep people from putting him on a pedestal. At the same time it reflected his genuine playfulness and the joy he discovered in the spiritual life.[40]

Once, a young priest asked him what prayer would be the most appropriate to say for a couple after a wedding Mass. Philip Neri thought for a moment and said, "A prayer for peace."

St. Francis de Sales, the seventeenth-century bishop of Geneva and renowned spiritual master, espoused a sensible, cheerful, and gentle spirituality. "When you encounter difficulties and contradictions, do not try to break them, but bend them with gentleness and time," he wrote. His humane approach to spiritual matters stood in contrast to some of the rigid practices of his day. So did his desire to help laypeople live a life of deep spirituality—at a time when "real" spirituality was thought to be the province of clerics. His classic text *Introduction to the Devout Life* was written specifically to help laypeople on their path to God.

Francis de Sales also knew how to use a joke to good effect. He was, for example, a great friend of St. Jane Frances de Chantal, a French noblewoman, and together, in 1610, they founded a religious order for women, the Visitation sisters. After Jane had decided to follow a strict religious life and remain unmarried after being widowed, she nevertheless continued to wear low-cut dresses showing off her décolletage. On the night of their first meeting, Francis de Sales took one look at her dress and quipped, "Madame, those who do not mean to entertain guests should take down their signboard!"*

More broadly, the saints also knew that a joyful nature was an effective tool in their work. Not long ago, I visited the shrine of St. Katharine Drexel, in the town of Bensalem, outside of Philadelphia.

---

* Michael O'Neill McGrath, a Salesian brother (Salesians follow the spirituality of St. Francis de Sales) offered an alternate version, which he was taught as a novice: "Madame, if you're not looking for another husband, take down the flags!"

I thought I knew all there was to know about this remarkable woman, but was surprised to find in the gift shop a refrigerator magnet with her smiling face and the quote, "We must attract them by joy." Later I tracked down the entire quote. Writing to the sisters in her order who were teaching children, she said, "We must attract them by joy in order to lead them to its source, the Heart of Christ."

Wisdom from St. Philip Neri

A heart filled with joy is more easily made perfect than one that is sad.

A glad spirit attains perfection more quickly than any other.

Cheerfulness strengthens the heart and makes us try harder to have a good life.

Saintly humor continues up until modern times. Perhaps the most well-known contemporary example is Blessed Pope John XXIII, who served as pope from 1958 to 1963. His most famous joke came when a journalist innocently asked him, "Your Holiness, how many people work in the Vatican?"

John paused, thought it over, and said, "About half of them."

Someone once asked John about the Italian habit of closing offices in the afternoon. "Your Holiness, we understand that the Vatican is closed in the afternoon, and people don't work then."

"Ah no!" said the pope. "The offices are closed in the afternoon. People don't work in the morning!"

Shortly after his election as pope, John was walking in the streets of Rome when a woman passed him and said to her friend, "My God, he's so fat!"

Overhearing her remark, he turned around and replied, "Madame, I trust you understand that the papal conclave is not exactly a beauty contest."

In the 1940s, when John was still an archbishop and the papal nuncio, or ambassador, in Paris, he was at an elegant dinner party, seated across from a woman wearing a low-cut dress that exposed a good deal of cleavage. Someone turned to him and said, "Your Excellency, what a scandal! Aren't you embarrassed that everyone is looking at that woman?"

And he said, "Oh no, everyone is looking at me, to see if *I'm* looking at her."

John XXIII is my avatar for holy humor. In fact, I was introduced to the life of this seminal figure in contemporary religious history not through any scholarly autobiography or learned lecture, but through a book called *Wit and Wisdom of Good Pope John* by Henri Fesquet, which I stumbled across in a retreat house. At the time I was supposed to be praying silently.

The passage that made me laugh in the retreat house (and draw pointed glances from the other, more silent retreatants) was a story that placed the pope in a Roman hospital called the Hospital of the Holy Spirit. Shortly after entering, he was introduced to the sister who ran the hospital.

"Holy Father," she exclaimed, flustered by his surprise visit, "I am the superior of the Holy Spirit."

"Well, I must say, you're lucky," said the pope, delighted. "I'm only the Vicar of Christ!"

Who couldn't love a pope who had a sense of humor? Who couldn't love a man who was so comfortable with himself that he made jokes about his height (which was short), his ears (which were big), and his weight (which was considerable). Born Angelo Roncalli, in the small town of Sotto il Monte, near Bergamo, after he was elected pope he met a little boy named Angelo and exclaimed, "That was my name too!" Then, conspiratorially, "But then they made me change it!"

His humor seemed to flow naturally from his joy. His joy made him comfortable enough to laugh at himself and poke fun at his office and invited others into his humorous outlook on the world. And that joy made him comfortable with the absurdities of the world. For his openness, generosity, warmth, and humor, "Good Pope John" was loved by many. When he died, a friend of mine was in a cab in Rome driven by a Jewish cab driver. "He was our pope too," the cab driver said.

There is something irresistible about a person in a position of authority with a self-deprecatory sense of humor. It instantly binds us to the person, perhaps because we see in him or her a reflection of what we could be, of what God wants us to be in the midst of our accomplishments: simple, humble, aware of our own limitations, and, of course, joyful.

Did St. Benedict Laugh?

Nearly all of the Benedictine priests, brothers, and sisters I know are joyful sorts. They are known in the Catholic world too for their gracious hospitality. So I was surprised to stumble upon warnings against laughter in the *Rule of St. Benedict,* the sixth-century document that guides life in Benedictine communities, written by the saint himself. I asked Lawrence S. Cunningham, an expert on monasticism and author of *A Brief History of the Saints,* to explain things. Was St. Benedict really against laughter?

> In various places in the *Rule of St. Benedict* are cautions against laughter in the cloister. In the wonderfully named Chapter 4 of the *Rule,* "Tools for Good Works," St. Benedict urges: "Prefer moderation in speech and speak no foolish chatter, nothing just to provoke laughter; do not love immoderate or boisterous laughter" (4:52–54). In Chapter 6, Benedict, discussing monastic speech, says: "We absolutely condemn in all places any vulgarity and

gossip and talk leading to laughter, and we do not permit a disciple to engage in words of that kind" (6:8). In the chapter on the steps of humility (7:9) he urges that "the tenth step of humility is that he is not given to ready laughter, for it is written: *Only a fool raises his voice in laughter* (Sirach 21:23)." To underscore this he adds: "The eleventh step of humility is that a monk speaks gently and without laughter . . ." (7:60).

What are we to make of his stern attitude toward laughter, which was repeated as a commonplace in later monastic literature? A few points are obvious. Benedict wanted his monks to be people of few words, and those words were to be sober ones in order to maintain a contemplative atmosphere in the monastery. Second, by quoting sacred Scripture he bowed to the wisdom of the inspired word of God, which often links laughter to foolishness. Finally, Benedict always uses the Latin word *risus,* which means not only laughter in general, but what we would call a "belly laugh," a practical joke, or even an act of mockery. Thus, the full weight of *risus* takes on the meaning of unrestrained laughter or, as the saint says, "boisterous laughter." If one reads the text carefully, Benedict's objections must have been to anything of the sort that disturbed the decorum of the community.

The Benedictines probably would not object to the kind of mirth praised in the famous quatrain of Hilaire Belloc, even though he wrote centuries after the saint had lived: "Wherever the Catholic sun doth shine / there's always laughter and good red wine. / At least I've always found it so. / *Benedicamus Domino*!"

The saints knew that there were some serious reasons for humor. But those insights are not simply the province of Christian spiritual masters. There is a Talmudic story, for example, of a rabbi meeting up with Elijah the prophet, who would answer questions for him about the "world to come."[41] The rabbi was in the marketplace when he came upon Elijah. He asked the prophet whether there were any in the marketplace who merited a place in the world to come. Perhaps the rabbi was hoping that Elijah would assure him that his piety and wisdom would earn him that reward.

Instead, Elijah pointed to two men and said, "Yes, those two." The rabbi approached the two men and asked them who they were and what they did. They replied, "We are jesters. We make sad people laugh. And when we see two people arguing, we make peace between them." A serious purpose indeed.

Likewise, in one Zen Buddhist tradition, according to Matt Weiner, the program director of the Interfaith Center of New York, there is an explicit emphasis on "foolishness." The Jodo Shinshu tradition, Weiner explained, was founded by Shinran in Japan in the thirteenth century. Shinran gradually came to the awareness that he probably would never become enlightened or perhaps even a good moral person. "That led to a philosophy of foolishness and of the foolish sage in his tradition," said Matt, who was raised Jewish and is now a student of Buddhism. Shinran later renamed himself Gotoku, which means "foolish, stubble-haired man."

Where does this foolishness lead? "Believing that we can become enlightened is foolishness," said Matt, "so the correct response is gratitude."

The Jesuit scholar Francis Clooney, who has written several books on world religions, spoke of the use of humor in Eastern traditions in a conversation. "There are fairly well developed categories in Indian literary theory about what is laughable or comic, in light of how human life itself is understood," he told me. "These larger insights would merit comparison with Greek understandings of comedy, and Christian insights into the comic side of reality—even the 'divine comedy.' If we move farther to the East, it seems that in the Chinese traditions, Confucius and Mencius both had a sense of

A Soul Waking Up

Jamal Rahman, a Sufi who was born in Bangladesh, is cofounder and cominister of the Interfaith Community Church in Seattle, Washington, cohost of Interfaith Talk Radio, and an adjunct faculty member at Seattle University, a Jesuit university. His book *The Fragrance of Faith: The Enlightened Heart of Islam*,[42] is an introduction to Islamic spirituality, which I have found most helpful in my quest to understand that faith tradition. Here is Sheik Rahman talking about laughter in his tradition:

> The beloved saints in Islam say that many of us are far too severe with ourselves and take life much too seriously. We need discipline and focus but also flexibility, spaciousness, and lots of laughter. A hidden smile from within knows that what is mortal and transient is also grounded in eternity. Truly all is well.
>
> The Persian mystic Hafiz points out that the Beloved's name is pure joy. The closer we come to Him, the more we are able to hear and feel God's laughter. If we don't laugh, it's because we are not yet blessed with higher awareness.
>
> "Isn't it strange?" remarks Rumi [a thirteenth-century poet], "that we are being dragged out of our fiery furnaces and smoky hell into paradise and the fragrance of the eternal rose garden, and all we are doing is howling and lamenting."
>
> The fourteenth-century Hafiz asks, "What is this precious love and laughter budding in our hearts?" Listen to his answer: "It is the glorious sound of a soul waking up!"

humor, while many Zen koans surely require a sense of humor, if one is to get their full impact."

Stories from a variety of religious traditions show that humor can serve some serious purposes. So let's look at a few reasons for humor in the spiritual life.

Chapter Four

Happiness Attracts

11½ Serious Reasons for Good Humor

Before beginning this chapter, a little caveat: I'm not advocating a mindless, idiotic happiness. As the Book of Ecclesiastes says, there is a time to weep and a time to mourn. You would be a robot if you weren't sad during a time of serious illness or at the death of a friend or family member, the loss of a job, or a sudden financial crisis in your life. Those are things to mourn and to grieve. But Ecclesiastes also says that there is a time to laugh. And sometimes laughter can be healthy even in the midst of sadness—as a way of lightening a heavy situation.

A few years ago the regional superior of the Jesuits in New York City was visiting the infirmary, where the sick and elderly priests and brothers live. The superior was talking about how the Jesuits in the area were getting older and older. "We have so many aging Jesuits," said the superior, "that there really isn't any place to put them. There isn't even room for anyone else here in the infirmary."

To which an elderly Jesuit shouted out, "Father, we're dying as fast as we can!"

Silly humor, as in this example, can sometimes help lighten sad situations. But it can deepen a person's spiritual life in a variety of other equally important ways. So let's look at eleven and a half serious reasons for humor in the spiritual life.

* * *

1. Humor evangelizes.

Joy, humor, and laughter show one's faith in God. For Christians, an essentially hopeful outlook shows people that you believe in the Resurrection, in the power of life over death, and in the power of love over hatred. Don't you think that after the Resurrection Jesus's disciples were joyful? "All will be well, and all will be well, and all manner of things will be well," as the fourteenth-century mystic Blessed Julian of Norwich said. For believers in general, humor shows your trust in God, who will ultimately make all things well. Joy reveals faith.

On a more practical level, Blessed Francis Xavier Seelos, a nineteenth-century Redemptorist priest, spoke of "holy hilarity" as a tool for spreading the gospel. Joy draws others to God. To paraphrase St. Teresa, why hide it?

When I was a Jesuit novice in Boston, the superior general of the Society of Jesus, Peter-Hans Kolvenbach, came to visit our novitiate. Before his visit, the novices were asked to come up with one question each to ask Father Kolvenbach. I thought long and hard about what I wanted to ask him. (Secretly I wanted to impress him too, which was probably not the best motivation for my question.) Since most religious orders are concerned about declining numbers, I decided to ask him the best way to increase "vocations."

The big day arrived, and so did he, clad in a simple black clerical suit with a black raincoat; he was accompanied by several other Jesuit officials from Rome and the superior of the Jesuits in New England. The tenor of the gathering seemed to match Kolvenbach's reputation as a rather serious leader. After the novice director greeted him formally, we moved into the living room. There we were invited to ask Father Kolvenbach our questions.

"Father," I said, "what's the best way to increase vocations?"

I expected him to say, "We have to do more recruiting in colleges or parishes," or "We have to do more advertising to get the word out about the Jesuits."

His response was as surprising as it was memorable. He said, "Live your own vocation joyfully!"

That's good advice for everyone. Joy attracts people to God. Why would anyone want to join a group of miserable people? A pithier way of expressing this came from Timothy M. Dolan, after his appointment as archbishop of New York in 2009. A *New York Times* reporter asked him about the declining number of vocations to the Catholic priesthood and wondered about his approach to that problem. Archbishop Dolan's answer: "Happiness attracts."

By the way, the superior general of the Jesuits is usually called "Father General" or, more simply, the "General." In the 1960s, another Father General, Pedro Arrupe, a Spaniard with a marvelous sense of humor, visited Xavier High School, a Jesuit school in New York City. At the time, all the boys at Xavier wore military uniforms and performed regular military drills. So when it was announced that Arrupe was coming to visit, the school decided that all the students would line the street, in uniform, as a way of giving Father General a special welcome.

A Jesuit friend of mine accompanying Arrupe told me that Father General's car drove down the street in between hundreds of students in uniform. Father General opened the door and stepped out onto the sidewalk. At that moment the students snapped to attention and saluted him.

Father Arrupe smiled and said to my friend, "Ha! Now I feel like a *real* general!"

2. Humor is a tool for humility.

We can tell jokes about ourselves to deflate our ego, which is always salutary—especially for anyone working in an official capacity in a religious institution, where it's easy to get puffed up. That goes for cardinals who wear silk robes and are called "Your Eminence."

That goes for priests, brothers, and sisters whom others think are holy simply because they're ordained or are in a religious order. That goes for preachers or rabbis whom others revere because they can recall verses of Scripture effortlessly. That goes for laypeople in parishes, schools, and hospitals who exercise a great deal of power over people's spiritual lives. Frankly, it goes for everyone.

All of us can get puffed up, and humor is a good way for people to remind themselves of their basic humanity, their essential poverty of spirit.

An Ecumenical Sense of Humor

A Lutheran pastor once told me that I needed to expand my repertoire of jokes. They couldn't all be about Catholics and Jesuits, he said.

"Are there any Lutheran jokes I could tell without offending anyone?" I asked.

"Are you kidding?" he said and then recounted his favorite:

> A Lutheran pastor is asleep one night when the phone rings. The fire department is calling to say that someone is about to jump off a roof. The pastor throws on his clothes, jumps in his car, and races to the house. When he arrives, a firefighter points to the man on his roof.
>
> "Don't jump!" yells the pastor.
>
> "Well, I'm going to," says the man. "I've got nothing to live for!"
>
> The pastor asks, "What about your family?"
>
> And the man says, "I've got none!"
>
> The pastor asks, "What about your friends?"
>
> The man says, "I've got none!"
>
> The pastor pauses for a long while and then says, "Well,

I'm sure we could be friends. I'll bet we have a lot in common."

"I doubt it," says the man on the roof.

The pastor thinks. "Well, do you believe in God?" he asks.

"Yes," says the man.

"See?" says the pastor. "We have that in common! Are you a Christian?"

"Yes," says the man.

"So am I!" says the pastor, delighted.

"Are you Lutheran by any chance?"

"Yes I am," he says.

"I'm a Lutheran pastor!" says the pastor. "We have so much in common!" Then he pauses and asks, "Which branch? Missouri Synod or Evangelical Lutheran?"

"Evangelical Lutheran," says the man.

Then the pastor says, "In that case, jump, you heretic!"

Humor brings us back down to earth and reminds us of our place in God's universe. "Angels can fly," wrote G. K. Chesterton, "because they can take themselves lightly."

For example, the Jesuit jokes I've recounted so far are fun to tell. I love the Society of Jesus and have professed my lifelong vows as a Jesuit. But lighthearted jokes remind me that Jesuits need to be careful about being too proud of their accomplishments or too focused on practical matters—the normal premise of the Jesuit joke.

One of the oldest is that of the three priests, a Franciscan, Dominican, and Jesuit, who are on retreat together. Suddenly they receive a mystical vision and find themselves at the nativity scene. They're kneeling before the manger, and the Dominican says to Mary, "Oh, the joy of seeing the Word made Flesh, of seeing the Incarnation of God, of seeing the union of the human and the divine!" The Franciscan says to Jesus, "Oh, the joy of seeing how the Son of

God identifies with the poor and chooses to be born in poverty and among the dear animals that he loves!" And the Jesuit puts his arm around St. Joseph and says, "Have you considered sending him to a Jesuit high school?"

Let me have too deep a sense of humor ever to be proud.
Let me know my absurdity before I act absurdly.
Let me realize that when I am humble I am most human, most truthful, and most worthy of your serious consideration.
—DANIEL LORD, AMERICAN JESUIT PRIEST

Humor reminds us not to take ourselves with such deadly seriousness. That goes for people at the very top. Once, when Pope John XXIII was in Rome he got a letter from a little boy named Bruno.

"Dear Pope," wrote Bruno, "I am undecided. I don't know if I want to be a policeman or a pope. What do you think?"

"My dear Bruno," wrote the pope, "if you want my opinion, learn to be a policeman, for that cannot be improvised. As regards being pope, anyone can become the pope. The proof is that I have become one. If you are ever in Rome, please stop by and I will be glad to talk this over with you."

Archbishop Fulton J. Sheen, the charismatic Catholic preacher whose television program *Life Is Worth Living* was a nationwide hit in the 1950s, was well-known for his own sense of humor. In one of his programs, he recalled Pope John telling him, "From all eternity God knew that I was going to be pope. He had eighty years to work on me. Why did he make me so ugly?"

Humility is also the best antidote for what you might call spiritual pride, which comes when you find yourself thinking, "I'm so holy!" Simply because you go to Mass every Sunday, donate a tenth of your salary to the church, are an elder in your congregation, or always attend the Shabbat (Sabbath) services at your synagogue does not mean that you are, ipso facto, holier than everyone else.

The saints and great spiritual masters were well aware the dangers of spiritual pride. In fact, some of them worked diligently to guard against it, especially since they were often acclaimed in their lifetime—as Mother Teresa was—as a "living saint." A key tool in their quest for humility was humor, as we've already seen with Pope John XXIII downplaying his election as pope and St. Teresa of Ávila humorously doubting her ability to describe prayer. The great Catholic theologian Karl Rahner noted that the one who laughs is the one who "does not adapt everything to himself, the one who is free from self."[43]*

And not just Catholics. One of the overriding themes of the book *The Wit of Martin Luther* is how Luther used humor to remind himself of the limitations of human knowledge when it comes to God. "Humor was for Luther," writes the Luther scholar Eric Gritsch, "the guard to prevent him from crossing the frontier to speculation about God and human life beyond its earthly existence." Humor served as a reminder of his own humanity and humility.

In non-Christian traditions, we have already mentioned the example of the Dalai Lama, a supremely joyful man who in his public lectures freely admits his own struggles in the spiritual life. He radiates humility. In the documentary film *Dalai Lama Renaissance,* he is shown sitting before an audience saying, "We don't even want a pain from a mosquito. *I* don't want it!" He laughingly tells how he tries to make peace with a mosquito's taking blood from him, time and again. He is human, like the rest of us. And toward the end of his talk he loses his train of thought and exclaims, "I forgot what I was saying. The mosquito took my idea!"

---

* Karl and Hugo Rahner were brothers. Both were German Jesuits. Jesuits used to joke that Karl's abstruse theological writings were so difficult to understand that Hugo had to translate them into German or that he read them in French.

* * *

3. Humor can help us recognize reality.

Humor can get right to the point. It puts things into perspective. St. Francis of Assisi is supposed to have said, "Preach the gospel at all times. Use words when necessary." That's clever and even funny. It's also a profound truth.

Sayings from the Book of Proverbs often use humor to communicate a point. "Like somebody who takes a passing dog by the ears is one who meddles in the quarrel of another."[44] That morsel of folk wisdom is conveyed through an amusing image.

Jesus often silenced his opponents with clever answers and humorous retorts, as when asked whether his followers should pay the traditional Roman tax.[45] In that instance, as in many others, his questioners were aiming to set a trap for Jesus. If he said yes, he would have been encouraging his fellow Jews to accept the Roman overlords. If he said no, he would have been guilty of sedition. So he simply said, "Give therefore to the emperor the things that are the emperor's, and to God the things that are God's." It's easy to imagine his onlookers smiling at that clever response and his opponents realizing that he had escaped their trap.

Humorous stories can accomplish the same thing; they communicate a truth in a way that a more serious explanation cannot. Here's an example from my own life.

A few years ago I was lamenting to my spiritual director how busy I was. At the time I was forever taking on more writing projects, saying yes to too many tasks, never refusing a request to do more at work, never turning down an invitation to lead a retreat, never declining an opportunity to speak at a parish, never saying no to any offer to be more "productive." Certainly I was productive, but I was also feeling overwhelmed by what seemed to be constant work. Rather than scold me or lecture me on workaholism, my spiritual director simply told me a story, which changed the way I live:[46]

> A man comes into his company's lunchroom one day and sits down next to his friend. He opens his lunch bag, pulls out a sandwich, opens the wrapping, and peers down. "Oh ugh," he says to his friend.
>
> "What's the matter?" asks his friend.
>
> "A cheese sandwich! I hate cheese sandwiches," he says and glumly starts choking it down. "They're awful. So dry."
>
> The next day he sits down next to the same friend and opens his lunch bag. "Oh, I can't believe it." he says, "Another cheese sandwich!" His friend shakes his head sympathetically and watches his friend grimace as he eats the sandwich.
>
> On the third day, the man once again sits down next to his friend and opens his lunch bag. "Oh, brother," he says. "Another cheese sandwich!"
>
> His friend says, "Boy, you really hate cheese sandwiches, don't you?"
>
> "Yes! I can't stand them!"
>
> Finally his friend says, "If you don't mind me asking something, why don't you just tell your wife to stop making you cheese sandwiches?"
>
> "Oh," says the man, "I'm not married."
>
> "Well then," said his friend, "who makes your cheese sandwiches every day?"
>
> "I do," he said.

That story, which made me laugh out loud, hit me like a bolt of lightning. Hearing it made me realize that, like the guy in the story, I was responsible for my own predicament. *I* was the one who was saying yes to every request for more work, who kept taking on more writing projects, and who refused to say no to any speaking gig, no matter how busy I was. I was making all those cheese sandwiches that I hated.

A funny story helped me to see this. My spiritual director could have talked for hours about the need to say no, about the need to avoid taking on too much work, and about the need to maintain a balance between action and contemplation, but his arguments wouldn't have made anywhere near the impression that that story did. Nor would it have been nearly as memorable. Humor opens us up to new insights; it blows the cobwebs out of our minds.

Humor—an amusing saying, a clever response, or a funny story—can be an effective tool for truth telling in a way that mere argumentation simply cannot. Humorous short stories and novels may do the same thing. The Catholic author Flannery O'Connor (1925–64), to take but one example, is known for her ability to make a point with her outlandish characters, bizarre plots, and overall absurd take on life. Once read, her stories, mainly set in the American South, are unforgettable. "Humor," said Margaret Silf, the British spiritual writer, "makes every message stick, whether it's the silly ad that you never forget or the joke that hammers home some important spiritual truth."

But humor has another connection to "reality," which was illuminated for me in a recent conversation with a friend who has a unique perspective on the matter. William A. Barry is a Jesuit priest, a clinical psychologist, a spiritual director, and a popular writer on prayer and spirituality. "Without a sense of humor you would be missing out on a whole lot of life!" he said. "You would be missing the way, for example, cats will jump on one another and play, the kind of playful humor that goes on between children and adults, and even some parts of the Bible. If you don't laugh at all that, you're missing something," said Father Barry. "Part of a healthy emotional life is being in touch with *all* of reality—not just the difficult parts."

* * *

4. Humor speaks truth to power.

A witty remark is a time-honored way to challenge the pompous, the puffed up, and the powerful. Jesus of Nazareth deployed humor to this end, exposing and defusing the arrogance of some of the religious authorities of his day with clever parables and amusing sallies. Humor is a weapon in the battle against the pride that infects most of us and sometimes infects our religious communities.

A friend's mother was once in the hospital at the same time the local bishop was. After his operation the bishop went around room to room visiting all the patients. When he visited my friend's mother, who was recovering from a difficult surgery, he said, unctuously, "Well dear, I know exactly how you feel."

And she replied, "Really? Did you have a hysterectomy too?"

A few months ago I mentioned that story to my friend, and he laughed and said, "You forgot the most important point! My mother and the bishop became friends. After she died, I invited him to preside at her funeral Mass, and he retold that story." He had learned to take himself not so seriously.

5. Humor shows courage.

As I mentioned, St. Lawrence showed his courage to his torturers during his martyrdom by saying, "I'm done on this side." It was both a pointed challenge to his executioners and a bold profession of faith. In that same vein, in the sixteenth century St. Thomas More, the onetime chancellor of England who had refused to accede to King Henry VIII's requests to recognize the king's divorce, was sentenced to death. As he climbed the steps to his beheading, he said to his executioner, "See me safe up: for in my coming down I can shift for myself."

Christian martyrs are often depicted as being calm in the face of death, a reaction that nonbelievers sometimes have a hard time understanding. But for martyrs, the threat of death at the hands of their persecutors means not only that they are closer to heaven, but that they are also following the example of Jesus. So it is sometimes possible for them to be not only brave, but also, occasionally, clever and even witty.

We might misunderstand humorous responses in that kind of situation as a simple deployment of wit, à la Oscar Wilde.* But these are more than epigrams. This type of wit shows a profound courage and conveys a deep theological truth. This kind of humor says, "I do not fear death," and, "I believe in God." It points to something beyond this world. It is a kind of prophetic humor.

6. Humor deepens our relationship with God.

One of the best ways of thinking about our relationship to God is as a close personal relationship or an intimate friendship. It's not a perfect analogy, but it can be quite helpful.

Like any relationship, for example, our relationship with God often starts with infatuation (as when everything about the spiritual life seems easy and wonderful); it goes through exciting times (when prayer is rich and worship is satisfying) and sometimes dry periods (when the spiritual life seems at a standstill). Like any friendship, our relationship with God requires that we devote time to it; it requires a willingness to listen, a tolerance for silence, and a desire for real honesty. All the things that we can say about friendship we can say, by analogy, about prayer.

Obviously, a relationship with God isn't *exactly* the same as a relationship with a friend. None of our friends created the world *ex nihilo* (though some act as if they had). But thinking about our relationship

* Oscar Wilde's last words, as he lay dying in a seedy hotel in Paris, were, "My wallpaper and I are fighting a duel to the death. One or the other of us has to go."

to God in these terms can help to show us where our spiritual life might be lacking.

For example, would you say that you were a good friend if you never spent time with your friends? Or if you never listened to them? If you were never honest with them? Yet some people approach their relationship with God in those ways. Again, the metaphor of friendship with God can help us see our spiritual life in a fresh way.

In that light, our relationship with God—like *any* relationship—can use some humor from time to time. That is, it's okay to be playful with God and accept that God might want to be playful with us.

But does the idea of a humorous or playful God have antecedents? Rabbi Burton Visotzky, professor of Midrash and interreligious studies at the Jewish Theological Seminary in New York, noted that although the Hebrew Bible often shows a stern God, the notion of a playful and loving God is also part of the Jewish tradition. "In a fifth-century Midrash in Israel," said Rabbi Visotzky, "the rabbis tell the story of God braiding Eve's hair in the Garden of Eden, like one who would help a bride. It is a charming and playful image of a loving God."

Once, when she was traveling to one of her convents, St. Teresa of Ávila was knocked off her donkey and fell into the mud, injuring her leg. "Lord," she said, "you couldn't have picked a worse time for this to happen. Why would you let this happen?"

And the response that she heard in prayer was, "That is how I treat my friends."

Teresa answered, "And that is why you have so few of them!"

This story, one of the most well-known about St. Teresa, is often told as a way of demonstrating her abundant humor. But it shows something else—her playful way of addressing God. Moreover, it shows the saint's assumption of God's own playfulness.

The Book of Isaiah says, "The LORD delights in you."[47] One of my spiritual directors used to quote that whenever I would tell him something wonderful or unexpected that happened to me. "The Lord takes delight in you, Jim!" he would say.

What a strange thing that was to hear! Previously, I had imagined God creating me, caring for me, maybe even taking an interest in my life, but certainly not *delighting* in me. But why not? Doesn't a parent delight in a child?

So here are a few questions to consider:

Can you allow yourself to think of God as playful?

Can you allow God to be playful with you?

Can you imagine a God who enters into a lighthearted relationship with you?

Can you imagine God delighting in you?

It is God's will . . . that we seek [God] willfully and busily . . . gladly and merrily without unskillful heaviness and vain sorrow.

—Blessed Julian of Norwich, *Revelations of Divine Love*

One of my favorite memories from my undergraduate days at the University of Pennsylvania is one of God's delight. Around October of our freshman year, with the practiced nose of impecunious college students, my roommate Brad and I discovered an off-campus event during which free food would be served on a Friday evening. Since both of us were on a limited budget, there was no question about trekking to a hotel far from our dorm on a cloudy fall day. "It's food and it's free," said Brad, with admirable clarity. As I dimly recall, it was a presentation on interfaith relations, something that neither of us had any interest in at the time.

After Brad and I found the hotel and stuffed ourselves with hors d'oeuvres, but before the scheduled presentations began, we slipped out of the conference and started the long walk back to our dorm under rapidly darkening skies. Then thunder rang out. Suddenly it started to pour.

"Uh oh," said Brad. Then the heavens opened. It was unlike any rain I had ever seen before or since; a torrential storm seemed to be coming from all directions. If pressed at the time, I would have sworn that it was coming up from the ground. Neither of us had an umbrella, as that was seen as distinctly "uncool."

After a few minutes of unsuccessfully trying to find cover, we started laughing uncontrollably. "My shoes are getting soaked!" I shouted over the din of the rain, pointing to my now-soaked Top-Siders. Brad smiled and simply took his off. So did I.

By the time we reached our dorm, the rain had stopped. When we appeared, barefoot, carrying our shoes, and soaked to the skin, our hall mates exploded in laughter. Soon we were all laughing, Brad and I the hardest.

Normally I would have been terribly embarrassed and overly concerned about how I appeared, but something about the event seemed so ridiculous, so outlandish, and Brad seemed so unconcerned with what others thought, that it was impossible not to experience delight.

At the time, our being caught in an unexpected downpour seemed a minor event, perhaps something silly that I would soon forget. Today, however, that small, ordinary incident is deeply invested with meaning for me: for Brad would die young, only a few years later. It reminds me of a young friend full of laughter, of a carefree attitude that allows you to enjoy yourself even in the rain. It also speaks to me of God's delight. It is this moment that I remember, more than any other, when I think of my friend Brad.

What other reason for getting caught in the rain was there, other than experiencing God's joy, which pours down on us like rain, watering our souls, replenishing our hearts, and helping us to grow in wisdom and love? In our shared delight, the Lord may have been delighting in both of us.

* * *

Can you also allow yourself to think that the wonderful or funny or unexpected things that surprise you are signs of God being playful with you?

Think about this in a slightly different way. Can you imagine God not simply loving you, but, as the British theologian James Alison often asks his readers to imagine, *liking* you? We've heard the phrase "God loves you" so often that it becomes a platitude—like wallpaper that we cease to notice once it's plastered in our room. We think, "Well, of course God loves me. That's just what God *does*." But thinking about God *liking* us is quite different. That word has a different energy around it—surprising, lighthearted, personal.

Here's another question: How do you show that you like a friend? Maybe you tell your friend outright. Or maybe you do something generous for him or her. But you also may be playful with your friend. So can you let yourself think of the funny things that happen to you not just as signs of God's love, but God's *like*?

Another way of looking at this is remembering that one of the oldest images of God is as a parent. Jesus refers to God as his father and even calls him *Abba,* a sort of affectionate Aramaic term, used even today in some parts of the Middle East, that may be fairly translated as "Daddy."

The traditional image of God as parent doesn't suit everyone (particularly those from abusive or severely dysfunctional families), but it can still be helpful as one image among many. Richard Leonard, a Jesuit priest and author, once said that when you imagine God as parent, you can imagine the best of all possible parents.

Using the metaphor of God as parent, then, you might ask yourself: Doesn't a parent sometimes enjoy being playful with a child? When you see a father throwing his child up in the air or a mother tickling her baby, you are seeing a human sign of this loving playfulness.

Look at God looking at you . . . and smiling.

—Anthony de Mello, Indian Jesuit priest

It is a wonder from the parents' perspective as well; playfulness is a gift for both parent and child. Indeed, one of the most delightful things about having two young nephews (now ages twelve and five) has been watching the progress of their intellectual, emotional, and spiritual development. They went from infants with tightly closed eyes, to babies exploring their surroundings, to toddlers learning to speak, and eventually to boys who carry on complicated conversations and, most astonishing of all, joke around. When my first nephew, Charles, made his first joke, it was a wonder to me—something of a shock even—and a vivid reminder that a sense of humor is a gift from God.

God is the One who delights in your own sense of humor and surprises you with life's funny moments. And in life's unexpected moments may be found signs of God's delight in your life. (We'll talk more about how to incorporate joy, humor, and laughter into your prayer in Chapter 9.)

Get Down Off Our Pedestal

In *God and the World,* Pope Benedict XVI says:

> I believe [God] has a great sense of humor. Sometimes he gives you something like a nudge and says, "Don't take yourself so seriously!" Humor is in fact an essential element in the mirth of creation. We can see how, in many matters in our lives, God wants to prod us into taking things a bit more lightly; to see the funny side of it; to get down off our pedestal and not to forget our sense of fun.[48]

7. Humor welcomes.

Hospitality is an important virtue in both the Old and New Testaments. In the Old Testament, Abraham and Sarah were rewarded for their hospitality toward three strangers with the gift of a son, which is my favorite story of biblical laughter.

In the Book of Genesis,[49] Abraham, age ninety-nine, is visited by three strangers. As part of a series of divine promises to the elderly man, God informs him that his almost-as-elderly wife, Sarah, will bear a child. Not surprisingly, Abraham laughs. A big laugh. Genesis describes it like this: "Then Abraham fell on his face and laughed, and said to himself, 'Can a child be born to a man who is a hundred years old? Will Sarah, who is ninety years old, bear a child?'"

Later on, Abraham and Sarah are visited by three mysterious strangers who turn out to be angels, or messengers of the Lord.* After Abraham offers them a meal, one of the visitors tells Abraham, again, that Sarah will soon conceive a child. This time Sarah herself overhears and laughs, probably even louder than Abraham first had!

Then the Lord asks Abraham why Sarah laughs at the thought of bearing a child and says, "Is anything too wonderful for the LORD?"

Sarah denies it, saying, "I did not laugh."

And the Lord answers, "Oh yes, you did laugh."

In time, Sarah has a child, and Abraham names him Isaac. But there's more to that name than meets the eye, because in Hebrew his name is Yitzhak, which means either "He laughs" or "He will laugh." Sarah rejoices in her good fortune. "God has brought laughter for me," she says. "Everyone who hears will laugh with me."

How wonderful! Commenting on this passage in his book *God*

---

* The relationship between the angels and "the Lord" is vague, according to the Oxford edition of the New Revised Standard Version of the Bible. The three may be individual angels; or they may be, taken together in their plurality, God. Or the third man may be "the Lord" and the other two his attendants. No matter what the interpretation, it is a striking story about hospitality in the ancient Near East and in the Jewish tradition.

Makes Me Laugh, Joseph Grassi says, "Faith in God concerns the humanly impossible; it is literally *ridiculous* in its root meaning, from the Latin *ridere* (to laugh)."

Sarah's story shows not only how laughter and hospitality are intimately bound together in the first Book of the Bible, but also how laughter is encoded into the spiritual DNA of the three great monotheistic religions, all of which recognize Abraham and Sarah as forebears in faith. In that foundational story is combined humor, hospitality, and holiness.

What is being rewarded is not only Abraham's and Sarah's faith, but their hospitality, a key virtue in the Bible. God encourages and rewards hospitality. A few Scripture scholars have even suggested that the real sin of Sodom and Gomorrah, and the reason that God condemned their inhabitants, was not their licentious or dissolute behavior, but their lack of hospitality.

In the New Testament, the act of welcoming Jesus into one's home was a sign of one's acceptance of Jesus. If a town didn't welcome the disciples, Jesus told them to leave that town and shake its dust off their feet.[50]

Jesus himself welcomed those who were outsiders into the community by forgiving their sins, healing them, and casting out demons. Jesus was always including people, welcoming, inviting, and bringing them in from the outside. As James Alison has noted, for Jesus there was no "other." All were welcome members of his community. By speaking to and healing "outsiders," those not part of the Jewish community, as well as eating at table with outcasts, Jesus was embodying God's hospitality.

Jesus's hospitality was the foundation of later patterns of Christian hospitality. In the Middle Ages, St. Benedict, in the set of rules for his religious order, gave his monks the dictum, *Hospes venit, Christus venit,* "The guest comes, Christ comes." For the Benedictines all guests were to be welcomed as Christ.

In the seventeenth century, St. Alphonsus Rodríguez, a Jesuit brother, worked as a porter, or doorkeeper, at the Jesuit college of

Sarah's Laugh

Here is the story of Sarah's laughter, from the Book of Genesis:

> [The angels who had been welcomed] said to [Abraham], "Where is your wife Sarah?" And he said, "There, in the tent." Then one said, "I will surely return to you in due season, and your wife Sarah shall have a son." And Sarah was listening at the tent entrance behind him. Now Abraham and Sarah were old, advanced in age; it had ceased to be with Sarah after the manner of women. So Sarah laughed to herself, saying, "After I have grown old, and my husband is old, shall I have pleasure?" The LORD said to Abraham, "Why did Sarah laugh, and say, 'Shall I indeed bear a child, now that I am old?' Is anything too wonderful for the LORD? At the set time I will return to you, in due season, and Sarah shall have a son." But Sarah denied, saying, "I did not laugh"; for she was afraid. He said, "Oh yes, you did laugh.". . .
>
> The LORD dealt with Sarah as he had said, and the LORD did for Sarah as he had promised. Sarah conceived and bore Abraham a son in his old age, at the time of which God had spoken to him. Abraham gave the name Isaac to his son whom Sarah bore him. And Abraham circumcised his son Isaac when he was eight days old, as God had commanded him. Abraham was a hundred years old when his son Isaac was born to him. Now Sarah said, "God has brought laughter for me; everyone who hears will laugh with me."

Majorca, in Spain. His job was to greet all the students, faculty, and visitors who rapped on the great wooden door. The humble Jesuit had a wonderful way of reminding himself to be cheerful and hospitable to all visitors, and—though he was not a Benedictine—welcome them as if they were Jesus himself. Upon hearing someone knocking on the door, he would say, "I'm coming, Lord!" Both Benedict and Alphonsus were repeating Jesus's hospitality to outcasts as well as Abraham and Sarah's earlier hospitality to the divine strangers who visited them.

Humor is a unique way of showing hospitality. Perhaps the easiest way to get people to feel at home is to make them laugh. You know that a social gathering is successful, and that people feel at home, when laughter breaks out. Humor helps people to relax, to feel comfortable, to let down their guard. Laughing with others tells them that you enjoy their presence. Humor welcomes. Here's an example from my own life.

During my Jesuit training I worked for two years with the Jesuit Refugee Service in Nairobi, Kenya. At the end of my first year I signed up for an eight-day retreat at the Jesuit retreat house in Nairobi. The spacious retreat house grounds are at the foot of the Ngong Hills, near the house of the author Isak Dinesen, the pen name of Karen Blixen, author of *Out of Africa*.

On the last day of the retreat, there was a celebratory dinner. After the meal, it was announced that everyone would speak about our experience of the retreat. What was it like? How had we experienced God? "Uh oh," I thought. Even though I had worked in Kenya for a year, I was still living in an unfamiliar culture and was worried about speaking publicly. Maybe I would say the wrong thing and inadvertently offend someone. As I uncomfortably shifted in my seat, one of the sisters urged me, "You first!"

When I looked around I realized that, oddly, the few other men—the priests and brothers on retreat—had already departed. I was the only man left. So I shyly stood up and saw fifty African sisters waiting for me to say something.

I blurted out, "I guess I'm the only man here."

From across the room an African sister called out, "And blessed are you among women!" Everyone laughed at this line from Scripture, and I felt right at home and could talk about my retreat with them.[51] Laughter had welcomed me.

8. Humor is healing.

Physicians, psychologists, and psychiatrists have shown how laughter helps the healing process in the physical body. Laughter releases endorphins, powerful chemicals that can relax the body, reduce stress, relieve feelings of frustration, and produce an overall feeling of well-being. Scientists know that endorphins also produce a natural analgesic, which serves as a barrier to pain. Researchers have also found that laughter causes enlargement of the inner lining of blood vessels, which increases blood flow and promotes a sense of physical well-being. Finally, laughter cleanses the body of the stress hormone cortisol.

For more on the intangible benefits of laughter, let's turn to an expert. Jordan Friedman is a professional "stress reducer" who lives in New York. As a child, he was diagnosed with a large brain tumor. After multiple brain surgeries, years of vision loss, and what he describes as "pretending to be normal," he became a public health expert who uses his experiences to help others to deal productively with life's challenges, changes, and crises. Now armed with a master's degree in public health, Friedman is a popular lecturer both in corporate conference rooms and on college campuses. He is also the author of *The Stress Manager's Manual.* Recently I asked him about the link between humor and laughter and a healthy emotional and spiritual life.

"Humor and laughter are potent and plentiful stress reducers and spirit boosters, because they simultaneously help us physically and emotionally," he said. As many in the field do, he pointed to Norman Cousins's now-classic book *Anatomy of an Illness,* in which the author chronicled the use of Marx Brothers films in the daily treatment of severe arthritis. "Laughter strengthens the immune function, decreases muscle tension, and increases our tolerance for pain. Humor breaks negative thought cycles and releases feelings of anxiety, sadness, and fear," said Friedman. Laughter helps even healthy bodies, say many doctors. Besides increasing endorphins and reducing cortisol, it can ease anxiety disorders, increase respiration, and even burn calories.

A cheerful heart is a good medicine,
but a downcast spirit dries up the bones.
—Proverbs 17:22

But the phenomenon is not simply a private one; it is communal, as he pointed out. "When we laugh with others, we feel more connected with them in the world. All of these benefits add up to a less burdened spirit and thus a greater ability to create, think clearly, solve problems, and help others."

Here's an example. The week before my ordination to the priesthood—the culmination of years of training—I got horribly sick. Just a few days before I was to travel to Boston for the ordination Mass, which my friends and family were planning to attend, I contracted a miserable virus. In the middle of one night, I grew so sick that an older priest named Vin had to accompany me to the hospital emergency room.

It was an exceedingly generous act. At that time Vin was about seventy years old and serving as the temporary superior of our Jesuit community. He had just returned from a grueling trip to eastern Europe, where he was training Jesuit and lay teachers. Though he was dog tired, Vin graciously volunteered to accompany me to the hospital and spend a few hours there with me.

In a taxicab on the way over, I grew furious. How could God "make" me sick during the week of my ordination? After all I had done for God, how could God do such a thing? Worse, what if I couldn't make the ordination Mass? What if I were too sick to attend? What if everybody showed up and I wasn't there?*

Once inside the emergency room, the hospital staff asked me to take off my clothes and don an embarrassingly revealing blue paper gown. Sitting on a metal table, cold, sick, and miserable, I felt ready to explode from frustration.

Finally, I said to Vin, "I'm sorry, but I need some emergency spiritual counseling. I have to ask you something."

Vin said, "Go ahead."

"I can't believe that this is happening! Why is God doing this to me?"

Vin looked at me levelly and said, with mock seriousness, "God is punishing you for all of your wicked sins!"

We both burst out in laughter. His joke helped me to laugh at myself and see how ridiculous I was being. God wasn't "doing" anything to me. I was just sick. Why should I be exempt from the human condition? Even Jesus had a human body and presumably got sick.

In a few days I felt much better and ended up perfectly healthy at my ordination ceremony. Vin's little joke, it seemed, helped me on the road to healing.

"If someone is trying to heal, humor offers a way to balance one's perspective," said Eileen Russell, the clinical psychologist who has written on the idea of resilience. "It's easy to become myopic about personal pain, and we can get stuck in negative ways of thinking. A sense of humor keeps you from going down too far."

Humor also helps us to endure suffering by giving us something of a break and reminding us that pain is not the last word for the one who believes in God. Having a friend encourage you to laugh during your time of suffering, pain, or struggle is a great grace. Is there anything more welcome than finally, after a period of trial, being able to laugh again?

---

* "What ifs" that cause us to worry about the future are usually a dead end in the spiritual life. So are "if onlys," when they prompt us to fret about the past. Although I knew that at the time, I couldn't keep myself from despairing.

In his book *The Wit of Martin Luther,* Eric W. Gritsch points out that Luther, who suffered at the hands of the Catholic Church (and also suffered from a variety of physical ailments),* used humor as a way of surviving from day to day. "There is overwhelming evidence from Luther's life and work," Gritsch writes, "to prove that for him at least, humor, next to music, was the most effective way to endure the trials of the penultimate life. In his way of thinking and being, smiling, laughing, and even mocking become the divinely inspired means of spiritual survival. Knowing of the happy end at the Last Day, Luther could remain cheerful in anticipating it." Simply put, humor gets us through life.

Humor may heal "bodies" in another way. If Christians take seriously St. Paul's beautiful image of the church as the "Body of Christ," we might consider that the same holds true for the Christian community. In the midst of some difficult times for churches, people could use, from time to time, some laughter.

That's not to say that one laughs *about* the pain or sin in church settings—like abuses of power, sexual abuse, or financial misconduct. Rather, humor gives us a much-needed break and so can help us heal. "Life brings many a difficulty with it," writes Bernard Häring. "Our heart sinks at the prospect of death. . . . But the joy of the Lord is our bulwark, our strength, our power."

Pastor Charles Hambrick-Stowe, a Protestant scholar and pastor of the First Congregational Church of Ridgefield, Con-

* According to Gritsch, Luther suffered from a variety of ailments, including kidney stones, gallstones, frequent insomnia, headaches, and angina. With his friends, he frequently used a certain "gallows humor" as a weapon against despair. In his last year of life he wrote an old colleague: "Farewell in the Lord, my Reverend Father! Both of us are old; perhaps in a short while we will have to be buried. My torturer, the [kidney] stone, would have killed me on St. John's Day, had God not decided differently. I prefer death to such a tyrant."

necticut, told me the story of an elderly woman, a "wonderful lady," whose husband was living with Alzheimer's. When one member of a couple suffers from this illness, it is always a difficult situation for the spouse. Still, she shared a funny story with a group of fellow church members and showed her ability to recognize humor admidst pain.

The woman said her husband had reached the point where he was unable to recognize her. One day she visited him in the nursing home and asked, "Do you know who I am?"

Her husband said, "You're my wife."

She was delighted that he had remembered.

Then he pointed to the nurses' station and said, "And I've got four more over there!"

Pastor Hambrick-Stowe said, "Whenever I tell that story, I also tell people that my mother had Alzheimer's, so they know that I'm not trying to make light of anything. But this church member was the kind of woman who even in the midst of tragedy could tell a funny story, and that helped her, and it helps me."

9. Humor fosters good human relations.

Humor is important not only for those who work in an official capacity in an institutional religion, but in any work environment. Humor fosters good human relations and so naturally helps in many social settings, particularly when the group is faced with a difficult task. In his parables, for example, Jesus used a little mirth to help people understand difficult topics.

Consider a more secular example of the use of humor in human relations. In Doris Kearns Goodwin's book *Team of Rivals,*[52] she details how Abraham Lincoln gathered together a very different group of men to form his Cabinet. On many occasions these men (some of whom had opposed one another in their former political lives) disagreed violently with each other, quarreled with one another, and even plotted against one another.

One way that Lincoln lightened the atmosphere or made a point in this contentious group, without offending anyone, was to tell a good joke or a "country story" to illustrate his point. In fact, on the last day of his life, after a long conversation about serious political matters, Lincoln sought to help his Cabinet relax with a few country stories. Humor can make for good social relations.

That goes for religious organizations too, where human interactions can be fraught with tension, since everyone tends to think that they are on "God's side"—and therefore correct. Once, before the Second Vatican Council, the great council of bishops and archbishops that would change the Catholic Church in the early 1960s, John XXIII picked up a preparatory document and saw a list of condemnations of theologians and theological propositions. He found it overly harsh. Rather than arguing with the men who wrote it or discussing his theological objections, he simply picked up a ruler, measured the document, and said, "Look, there are thirty centimeters of condemnations here!"

Pastor Hambrick-Stowe told me that he prefers to run meetings with a healthy amount of humor—coming from him. "When I used to work at a seminary one of the secretaries would say, 'All I hear from your meetings is laughter!' The laughter pierced the walls, even if the words didn't," he said. "But it helps in meetings not to take yourself so seriously. It takes a bit of ego strength, but it helps everyone to relax."

Humor reduces stress, the number one reason for workers' compensation claims. It may also help in encouraging creativity and flexibility on the job. In the 1980s, the *New York Times* published an article entitled, "Humor Found to Aid Problem-Solving,"[53] in which the reporter, Daniel Goleman, summarized a number of psychological studies suggesting that telling jokes that put people in a good mood enables them to "think through" problems with greater ingenuity. (Goleman, who later wrote *Emotional Intelligence,* reported on behavioral sciences for many years at the *Times.*)

"Any joke that makes you feel good is likely to help you think more broadly and creatively," said Alice M. Isen, a psychologist then working at the University of Maryland. Another study found that people who had watched a comic movie were better able to make connections and see complex interactions. "They think of things they ordinarily would not and have access to a broader range of mental material. And the more ideas present in your mind, the more ways you see to connect things; you're able to see more solutions," said Isen. More recently, Eileen Russell, the clinical psychologist, told me, "When we're in a negative frame of mind, we're much more conservative in our problem solving."

Humor helps in all social settings, even the most intimate ones. Another psychologist, John Gottman, who specializes in marriage and parenting, notes that for couples who are married for more than seven years, the most consistent predictor of divorce is the absence of laughter. "Our marriages are only as good as our histories of laughter together."[54]

Now, this is an area that you might not think I know much about—I'm a celibate priest, after all—but it's very easy to notice in married friends. One of my married friends recently told me that humor between spouses (or boyfriends and girlfriends, for that matter) can be a powerful form of affection. The playful teasing humor of a couple, gently poking fun at one another's habits or foibles, is a delight to see, particularly among couples who have been together for long periods of time. Sharing a laugh can be an act of love.

Humor sometimes both depends on and builds relationships. Perhaps the person who "gets" our jokes the best is the one with whom we have shared the most. As well, humor can cement the bonds of friendship and love in often playful and highly personal ways.

Funny enough, this point was beautifully elaborated in an unexpected way not long ago, when I was giving a lecture at Yale University. I had been invited to speak at More House, the center for

Catholic students on campus. During my talk, I touched on the idea of humor as a way of building community and fostering good social relations. Afterward I signed a few books and chatted with the students and faculty who attended the lecture. Around eight o'clock, the Catholic chaplain motioned that it was time for dinner at a local haunt in New Haven with his staff, some friends, and a few university students.

On that cold and rainy night, the crowd of us huddled under umbrellas. Suddenly, one of the students I had met earlier appeared before me, breathless after running to catch up with us. "Father Martin," he said, "I was thinking about what you said about humor and community." Then, to my surprise, he opened his mouth and declaimed an almost letter-perfect disquisition on the topic. That he was able to do so with such clarity made me laugh out loud.

"That's wonderful!" I said to Griffin Oleynick, age twenty-four, a graduate student in Italian literature. "Will you write that up so that I can include it in my book on humor?"

"Sure," he said cheerfully.

A few weeks later, he sent me this summary of the connection between humor and community, which you should imagine delivered on a rainy night as our group splashed through puddles. I've edited it only slightly:

> Humor and community are intimately linked. In an intuitive way, we get the feeling that jokes are best enjoyed in the company of friends. We tell them at school, at work, at the bar, and at home. They demonstrate intimacy, trust, and a sense of togetherness among those who both tell jokes and listen to them. Thus one of the most important elements of humor is the intimate connection it fosters among the members of a community. Through jokes we also show our affection for the people who are most important in our lives. By joking with other people we are, in effect, taking care of them and

simultaneously telling them that we love them. And by inviting more people to share the same joke, our community expands and becomes more open to the presence of others.

Jokes affirm a group's identity and, at the same time, make that community far richer by attracting new members. Yet the importance of humor extends farther. Jokes and humor may also be viewed as evidence of the changes that occur in the community over time. They point to a shared history, a common past that consists of a litany of dangers, trials, and occasional bouts of real suffering and genuine hardship. Humor does more than simply "smooth over" or "take the edge off" these rough times. It literally reverses the sentiment of despair into its opposite: hope. Humor thus performs the Janus-like task of looking backwards and forwards in time. It recalls the past, and it sets it squarely before our gaze. Yet humor, the language of hope and joy, turns our eyes even more resolutely toward the future. By telling a joke we affirm that our relationships are vitally healthy and ongoing, and thus open to change, to further development, to continual deepening—in short, jokes open our lives and our communities to God.

10. Humor opens our minds.

When we laugh, we release endorphins, which helps us to relax. Psychologists say that when we relax and feel less threatened, we are more able to listen and learn. It's the opposite of the fight-or-flight response, in which a real or perceived threat increases stress, builds up tension, and makes it more difficult to listen. By relaxing listeners, laughter can therefore help to get a message across. And, as mentioned above, it may help us think more "broadly" or creatively.

Likewise, laughter can signal a sudden spiritual insight. Often, in spiritual direction (that is, the practice of talking about a person's prayer life) when people finally realize how foolish or sinful or selfish they have been acting, they laugh. Why do they laugh? It's funny to be reminded of how human we are, and it's joyful to know that we have been given insight by God. It's a laugh of recognition. Let me tell you two stories about that.

Not long ago at a retreat, an elderly woman (I'll keep the details vague) told me that she had a hard time praying with her imagination. St. Ignatius Loyola encouraged people to enter imaginatively into Scripture scenes as one way of prayer. Visibly discouraged, she said that she had tried using her imagination in prayer, but had given up, admitting that she simply was too literal-minded. "I simply don't have an imagination," she said sadly. Others seemed to be able to do this kind of prayer, but not her.

Then I had an inspiration. A question came to mind that seemed risky but worth asking. "Has your imagination ever led you to think about sex?" I asked.

She let out a booming laugh, seemingly from the bottom of her soul. She laughed and laughed and laughed. "Yes, it has!" she said finally.

"Well, then, I guess you *do* have an imagination!" I said. Then we both laughed. Later during that retreat she was able to pray with her imagination and pictured herself speaking with Jesus, which delighted her. Her laughter betokened a sort of release, a newfound freedom. It was a sign of God's presence.

On another retreat I was giving spiritual direction to an older man who was practical, hardworking, and efficient. (Again, I am changing some details.) He had spent many years working diligently at his job. For him life was about being productive. But now that he was getting older, he was becoming frustrated. As aging had slowed him down, he felt less "productive." It was difficult even to be on retreat, because he didn't think that *that* was productive. Part of his problem, in both prayer and daily life, was an overemphasis on "results."

Unlike the retreatant I just mentioned, this man had no trouble praying imaginatively and in fact enjoyed it. So I asked him to pray using the image of Jesus as a young man during the period between the ages of twelve and thirty, before he had started his public ministry. During those years Jesus was, as far as we know, not preaching or performing any miracles. He was simply working in a carpentry shop in Nazareth, plying his trade and living a simple life.

At one point, as he imagined watching Jesus working in the carpentry shop, he found himself saying to Jesus, "Why don't you start healing people *now*? You're wasting all this time! You're not being very efficient!"

When he recounted this to me, I said, "You told Jesus that he wasn't productive?"

Then he smiled and began to laugh.

In that imaginative exercise, God seemed to have revealed to him that productivity wasn't the only goal in life. That insight let him relax, pray in a more relaxed way, and ultimately see that it was okay for him to be a "human being" from time to time instead of just a "human doing."

With both of these people, laughter was a sign of their being freed from old ways of thinking, from being bound to old habits. It was a sign of God's liberation.

11. Humor is fun.

There may be no better reason for humor than that it's fun. Not everything has to have a purpose. That is, God may be giving us humor as an outright gift.

It reminds me of the story, perhaps apocryphal, of the composer Franz Schubert. Once he sat down and played a new composition for a friend. Afterward the friend said, "But what does it mean?" Schubert sat down, played the piece again, and said, "*That's* what it means!" Joy, humor, and laughter are their own rewards.

Fun—a word you don't hear much in church—is also a foretaste of heaven and, for Christians, an important spiritual goal. "The entire message of the gospel should result in joy," said the Reverend Ann Kansfield, pastor of Greenpoint Church in Brooklyn, New York, a Dutch Reformed Protestant congregation.

"What else can we do but be full of joy at the news that God loves us, that God forgives us, and that God saves us from ourselves?" said Kansfield. "This is not a dogma of sadness and pain, but freedom and joy. And we ought to respond as Sarah did—with laughter. Because if God can forgive someone like me, then the least I can do is to respond with joy and gratitude!"

The saints understood this, and I would bet that the man whose first miracle was to turn water into wine at the wedding feast of Cana understood the need to have some high spirits in life.

11½. Humor is often practical.

Here's my half reason, which is not exactly a spiritual one. Humor can serve some eminently practical purposes too. It might even save you some money. To that end, one of my favorite real-life stories.

My father's cousin, named Bernie, lived in Philadelphia, but owned a small store on the coast of southern New Jersey (affectionately called "the shore.") One evening he was speeding down the highway, en route to his store. He was late for an appointment. It was also the last day of the month, the time when police officers were eager to make their monthly "quota" of citations for speeding tickets. So Bernie knew that the police would be especially vigilant to catch anyone speeding. Nonetheless, he was in a hurry, so he went far over the speed limit, almost eighty miles an hour.

Sure enough, not long after he crossed into New Jersey he saw a flashing red light in his rearview mirror. Bernie sighed and pulled over. The officer strode up to the car and motioned for Bernie to roll down his window. "I've been waiting for you all day!" said the pleased officer.

"Well," said Bernie, "I got here as fast as I could!"

The officer laughed so hard that he didn't give Bernie a ticket.

Joy, humor, and laughter should be part of everyone's spiritual life. They are gifts from God and help us enjoy creation. "A good laugh is a sign of love," said Karl Rahner. "It may be said to give us a glimpse of, or a first lesson in, the love that God bears for every one of us."

Chapter Five

I Awoke

How Vocation, Service, and Love Can Lead to Joy

In the previous few chapters, we've been looking at ways to find joy in everyday life—by being awake, aware, and attentive. But there is a danger. You could falsely assume that that joy is something that simply "happens" in life or something you just stumble upon. But joy is often the result of specific choices and can flow from the way you lead your life. That is, joy is often the result of your actions.

So let's look at joy as an outgrowth of specific areas in our lives: vocation, service, and love.

Vocation is an often misunderstood term. Some people still think the only people who have vocations are those in the clergy or who work for overtly religious organizations. But everyone has a vocation. The word comes from the Latin *vocare,* meaning "to call," and so vocation is something that you are called to.

Even the idea of a "call" is misunderstood. When people hear that a person felt "called" to the priesthood or life in a religious order, they occasionally think that it means hearing voices. (When the Jesuits phoned to tell me that I had been accepted into the novitiate, my sister quipped, "Oh, is that what they mean by *getting the call*?")

But most of the time the call manifests itself as a simple human desire. A medical student, for instance, may have discovered her interest in medicine when she first dissected a frog in junior high school, or found herself transfixed by a television series that featured doctors, or had a chance interaction with a family physician willing to talk to her about her work. At any of these points she might have said to herself, "Gee, this seems really interesting!" Likewise, a teacher may have intuited his vocation by realizing how much he liked being in the classroom, or how much he enjoyed tutoring younger students after school, or how much fun it was to help the teacher in class. In both of these situations, the person is awakening to a desire within. Vocations start with a desire, a simple heartfelt attraction to something you like.

Two other examples are taken not from the professional world, but the personal. A husband and a wife are drawn to one another through desires that are physical, emotional, and spiritual. Likewise, friends are drawn to one another out of mutual attraction. In both of these cases, people find their vocations to be spouses and friends.

But vocation is bigger than what you do, that is, your work, your job, or even your career. It's about who you are. Each of us has a unique vocation to become the person we are meant to be.

That may sound confusing, even a bit abstract, but it's as simple and as practical as this: God desires for us to be the freest, most mature, most loving, most alive person we can be. As the second-century theologian St. Irenaeus said, "The glory of God is the human person fully alive!"* In other words, God wants us to be our best selves. Our ultimate vocation is to become the person God wants us to be. And the first step in this journey is recognizing that our deepest desires—for satisfying work, for supportive community, and for healthy love—are holy desires, planted within us by God for our own happiness.

So desire is an important part of the spiritual life. Where does desire come from? Well, I believe that our deepest desires, our most

* "*Gloria Dei vivens homo!*" The next sentence of Irenaeus's famous insight is: "And the life of the human person is the vision of God."

heartfelt longings—not simply our surface wants and selfish needs—come from God. In our deepest longings we hear echoes of God's longing for us. And the more we can follow those deep-down desires, those that God places within us for our happiness, the more joyful we will find ourselves.

Of course distinguishing between our surface wants and deep desires requires some careful discernment. Just because I "want" something doesn't mean it's good for me. Christopher Ruddy, a professor of theology at the Catholic University of America, recently put it this way to me: "Another Quarter Pounder sometimes seems like a good idea—but I always regret it later. Only in hindsight do we see how God would not let us settle for our well-intentioned but limited desires, but called us—sometimes weeping and kicking—to something more enduring and satisfying."

The most lasting joy comes from following those deep desires and heartfelt longings that bring us closer to God. It makes sense if you think about it, because when we are acting in concert with what we feel God desires for us, things will feel in sync. St. Ignatius Loyola often spoke of feelings of "consolation" that come when we follow our deepest, holiest desires. In coming to know ourselves as capable of being moved by God's holy desires, and in choosing to strive to follow those invitations the best we can, we feel ourselves moving closer to God in trust, in hope, and in confidence. All this leads to joy. In other words, when we do what we are made for, we find joy.

Here's an example from my own life. During my time in Nairobi working with the Jesuit Refugee Service, I ended up getting too little sleep and working too many hours, and I came down with mononucleosis. As I lay on my sickbed, depressed, I started to wonder whether I should return home to the States. Maybe I wasn't cut out for this kind of work.

But after recuperating, I found myself in what was the best job I've ever had: helping refugees from all over East Africa—Uganda, Sudan, Ethiopia, Rwanda, Burundi, and Somalia—start small businesses to help support themselves. Many of the refugees brought with them from their home countries incredible creative skills. So, for example, we sponsored Rwandan women who made beautiful sisal baskets, Ugandan men who created beautiful oil paintings, and Ethiopian women who embroidered gorgeously colored shirts.

In time we opened up a little shop on the outskirts of a slum, where we could market some of these refugee-made handicrafts to expatriates and wealthier Kenyans. It dawned on me that the work was a marvelously unexpected use of my earlier training in business, my enthusiasm for arts and crafts—and even my pushy personality, which helped us sell to customers reluctant to part with their money. It seemed that God was using all of the talents I brought to Africa, talents I thought I would never use again. Who could have guessed when I was studying accounting and marketing that I would be using them in service of African refugees rather than corporate America? As the saying goes, God writes straight with crooked lines.

In this I discovered immense joy. It seemed I was in precisely the right place—and what a wonderful experience that was, after years of being miserable in the corporate world, where I felt like a square peg in a round hole. Although business is a terrific vocation for some people, it wasn't for me. It had taken a while to discover my own vocation in life, but once I did, I was happy—and I had never been happier "on the job" than when I was working with the refugees. Working in Nairobi helped me to see how joy can flow naturally from discovering your vocation.

St. Thomas Aquinas goes even farther. He suggests that when we discover something for which we are made, it not only leads to joy; it "expands" us. This is from his comprehensive work of theology, the *Summa Theologica:*

> Now expansion denotes a kind of movement toward breadth; and it belongs to pleasure in respect of the two things requisite for pleasure. One of these is on the part of the apprehensive power, which is cognizant of the conjunction with some suitable good. As a result of this apprehension, a person per-

> ceives that he has attained a certain perfection, which is a magnitude of the spiritual order: and in this respect a person's mind is said to be magnified or expanded by pleasure.[55]

When St. Thomas is talking about "apprehending" something, he's talking about understanding it in the most profound way. So when individuals see that they have moved toward a "suitable good" (in this case, the life they were meant for), they not only experience pleasure, but a certain "expansion." Thus, discovering and living out our vocation, what God wants us to do and become, leads to joy. Sometimes this achievement comes quickly and relatively easily; other times, slowly and only with difficulty. But it always leads to joy.

Often overlooked in some religious circles is the notion that following your vocational desires leads not only to joy, but to fun too. Several years ago, for example, I spent a summer in Milford, Ohio, at a Jesuit retreat house learning how to direct retreats, along with two Jesuit friends. It was an inordinately busy schedule. Kevin, Dave, and I spent the mornings in classes studying the varieties of ways that people pray and the subtle techniques of spiritual direction. "Team meetings" with the other spiritual directors took place at noon. From twelve-thirty to one we gulped down a hurried lunch. Then came three or four hours of giving spiritual direction to people on retreat. Mass was at five, where we were sometimes expected to preach. After dinner, the three of us were left to ourselves, and we spent the time watching movies (we saw everything that summer, no matter how cheesy), renting videos, and consuming an inordinate amount of ice cream at a Cincinnati hangout called Graeter's.

If the nights were relaxing, the days were a riot of activity. One morning the director of the program told us in solemn tones that if we wanted to be good spiritual directors, we needed to lead a contemplative life. We needed sufficient time in our days for quiet and prayer. At lunch, after we gobbled down a colossal meal of stuffed peppers, rice, and ice cream, the three of us hurried to meet with our retreatants. As we sprinted down the hallway of the retreat house, Kevin laughed, "This is so *contemplative*!"

That summer I realized not only how lucky I was to be doing this kind of work, how happy I was to have good Jesuit friends, and how a deep-down joy had filled my life, but what *fun* it all was. And how this fun was possible only because of responding to God's "call."

Service IS ANOTHER PART of life that is intimately connected to joy.

A quote I have long pondered over is one from the Indian writer and Nobel laureate Rabindranath Tagore (1861–1941). I found it in a book of quotations, randomly, before I entered the Jesuits, and it made a deep impression on me. It seemed to speak to a part of me that was ready to hear, but didn't understand. And I didn't begin to "apprehend" it until many years later. Tagore wrote:

> I slept and dreamt that life was joy. I awoke and saw that life was service. I acted and behold, service was joy.

What does that mean? For me, it seems to mean that in a sleeping, or unaware, state we might blindly believe that life should simply be joyful. We wonder, "Why can't I be happy all the time?" But looking around quickly shows us that life not is always like this; indeed, it is often filled with great suffering.

Awaking from our slumber, we see that an important aspect of life is service. Much of life is about doing things for other people and sometimes doing things we'd rather not do, whether out of laziness, fear, or resentment over having so many responsibilities. But in acting out of service—for religious reasons or otherwise—we discover a unique joy that often comes only with helping others.

That probably sounds Pollyannaish, as if I'm trying to lure you into a life of selfless service by promising you joy. And it's true that not every act of service is joyful.

When I was a Jesuit novice, for instance, I worked in a homeless shelter in Boston, and from time to time I would work in the kitchen. One day, I spent hours making a huge tub of fresh mashed potatoes for the guests of the shelter. Then I spent another hour ladling out gravy on top of the mashed potatoes for the men waiting in line. After that, I sat down next to one of the men, who was very grumpy that day—not surprising for an indigent man forced to live outdoors in the frigid New England winter—and spent an hour listening to him talk about his problems.

At the end of a long day, I helped clean the kitchen, sweep the floors, and replace the pots and pans on the appropriate shelves. After I was finished, I bade farewell to my fellow volunteers, put on my coat, and walked out the door. There was that same man I'd listened to for an hour, leaning against the brick wall of the homeless shelter, calmly smoking a cigarette.

"How about some money?" he asked.

Maybe he didn't remember me, I thought. But I had just seen him a few minutes before. I told him I was sorry, but I didn't have any cash—which was true, since as novices we had almost no money to ourselves.

"Screw you!" said the fellow with whom I'd spent all that time.

I didn't feel very joyful then, but that marks the exception. Over the past twenty-two years as a Jesuit, I have worked in a variety of what you might call service-related positions. While a novice in Boston, beside the time at the homeless shelter, I worked in a hospital for the seriously ill. Also during my novitiate, I worked with Mother Teresa's sisters in the slums of Kingston, Jamaica, in a hospice for the sick and dying. During philosophy studies in Chicago, I worked with gang members and at a community center helping unemployed men and women find jobs. After that came my two years in Kenya with refugees. That work was probably the most concentrated time spent in "service." It would take me into some of the worst slums in the world and introduce me to some people who were certainly the poorest of the poor, and yet whose great faith astonished me.

Later, during my theology studies in Cambridge, Massachusetts,

I worked as a prison chaplain, spending time with men and women from poor backgrounds who had sometimes committed terrible crimes—though most were convicted not for violent crimes, but for possession of narcotics—and who were desperate for someone to talk to. And since ordination I continue to do service in the form of sacramental ministry like hearing confessions, presiding at funerals, and accompanying people in difficult times.

These works all brought me joy. Maybe not all the time—but what work does? It would be like asking parents, "Do your children always bring you joy?" They would probably laugh and say, "Not all the time!" But then they would smile and say yes.

Why does service lead to joy? Why was Tagore right? Let me suggest a few reasons.

First, service takes us out of ourselves. So much of our contemporary lives is self-centered. (This would have surprised men and women from centuries past, whose lives were more focused on the family and the larger community.) It's an almost unavoidable aspect of our culture, which often encourages us to concentrate almost exclusively on our own needs. On top of that, there is something in human nature, particularly in our more childish moments, that tempts us to focus exclusively on our physical and emotional needs.

Of course some self-care is important. Jesus asked us to love others as ourselves. But if you don't love yourself, you can't follow Jesus's injunction. One of my theology professors, James F. Keenan, S.J., used to speak of a triad of Christian love: love of God, love of neighbor, and love of self. And loving yourself includes caring for yourself.

Taken to the extreme, however, this can lead to a complete focus on oneself. Solipsism. Narcissism. Selfishness. And I'm sure you've met people who are utterly focused on themselves, concerned only with their own needs, complaining whenever their own small world is intruded upon. Those people generally are unhappy.

Recently a friend told me an incredible story of solipsism. Rick Curry is a Jesuit priest as well as talented actor and teacher who was born without a right arm. He has worked for many years with the disabled and founded the National Theatre Workshop of the Handicapped, which helps to train disabled actors. One day, he met a Jesuit friend who had broken his right arm. Rick asked what happened. His friend described in great detail his accident and then said, with no trace of irony, "You have no idea how inconvenient it is not to be able to use your right arm!" This is the extreme of self-focus.

Service liberates us from that self-enclosed prison. It broadens our perspectives by reminding us that everyone struggles and that no life is free of pain. It also helps us to move beyond our own problems. It makes us "other-directed." Service orients us outward in a healthy way.

Second, service to the poor helps to remind us of what we already have in life and helps to increase our gratitude. This became evident to me in Kenya. One of the clearest explanations of this phenomenon comes from a short book called *Dialogue of Life: A Christian Among Allah's Poor*. It is the memoir of Bob McCahill, a Maryknoll missionary priest who worked for many years among the Muslim poor of Bangladesh. In response to the question about how Christian religious personnel are "evangelized" by the poor, McCahill speaks eloquently about how much one receives when one works with the poor. Many of these reflections could apply to working with any person in great need:

> It seems to me that the poor evangelize us by giving us various types of good example. They instruct us in patience by their patience under adversity. They edify us by their uncomplaining struggles. They inspire us by undergoing suffering without becoming bitter. They encourage us to face our own problems more bravely by grappling with the pain in their lives. They teach us about the simplicity with which one can live a human life. They offer us a model for prayer life by their dependence on God: that is, in times of great need they look to God before all else. They do not appeal

> to God secondly or lastly after other possibilities have failed them. When we witness their efforts to survive with dignity amidst the hardships they constantly encounter, they help us to put into perspective our own overblown problems. Through the struggling poor we begin to understand how good God is to us and how stingy we are with our thanksgiving to God. If we think about them deeply enough, they put us to shame, for, though they are oppressed, they can still laugh and sing.

Of course the poor with whom we work are not simply there to "do" something for us. McCahill's book is primarily about friendship and love, not instrumentality. But working in any sort of service—with a sick person, with a lonely shut-in, in an organization that deals with the underprivileged—reminds us to be grateful for what we have. This gratitude can ground us in a confidence in the God who cares for us, which leads to the joy that comes from trust.

Third, service brings us into contact with people in new ways, and this enables us to meet God in new ways. In helping others, we move out of our own comfort zones into unexpected places of vulnerability, where it is often easier to meet God. This is not to say that God forces us to become vulnerable, but rather that, when we are in unfamiliar places and our defenses are down, it may be easier for God to break in. Service, which often can be profoundly disconcerting—say, when you're caring for a sick relative—can lead us to God in new ways, and often to joy.

Those in need of service who have themselves accepted the reality of their situation are often carriers of joy. And there are few things in life more astonishing than the good spirits maintained by those facing difficulties in life. One woman I met on a pilgrimage to Lourdes, the French shrine, whose body was crippled with a muscle-wasting disease, listened to my sympathetic remarks about her illness and then said, "Oh, it's not so bad!" Not just her faith, but her good humor filled me with joy.

Bob McCahill closes his meditation on the poor by saying, "Still, the safest answer to give to the question 'How do the poor evangelize us?' is to recall that God is with them. God is a mystery to us, and God's way of working through the poor is beyond our analysis."

Fourth and finally, service can be fun. I might add to Tagore's quote: "I worked and found that service was fun." This is an often ignored piece of spiritual wisdom. In Kenya, I felt that when I was helping others and making a difference, my life was not only purposeful, but fun. How much more enjoyable could life be than laughing with the Ugandan refugee who had sold her first embroidered shirt, or delighting with the group of Ethiopians over the opening of a restaurant in a slum?

The refugees themselves were fun to be around. Perhaps that sounds odd to say about people whose lives—lived in squalid slums far from home, haunted by memories of family members killed or wounded in their war-torn homes—seemed far from "fun," but it was true. Their beguiling lightheartedness and sunny humor made my life fun. They often, for example, encouraged me to laugh at myself.

Early on in my time in Kenya, I met a Ugandan refugee named Khadija, who was pregnant. After I helped her with her small business (making straw mats), she told me that if her baby was a boy she would name him after me. Imagining this to be simply a polite gesture and that she couldn't possibly be serious, I thanked her.

A few months later, Khadija popped by the office with a tiny infant tied to her back with a colorful cloth. With a deft motion she untied the cloth, cradled the baby in her arms, and handed him to me. "This is James Martin," she said. I was so stunned that I laughed out loud.

After I thanked her profusely, Khadija told me that since the baby's baptism was approaching, she could use money for a few things, specifically, a baptismal garment and a little party afterward. Needless to say, I chipped in, taking the money from my small Jesuit stipend. A few weeks later, I not only joined her at the church for James Martin's baptism, but hosted the party at our Jesuit community.

Surprisingly, a few weeks later another Ugandan refugee, named Irene, made the same announcement and request. Her soon-to-be-born baby would be called James Martin and could she please have some money for a baptism?

Soon afterward I was telling this story to Alice, another Ugandan refugee who had a delicious sense of humor and never tired of poking fun at my naïveté. She shook her head back and forth when I got to the part about giving Irene some money.

"Brother Jim," she said to me with a droll smile. "If Irene and Khadija name their babies James Martin, and if you give Khadija and Irene money for baby clothes, then surely, Brother, don't you see that soon there will be many, many babies in Nairobi named James Martin?" We both roared with laughter.

Another source of joy is *love*. This shouldn't surprise anyone with any knowledge of the human condition. Just talk to any people who have recently fallen in love; they are usually bursting with joy! Or spend time with two people about to get married; their delight is usually palpable. (That is, if they're not freaking out about the wedding plans.) Joy is one of the most obvious outgrowths of a loving relationship between two people. "Every day is a gift," said a young groom to me recently, a few days before his wedding.

Couples who've been married for several years know that married life isn't always joyful. Stresses and strains regarding children, money, and careers can make married life distinctly unjoyful. But the underlying love between husband and wife can lead to a deep-down joy.

But I'm not talking simply about romantic love. The love between friends is a true source of joy as well. Simply spending time with a close friend, doing the simplest and most ordinary things together, can lead to extraordinary joy.

None of this should be surprising, nor do I need to go on at length about how joy flows from friendship and love. What might be surprising, however, is the way the Bible includes stories that point to joy as an outgrowth of love.

Gerald O'Collins, whom I quoted earlier, is a Jesuit priest and a professor at the Pontifical Gregorian University in Rome and the author of over thirty books on Scripture and the spiritual life. In his book *Following the Way,* a series of meditations on the parables of Jesus, O'Collins reminds us that over and over again Jesus brings into his preaching a memorable image: the celebratory feast.

In the parable of the prodigal son, for example, the homecoming of the young son leads immediately to a family celebration. The father, exceedingly grateful for the unexpected return of his son, is so joyful that he rushes out to greet him. He showers the son with kisses. (This is *before* the son's apology, by the way.) Then, in celebration of his long-lost son's return, he plans to gather together all of his friends and family for what O'Collins calls a "feast of joy."

Jesus goes so far as to describe the father rebuking the older son, who refuses to forgive his formerly wayward brother and to share in his father's delight at his brother's repentance. "We had to celebrate and rejoice," says the father to the elder son, "because this brother of yours was dead and has come to life; he was lost and has been found."[56]

What O'Collins says about this parable made a deep impression on me when I first read it:

> Jesus reminds us how joy, even indescribable joy, is woven into the very texture of love. Joy inevitably accompanies real love and all those occasions which in a particular way celebrate and express our love for one another: a birth, baptism, a bar mitzvah, a wedding, an ordination, and even a funeral. We happily join our special friends or take part in family reunions. There is no more obvious spin-off from love than joy.

The parable of the prodigal son, as many Scripture commentators have noted, could just as easily be called the parable of the prodigal father. The father is "prodigal" in the sense of being lavishly generous with his love—something that undoubtedly surprises both of his sons, and surprises us.

Recently, I was on retreat with the Jesuits of my "province," in other words, the geographical region of which I am a member. Our regional superior invited us to Fairfield University, in Connecticut, where we were to spend one week of silent prayer. Before the retreat, I was worried that the gathering would turn out to be a series of discussions, meetings, and conferences rather than an actual silent retreat. (We Jesuits can be a talkative bunch.)

My fears were unfounded. The hundred or so Jesuits gathered for a brief reflection each morning, followed by Mass. For the rest of the day (except for meals—which were also in silence, to facilitate our prayer) we were free to pray where and when we wished. People unfamiliar with retreats may laugh at the notion of a hundred friends convening in a single place and not talking; but praying together with a group of people can be a powerful experience of community and friendship.

One sunny morning, I was sitting on a wooden bench in a stone plaza outside the campus chapel, waiting for Mass to begin. As I sat under the sunny sky, I watched dozens of individual Jesuits walk into the chapel: this one who had been a friend during a difficult time, this one whom I'd known for my entire Jesuit life, this one whom I'd studied with, this one who had helped me through a tough patch, this one who had been my spiritual director, this one who had been a kind community superior, this one who had been a wonderful source of laughter, and on and on. Into the chapel they walked. And so the chapel became for me a symbol of God's love for me, expressed through my brother Jesuits of the last twenty years. Suddenly I was filled with great joy about my Jesuit vocation. Recognizing the love that they had shown me led to my own joy.

And it surprised me! Perhaps as much as the prodigal son was surprised by his own good fortune at God's prodigal love. As Gerald O'Collins writes, "The last word about the divine love is that it will surprise us with joy—both in this life and in the life to come. Jesus has much to say about the boundless joy that our loving God holds out to us."

The closer one moves to God, the more one experiences a sense of deep joy. So for those following their heartfelt desires and living out their vocation, there will be joy. For those following God's call to care for the least of our brothers and sisters, there will be joy. And for those following God's invitation to love one another, there will be joy.

Joy is often an outgrowth not simply of following our vocation in life, but of helping those in need and of loving one another. So joy is not a selfish thing to seek, but a selfless thing to find.

A Study in Joy: The Visitation

Earlier we looked carefully at the use of joy in one particular biblical passage, Psalm 65, in which the hills were said to "gird themselves with joy." Now I would like to look at one of my favorite passages from the New Testament.

In the first chapter of the Gospel of Luke, the angel Gabriel appears to a young girl named Mary, who lives in the small town of Nazareth. The angel announces the birth of a son, to be named Jesus. Not surprisingly, Mary is at first fearful, and then doubtful. "How can this be," she says, "since I am a virgin?"*

In response, the angel offers an obscure answer. "The power of the Most High will overshadow you." Then, as if to remind Mary of God's power, he says, in effect, look at what God has already done. Her cousin Elizabeth is already pregnant, says the angel, even though

* Here's something I have always found mildly amusing. Earlier in Luke, Zechariah, the father of John the Baptist, encounters an angel one day while worshipping in the synagogue. He too is told of the upcoming birth of a son. Like Mary, Zechariah doubts. "How will I know that this is so? For I am an old man, and my wife is getting on in years" (1:18). In response to *his* doubting, he is struck dumb by the angel, while Mary's doubt prompts a kindly response from the angel. Zechariah is silenced by God; he can't speak until his son is born. It's the same angel too. Why the two different responses to doubt? Either Gabriel was having a bad day or he is gentler with women.

the elderly woman was thought to have been unable to conceive. "For nothing will be impossible with God," says Gabriel.

Seemingly satisfied with this answer and overcoming her initial fear and doubt, the young woman assents. "Let it be with me according to your word," Mary says.

This passage in the Gospel of Luke, called the Annunciation, is one of the most beautiful in the entire New Testament. It is also one of the most mysterious. Like many passages from Scripture it seems to raise as many questions as it answers.

For example, did an angel appear to Mary in precisely this way? Perhaps. After all, nothing is impossible with God. (If God could create the universe from nothing, then sending an angel to a young woman seems relatively easy.) Did her encounter with the transcendent mystery of God happen in another way—say, in a dream? Or was a meeting with an angel the best way that Mary could communicate an incommunicable story?

Who can say? We do not have access to Mary's inner life. As the esteemed Scripture scholar Joseph Fitzmyer, S.J., writes about this passage: "What really happened? We shall never know." The story of the Annunciation, beloved as it is, can seem completely removed from our human experience.

The next part of the story, however, may be easier to understand. "Mary set out and went with haste to a Judean town in the hill country." She is going to visit her cousin Elizabeth. This part of the tale, which I would like to focus on, is called the Visitation.

Why is Mary portrayed as traveling to the hill country? Several reasons suggest themselves. First, Elizabeth is elderly and so will need some help in childbirth. It would be natural for a young woman, once she heard news of her older cousin's pregnancy, to visit her. Perhaps Mary's parents even encouraged her to visit Elizabeth as part of her familial duties. On the other hand, the last verse of the passage, which says that Mary stayed for only three months, implies that she apparently left at the time of Elizabeth's greatest need—though perhaps Mary left as her own pregnancy was progressing.

Another possible reason for her journey is that Mary may have been frightened. Perhaps terrified by her strange encounter with the divine (in whatever way it occurred), she may have sought out the advice of an older woman. She may have had a close relationship with Elizabeth and felt the need to discuss her situation with her older cousin.

Perhaps at the time she felt closer to Elizabeth than to her parents. Who knows how Mary's parents responded to her situation? In Jewish law Joseph, to whom she was betrothed (a formal arrangement somewhere between engagement and marriage), would have been well within his rights to divorce her upon hearing of the pregnancy. Likewise, Mary's parents could be forgiven if they were not thrilled by her news, at least initially. Perhaps Mary's parents even sent their daughter away for her own good, until any scandal died down. Or the young woman may have feared her parents' reaction to what she knew would sound outlandish, ridiculous, even blasphemous.

Both concern for Elizabeth and her own fear may have motivated Mary's "haste" to visit "the hill country" of Judea. You can imagine her journeying to help a relative, to meet with someone who might help her make sense of her mysterious encounter and strange predicament, or simply to seek counsel from a wise, older woman.

But there is another possibility—*joy*. For the first words out of Mary's mouth when she meets Elizabeth are a jubilant song of praise. "My soul magnifies the Lord," says Mary, "and my spirit rejoices in God my Savior."

There are few more beautiful words in the entire Bible. The following verses have often been set to music and sometimes are called by the first word of the Latin translation of Mary's song, the *Magnificat*. "*Magnificat anima mea . . .*"

Mary is happy. The young Galilean woman, like most women then and now upon hearing such news, was filled with joy at the prospect of giving birth to a child. And she is filled with joy at the sight of Elizabeth, who is also expecting a child. Both of them are joyful at God's activity.

This is not so far from our own experience—man and woman

alike. Think of occasions when both you and a friend, or you and someone in your family, have received good news at the same time. Is there anything more joyous? Perhaps you have both passed a difficult course in school, you've both gotten into the college of your choice, or you've both received a promotion. How exciting it is to celebrate together! You want to be with your friend, to rush right over and share your dual joy. So Mary sets out "with haste." And on greeting Elizabeth she opens her mouth in praise.

Mary is filled with joy,* first, for what God has done for her. "For he has looked with favor on the lowliness of his servant," she says. "Surely, from now on all generations will call me blessed; for the Mighty One has done great things for me." Like many of us in times of good news, we feel as though we are bursting with joy and want to declare praise to God. If we receive a promotion, fall in love, find out that we are going to become parents, or get a good diagnosis from the doctor, we want to sing, with Mary, "My spirit rejoices in God my Savior."

Joy is the simplest form of gratitude.

—Karl Barth

But Mary is not only happy for herself; she is also grateful for what this means for Israel, for God's people. Her song now widens to include the larger community. God has reversed the fortunes of those who were suffering. God has heard the cries of the poor, those who were hoping for some sort of salvation. "He has scattered the proud in the thoughts of their hearts," she says. "He has brought down the powerful from their thrones, and lifted up the lowly; he has filled the hungry with good things, and sent the rich away empty." Who isn't joyful when they finally see things set right?

Mary's *Magnificat* is often used by Christians who work with the

* On a literal level as well you might say that she is "filled" with joy, for she is filled with Jesus.

poor and advocate on their behalf as a way of pointing to another reality: what the kingdom of God is like. In the kingdom of God, one of Jesus's favorite themes, things are finally made right; the lowly are lifted up, the proud are cast down from their thrones, the rich are sent away empty. In Jesus's ministry, a similar reversal of fortune happens, one that he himself brings about on earth: the blind see, the lame walk, the deaf hear.

God reverses things and upends our usual expectations, so that those who had been on the bottom are on the top. God has fulfilled his promises to his people. So Mary, a poor woman, is joyful.

Mary praises what God has done. Often the Hebrew and Christian Scriptures point to a hopeful future, based on the past. God has done this, and so God will do this in the future. The angel Gabriel says something of the same to Mary. Look what God has already done for Elizabeth. Fear not!

Scripture scholars note that the *Magnificat* is based largely on Hannah's prayer in 1 Samuel.[57] Mary's praise hews very closely to that of Hannah's, often called the "Song of Hannah." Thought to be barren, Hannah has given birth to Samuel. "My heart exults in the LORD; my strength is exalted in my God," she says. As in the *Magnificat,* Hannah goes on to praise God for reversing the fortunes of his people. "[The LORD] raises up the poor from the dust; he lifts the needy from the ash heap, to make them sit with princes and inherit a seat of honor."

What, then, are we to make of Mary's *Magnificat*? Did Luke simply place it in her mouth at that point in his narrative to link the story of Jesus to that of Samuel, an Old Testament figure? Perhaps. Some scholars even posit that the story was originally associated with Elizabeth, the older woman in the story, thought to have been barren.

But there is also the distinct possibility that Mary (and Elizabeth) knew the song of Hannah. A devout Jewish woman might have known of the story of a strong woman from her religious tradition. It would have been natural for her to make use of familiar images and language in her daily life, as it would be today for someone familiar with Scripture.

Mary is not the only one who is joyful. Elizabeth too seems overwhelmed not only by her own unexpected pregnancy, but by this amazing visit. When she first hears the voice of Mary, she exclaims with a loud cry: "Blessed are you among women, and blessed is the fruit of your womb. And why has this happened to me, that the mother of my Lord comes to me? For as soon as I heard the sound of your greeting, the child in my womb leaped for joy."

The child leaps for joy! Mothers know of the experience of a child moving—sometimes, mothers say, it feels like jumping—in their wombs. What a beautiful image is presented to us in Luke's Gospel. At the sound of Mary's voice, something literally stirs within Elizabeth. The child of course is John the Baptist, the cousin of Jesus, who will prepare the way for Jesus.

The baby's leap is a marvelous response to anyone who thinks that religion is about being gloomy. The Greek word used here is *agalliasis,* sometimes translated "exaltation." As another translation has it, the baby "leaped with gladness."[58] It is the same word used by Mary a few lines later, when she says that her own spirit "rejoices."

"The context makes clear that by leaping John recognizes his Lord, Jesus," says one commentator. "John's joy is the most appropriate response to God's fulfillment of promise in Jesus."[59] Joy is the response to the good news.

Mary is joyful. Elizabeth is joyful. Even the baby John leaps for joy.

Joy virtually *leaps* off the page in this story of the Visitation and in Mary's great *Magnificat.* Other Bible stories also reveal great joy, if we know where to look for it.

The Visitation and the *Magnificat* (Luke 1:39–56)

In those days Mary set out and went with haste to a Judean town in the hill country, where she entered the house of

Zechariah and greeted Elizabeth. When Elizabeth heard Mary's greeting, the child leaped in her womb. And Elizabeth was filled with the Holy Spirit and exclaimed with a loud cry, "Blessed are you among women, and blessed is the fruit of your womb. And why has this happened to me, that the mother of my Lord comes to me? For as soon as I heard the sound of your greeting, the child in my womb leaped for joy. And blessed is she who believed that there would be a fulfillment of what was spoken to her by the Lord."

And Mary said,

"My soul magnifies the Lord,
and my spirit rejoices in God my Savior,
for he has looked with favor on the lowliness of his servant.
Surely, from now on all generations will call me blessed;
for the Mighty One has done great things for me,
and holy is his name.
His mercy is for those who fear him
from generation to generation.
He has shown strength with his arm;
he has scattered the proud in the thoughts of their hearts.
He has brought down the powerful from their thrones,
and lifted up the lowly;
he has filled the hungry with good things,
and sent the rich away empty.
He has helped his servant Israel,
in remembrance of his mercy,
according to the promise he made to our ancestors,
to Abraham and to his descendants forever."

And Mary remained with her about three months and then returned to her home.

Chapter Six

Laughing in Church

Recovering Levity in the Community of Believers

Let's concentrate on one specific place where we need humor and laughter—religious institutions. In this chapter let's look at the use and presence of lightheartedness within churches and synagogues. I'll use the Catholic Church as my prime example, but you can easily apply these lessons to any denomination or religion, because they can all use a dose of joy.

Despite the seriousness of the call to preach the gospel; despite the ancient traditions of Christianity; despite the place of suffering in Christian spirituality; despite the sober writings of the church fathers; despite the grave issues that have faced the church throughout history; despite the fallout from some painful recent history, like the sexual abuse crisis in the Catholic Church; and despite widespread theological divisions that keep Christians separated, churches can still be, from time to time, very funny places.

For that we should be grateful. Thank God for salt, leaven, and light.* Thank God for salt in bland times, for leaven in flat times, for light in dark times. Humor is salt, light, and leaven. Humor is a gift to the church.

---

* Salt, light, and leaven are Gospel images. "If salt has lost its taste . . . it is no longer good for anything," says Jesus (Matt. 5:13). "Let your light shine before others," he says (Matt. 5:16). And although leaven (or yeast) is used negatively in his warning to beware of the "leaven of the Pharisees" (in one translation of Mark 8:15), normally it is used positively, as in the parable of the growth of the kingdom (Matt. 13:33; Luke 13:20–21). Today the image of leaven is used to show how even one or a few people can enliven an entire community, or the world.

It's Listening!

Real-life stories are often funnier than jokes. Here is one that features two friends. One was an elderly priest, renowned for his spiritual direction skills. The other was my friend Kevin, who was, at the time, a novice. The two met at a Jesuit gathering.

The priest asked, "So, Kevin, where are you from?"

"Boston," Kevin said. Then Kevin decided to ask this revered spiritual director an important question. "Father," said Kevin, "what would you say is the most important part of spiritual direction?"

The priest answered, "That's easy, Kevin. It's listening. You have to be a good listener. Listening is the key to being a good spiritual director."

"Thanks, Father. That's really helpful," Kevin said.

And the priest asked, "So, Kevin, where are you from?"

For all its dignity and grandeur and gravity, the Christian church is, like any institution, manifestly human. With that humanity comes some laughter, both intentional and unintentional. This is a gift from God, who wants us to enjoy ourselves, to appreciate the absurdities of life, and not to take ourselves so seriously, particularly in religious institutions, where it's easy to become deadly serious.

Is it any wonder that many people find religious settings stultifying? "The lack of humour and irritability into which we in the contemporary Church and contemporary theology have so often slipped is perhaps one of the most serious objections which can be brought against present-day Christianity," wrote Cardinal Walter Kasper, a German theologian and a Vatican official.[60]

Levity is still considered excessive in some churches. (Believe me, I've visited them and worshipped in them.) And when bishops, priests, sisters, brothers, ministers, pastors, elders, pastoral associates, music ministers, hospital chaplains, directors of religious education, and religious education teachers act as if they have the weight of the world on their shoulders, that no job is as difficult as theirs, and that they alone are responsible for doing God's work, then we're in trouble.

As mentioned in Chapter 2, there are several historical reasons for this downplaying of humor in church circles. John W. O'Malley, a distinguished Jesuit scholar and the dean of American Catholic historians, told me recently: "In strictly ecclesiastical or 'churchy' circles, humor has never, ever been a big thing. However, in the late Middle Ages and Renaissance, humor *about* religion was widespread in literature, for example, Boccaccio's *Decameron,* Chaucer's *Canterbury Tales,* Erasmus's colloquies and *Praise of Folly,* even Thomas More's *Utopia* (which is not exactly humor, but is seriously lighthearted). But the Reformation controversies suppressed all that, pretty much ever since, though people like G. K. Chesterton tried to get a little bounce back in things." That humor has never been a "big thing" in ecclesial circles has been my experience as well.

Groucho Marx was once in a hotel lobby (or stepping off a train, or having lunch, depending on the story) when a priest, in his clerical collar, rushed over to see the great film comedian. "Thank you, Groucho, for bringing so much joy and laughter into people's lives!" he said.

"Thank you," Groucho replied, "for taking so much joy and laughter out of them."

It's not just a Catholic problem. The Reverend Martin Marty, a distinguished Protestant theologian and the author of many books and over five thousand scholarly articles, told me that certain aspects of the Protestant tradition have always struck him as "grim." In a recent interview Marty said, "*Hilaritas* is not characteristic of the Protestant ethos."

Professor Marty sees that as ironic, since Martin Luther, about whom Marty has written extensively, often stressed the value of "play" in his writings.* He was also fond of the occasional witticism. In one of the sayings later collected in Luther's *Table Talk,* one of his friends recounts Luther's amusing way of preparing to deliver a particular homily. "Tomorrow I have to lecture on the drunkenness of Noah,"[61] said the great man, "so I should drink enough this evening to be able to talk about that wickedness as one who knows by experience." To underline his humor, I should add that I first read this in Eric Gritsch's book, entitled *The Wit of Martin Luther.*

Ironically, Professor Marty said that his own career could be attributed to a taste for mirth. While studying at Concordia Seminary in Missouri, he and his friends playfully concocted a fictional scholar named Franz Bibfeldt, whose fake name and spurious accomplishments they attempted to place in as many academic settings as they could—student newspapers, the school's library card catalog, and so on.

In response to these shenanigans, the dean called him into his office for a scolding. He told Marty that someone with such frivolity could never be a good Protestant scholar and sent him to work with a pastor at a church. But the pastor of that church told the young man that all his assistants studied for their doctorates. So that's what Marty did. "So my whole professional life was thanks to a prank!" he told me.

Today you can find on the Internet references to the work of the wholly fictional Professor Bibfeldt, including a book penned by Marty and a friend with the wonderfully serious title *The Unrelieved Paradox: Studies in the Theology of Franz Bibfeldt.* Among the fanciful articles is "Franz Bibfeldt and the Future of Political Theology."

"And I'm *still* accused of not being serious enough!" said one of the country's greatest scholars of religion. "I have a real taste for humor."

Professor Marty, who is also the author of *Righteous Empire: The Protestant Experience in America,* surmises that the American Protes-

* One of Professor Marty's most well-known books is his short biography *Martin Luther.* When the book was published, I offered to review it for *America* magazine, in order that we might have the chance of titling the review "James Martin on Martin Marty on Martin Luther."

tant tradition's emphasis on seriousness may relate to the belief that what you do needs to "add up" to something. Of course, he said, there are many Protestants who are lighthearted, humorous, and joyful. But overall he detects a certain grimness in parts of the Protestant DNA. "After all," he told me, "we talk about the Protestant work ethic, not the Protestant play ethic."

Pastor Charles Hambrick-Stowe agreed, suggesting that this seriousness may be ingrained in aspects of the American Protestant tradition. "Perhaps a great deal of this comes from our Puritan background," he said. "After all, Cotton Mather talked about the dangers of humor and noted that nowhere in Scripture does it say that Jesus smiled. But the absence of evidence isn't evidence of absence." Hambrick-Stowe laughingly recalled H. L. Mencken's acid definition of Puritanism as the "haunting fear that someone, somewhere, may be happy."

Pastor Hambrick-Stowe has a range of experience in a variety of Protestant traditions. He has taught both at the General Reformed Seminary, a Methodist institution in Pennsylvania, and at the Pittsburgh Theological Seminary, affiliated with the Presbyterian Church (USA). Hambrick-Stowe has also taught church history at the Baptist-run Northern Seminary in Lombard, Illinois. He is an excellent person to address the topic of humor in American Protestantism.

Hambrick-Stowe agreed with Professor Marty about the over-emphasis on what he called the "grim, dour, and rigid" brand of some Protestant traditions. "Too many thou-shalt-nots," he said.

"Then why do I know so many joyful Protestants?" I asked.

In response he pointed to an interesting historical development that helped to usher in a more joyful form of American Protestantism. In the aftermath of the Civil War and the rise of industrialization in the late nineteenth century, many Protestant denominations began to realize that the center of people's lives was moving away from the church. This led to a growing awareness of the need to link the life of the local church with the everyday "social" life of the congregation. "This is when you had churches building social halls, gymnasiums, church parlors, and even bowling alleys, where all sorts of groups could meet," he said. "Pianos started to appear in social halls, and not just for the singing of religious songs. You had a greater emphasis on fellowship and youth groups." As a result, said Hambrick-Stowe, what was injected into American Protestant culture was both "fellowship and fun."

Even with these relatively recent developments, and even if many priests and ministers admit the need for joy, many religious institutions still seem to find little room for a smile, a joke, laughter, or the occasional measure of silliness. But God, I would suggest, may think otherwise.

Why do I believe this? Because God relentlessly introduces into even the most serious of situations—whether we like it or not—joy, humor, and laughter. God brings this into churches and synagogues through our humanity on a regular basis, which is something that we should rejoice about. God seems to be in favor of excessive levity.

Some of God's levity comes in the form of unintentionally funny events. God breaks into our deadly serious religions with divine humor. Let me start with the community I know best: Catholics.

Catholics do some risible things quite unintentionally. In some parishes in recent years, for example, the Christmas Eve Midnight Mass is celebrated at four o'clock in the afternoon to accommodate families with children. And so a question that used to be a joke is one no longer: "What time is your Midnight Mass?"

Even our use of Scripture can prompt a smile, if we're open to looking at ourselves with a humorous eye. Whenever I read the Gospel passage in which Jesus says, "Call no one your father,"[62] I have to suppress a smile. Soon after my ordination I preached on that reading. On the way out of the church one woman said, "I really enjoyed your homily, especially that part about not calling any man your father . . . Father." I'm not sure if she was kidding or not.

And I always perk up when the priest on Ash Wednesday reads the Gospel passage that says, "And whenever you fast, do not look dismal,

Laugh On!

The vast compendium of the lives of the saints recorded by the redoubtable Reverend Alban Butler, an English Catholic priest (1711–73), is typically called *Butler's Lives of the Saints* or, more simply, *Butler's*. The four-volume work, which has been revised and updated, took the hardworking priest thirty years to complete. Some of his descriptions focus on ascetical practices and gruesome martyrdoms, but occasionally some hilarity breaks through, as it does in the case of Blessed Jordan of Saxony, a twelfth-century cleric who was the second superior of the Dominican order (after St. Dominic himself). Here Butler describes what happened one night in a Dominican community during evening prayer in the company of some of the young novices.

> One of the young men under emotional strain began to giggle, and all the others followed suit. One of the brothers, greatly shocked, made gestures to try to stop them. Jordan finished the [prayer] and gave the blessing; then, addressing the brother, he asked, "Who made you novice master?" And turning to the young men, he said, "Laugh on! You may well laugh, for you have escaped from the Devil, who formerly held you in bondage. Laugh away, dear sons!"[63]

like the hypocrites, . . . but . . . wash your face, so that your fasting may be seen not by others."[64] What does the priest do next? He asks parishioners to come forward to smear ashes on their foreheads, dirtying their faces so that everyone can see that they are doing penance.*

* A few years ago as I was distributing ashes I said to a well-coiffed Manhattan matron, "You are dust, and to dust you shall return." As I prepared to rub the ashes on her forehead, she said, "Watch the hair!"

Surprise!

During the Communist regime in the Soviet Union, Jesuit priests and brothers were forced to live "underground." Men joined the Jesuits and did their training one-on-one with another underground Jesuit, all the while carrying on their "normal" lives.

After the fall of the Soviet Union, one young Estonian man decided it was time to tell his family that he was, in fact, a Jesuit priest. His family was gathered for a big meal when he finally announced to them his vocation as a Jesuit. There were various reactions, but that of his younger brother was the most unexpected: "Me, too!"

Funny things that happen in church settings may seem doubly funny because we're sometimes told that, unless the sermon includes jokes, we're not supposed to laugh in church. Church art, as I've mentioned, underlines that. Think of all the stained-glass windows, statues, and mosaic you see in Catholic churches. And perhaps the most frequent image of Jesus in the Catholic Church is of him hanging on the cross. Even images of Jesus *after* the Resurrection make him look serious.

Imagery in some Protestant churches is often similar. Not a few feature a stained-glass window of a grim-faced Jesus with his hands clasped in prayer in the Garden of Gethsemane, hardly a cheerful topic or, as in Catholic churches, on the cross. Did Jesus ever smile? Not if you trust church art.

Of course sometimes including humor in religious settings is inappropriate. Silliness can distract us from paying attention to something important, and jokes can be offensive if delivered at the wrong time. Much of religion *does* address serious topics—suffering, illness, death, sin, hatred, injustice, war, violence—that deserve to be taken seriously. But flashes of humor may be signs that God wants us to relax. God may be injecting humor at these moments to save us from deadly seriousness.

Children are adept at reminding us not to take ourselves so seriously in church. My sister's friend is Catholic and her husband is Jewish. The mother brought her six-year-old son to church regularly. One Sunday the little boy was listening to a particularly dull homily and asked his mother, "Can we leave now?"

The mother said, "No. The Mass is only half finished."

And he said, "Well, I'm only half Catholic. Let's go!"*

For the Catholic clergy, the most popular stories of this genre concern snafus during Mass. Priests treasure these tales, not only because they remind them that priests aren't perfect—as if they needed any reminder—but also that even the most devoted priests can make a mistake or commit a faux pas without the world ending.

Some stories are clearly apocryphal. Like the supposedly true story of the nervous priest during his first Mass who says, with great devotion, not, "This is the Lamb of God," but "This is the Leg of Lamb." I've heard that story dozens of times from people who swear it is true, but when you ask them, it always turns out that they heard it from someone else. But I've heard stories that have happened to close friends, and I've been an eyewitness to ecclesial events of memorable absurdity.

One priest friend recounted the story of his first wedding, which he performed shortly after his ordination. My friend had borrowed the marriage rites book, the guide containing the script of marriage ceremony, from an elderly Jesuit. The old Jesuit had written

* Professor Maureen O'Connell told me the story of a friend who had prepared what she thought was a good meal for her two children. In this house, each child takes turns saying grace. That evening, her five-year-old son took one look at his plate, put his head in his hands, and said, "Jesus Christ, help me. This looks nasty."

A Confession

An elderly man walks into a confessional.

MAN: "Father, I'm a ninety-five-year-old widower, I have many children and grandchildren, and yesterday I went out on a date with a twenty-five-year-old supermodel!"

PRIEST: "Well, that doesn't sound like a sin. You should know that as a Catholic. Dating is not a sin."

MAN: "Oh, I'm not Catholic, Father. I'm Jewish."

PRIEST: "So why are you telling me all this?"

MAN: "I'm ninety-five years old! I'm telling everybody!"

little notations in pencil, because the rites book includes all of the words needed for the wedding Mass, but not what you might call the "stage directions." So alongside the script for the marriage vows the old priest had scribbled helpful directions like, "Turn to the bride," "Turn to the groom," "Go back to the presider's chair," "Take the rings from the best man." He also wrote directions for the congregation that aren't included in the book, like saying, "Please stand" or "Please kneel."

All was going smoothly until my newly ordained friend reached the end of the vows. There was a little notation that added something that most priests say, but is not included in the official Catholic rites.

The penciled-in note said, "You may now kiss the bride."

My friend found that baffling. But who was he to argue with the elderly priest, who had done more weddings than he had? So my friend stopped, closed his book, leaned down, and kissed the bride.

She stood there dumbstruck, and everybody burst out laughing. Finally, he said to the groom, "Uh, I think *you* were supposed to do that!"*

* Several early readers of this book wrote, "That's impossible!" or "Really?" I assure you, I know the priest in question.

God is in favor of some excessive levity from time to time. And no matter how hard some people try to turn the church into a deadly serious place, the Holy Spirit enlivens and inspires it.

Religious groups often have their own funny lingo too, which can help bind the community together in a lighthearted way, with a shared inside joke. Protestants refer to the "frozen chosen"; Catholics, to the "smells and bells" and "A&P Catholics" or "CAPE Catholics."* Catholic religious orders like the Franciscans, Dominicans, and Jesuits have their own lingo too, which can serve as a cohesive element. When something goes wrong in the Jesuits we call it a "Tarbo," which is similar to "Fubar," army lingo for "Fouled Up Beyond All Recognition."† Tarbo stands for "Typical Affair Run by Ours," shorthand for anything that goes wrong in a typically Jesuit way.‡

A classic Tarbo is the true story about a statue of St. Ignatius Loyola located in the Jesuit headquarters in Rome. Prominently displayed in a hallway is a huge bronze statue of the Jesuit founder raising his arm heavenward and clasping a book—his traditional pose. On the statue's marble pedestal is one of his most famous expressions, words he is supposed to have said to the great Jesuit missionary St. Francis Xavier before he left on his far-flung travels to Africa, India, and Japan: "Go set the world aflame." "*Ite inflammate omnia*" says the legend inscribed on the pedestal. Next to the statue, firmly affixed to the wall, is a fire extinguisher. Classic Tarbo.

There are also shorthand phrases for longer jokes. One old

* "Smells and bells" refers to a Solemn High Mass with incense (smells) and the ringing of bells. "A&P Catholics" attend Mass only on Ash Wednesday and Palm Sunday, though the reference to the previously omnipresent supermarket chain may be lost on many people who have never seen an A&P store. "CAPE Catholics" attend Mass only on Christmas, Ash Wednesday, Palm Sunday, and Easter.

† However, in the army they don't say "fouled."

‡ "Ours" is an old way to refer to Jesuits, as in "Is he one of Ours?" or "Ours don't really do that."

The Contented Fisherman

Jesus wasn't the only religious figure who told humorous stories. Many great spiritual masters have freely used stories with comic characters and funny endings to make a serious point. The Indian Jesuit Anthony de Mello was renowned for his use of clever fables that combine Christian insights with Eastern settings. Here is one of my favorites, from his book *The Song of the Bird:*

> The rich industrialist from the North was horrified to find the Southern fisherman lying lazily beside his boat, smoking a pipe.
>
> "Why aren't you out fishing?" said the industrialist.
>
> "Because I have caught enough fish for the day," said the fisherman.
>
> "Why don't you catch some more?"
>
> "What would I do with them?"
>
> "You could earn more money," was the industrialist's reply. "With that you could have a motor fixed to your boat . . . and catch more fish. Then you would make enough to buy nylon nets. These would bring you more fish and more money. Soon you would have enough money to buy two boats . . . maybe even a fleet of boats. Then you would be a rich man like me."
>
> "What would I do then?" asked the fisherman.
>
> "Then you could really enjoy life."
>
> "What do you think I am doing right now?"

standby is the story of the young novice who walks into a lavish Jesuit dining room on the Feast of St. Ignatius. It is typically the occasion for the biggest dinner of the year. The young Jesuit sees a buffet with filet mignon and says, "If this is poverty, bring on chastity!" Because we Jesuits all know this joke, when we see something not in keeping with our simple lifestyle, all someone has to say is, "Bring on chastity," and everyone gets it.

The effectiveness of a good joke in communicating a deep truth is often ignored. Some of Jesus's parables read like little jokes, and because they say a lot with an economy of words, they easily imprint themselves on hearers' minds.

Note how the punch line from the joke above, "Bring on chastity," carries meaning. It says that members of religious orders need to be careful about not living too extravagantly. It says that if religious orders are hypocritical about poverty, they will confuse those on the outside. It also says, implicitly, that younger men may not be interested in a group that professes one thing and does another. It says all these things about the institution and does so in a lighthearted way.

Jokes can be powerful carriers of meaning. They therefore can be of service to religious institutions, which need to be open to self-critique if they are to grow.

God's humor can also illumine truths about religious institutions that may otherwise go unnoticed. Rabbi Daniel Polish recently told me a story about a Jewish worship service. At an inner-city synagogue he was serving in Los Angeles, the congregation participated in a familiar Jewish custom. On Friday evenings, as they sang a traditional song that "welcomed the Sabbath queen," they rose and faced the rear doors to "greet" her. On this particular Friday as they rose and turned toward the rear, one of the doors was flung open and there, waiting to reciprocate their greeting, was a bag lady, a regular attendee, arriving late for worship. Their collective amazement was no less then her own. Prior to this night, said Rabbi Polish, he would occasionally look out over the congregation during other services and catch sight of this disheveled woman seated next to some of the wealthiest and most influential in the city.

I asked the rabbi whether he felt that God was being playful during that Friday night service. In response, he adverted to the way that events like this lead to humility, which leads to intimacy:

> It didn't feel that G-d was playing with me as much as helping me put myself back into perspective. I think a danger for all clergy is that we can come to take ourselves a little too seriously. . . . On the occasions when it was my privilege to see the bag lady and the rainmaker next to each other, I felt a terrific intimacy with G-d, feeling we had a lovely secret that only we two were aware of. And it now makes me wonder how many such secrets G-d shares with countless others all the time.

When those in official capacities in religious institutions begin to swell up with spiritual pride ("I am holier than you are"), humor can offer an antidote. Self-deprecating humor fosters humility among those who may need it most.

Rabbi Burton Visotzky told me that the great twentieth-century Talmudic scholar Rabbi Louis Ginzberg was once asked if there was humor in the Talmud. "Of course," said Rabbi Ginzberg. "The Talmud says that rabbis bring peace into the world, and this hasn't happened yet!"

As a Catholic priest, it is difficult not to get a swelled head when people tell you that you've helped them with their spiritual lives, that they love your homilies, that you celebrate Mass so beautifully, and so on. One woman once said to me, "When you say Mass it's like I'm watching *Jesus*!" Occasionally very elderly or very pious people kiss my hand when they leave Mass.

One friend told me the (true) story of a powerful Catholic cardinal who was invited to a large civic banquet many decades ago. Because of his stature he was always given a prominent place at the head table. But because of a mix-up, he was seated with "everyone else" at the banquet. The person in charge rushed over, apologized profusely, and said that certainly the cardinal should have been placed, as usual, at the head table. The cardinal glowered at him and said, "Son, where I am *is* the head table."

Humility is not always the default mode for religious leaders, but it should be. Think of people like Pope John XXIII, who consistently referred to his "peasant" upbringing, or Mother Teresa, who, though strong-willed, called herself "a pencil in God's hand." St. Ignatius Loyola often signed his letters, "Poor in Christ." And he meant it. Jesus himself told his followers that the greatest among them was the one who served.[65] Christian religious leaders need to be reminded of this daily.

Pomposity is a danger when you are perceived to have power over people. For better or worse, you are a representative of a religious body, and this confers authority on you, and some power as well. It can lead to pride.

Timothy Radcliffe, the former superior general of the Dominican order, once recounted the tale of an elderly Benedictine monk receiving Eucharist. When the eucharistic minister said, "The body of Christ," he said, "Yes, I know." Catholics can get so puffed up that even when standing in front of the Eucharist, it's all about us.

For the priest, minister, or rabbi, spiritual pride is a special danger. "When we take ourselves too seriously, we are at the risk of taking other things, including God, too lightly," said Margaret Silf in a recent letter.

During my time working with refugees in Kenya, I was exposed to the humor of the poor, which was a great blessing when I started to take myself too seriously. One Rwandan refugee in particular helped me to laugh at myself frequently. Her name was Gaudiosa, which means "joyful."

Along with several other Rwandan refugees Gauddy, as everyone called her, had started a small sewing shop, which later became the Splendid Tailoring Shop and School, located in a dilapidated concrete building off a rutted dirt road in one of the worst slums of Nairobi. There Gauddy and her friends sewed dresses, shirts, and pants, while running a small school. Funding came from the Jesuit Refugee Service, part of the "income-generating activities" we sponsored in Nairobi.

One of the biggest customers for refugee-made handicrafts like Gauddy's was the U.S. Embassy in downtown Nairobi. In the weeks before Christmas and Easter, the embassy graciously allowed us to take over a conference room to market our wares. We would invariably do very well, selling out nearly all our stock. During one trip I asked some of the embassy staff if they would like to visit our shop. Some were skittish about venturing into the slums, but they eventually agreed, as long as I promised to be their escort.

The next week I asked Gauddy if she would be willing to make a presentation to the embassy staff, which would number about twenty people. But I anticipated one "problem." Gauddy was a successful businesswoman. The vast majority of the refugees we helped, however, were desperately poor. I was going to gently suggest to Gauddy, a savvy, well-dressed woman, that perhaps she shouldn't dress too nicely, so that the embassy staff wouldn't think that we were aiding "wealthy" refugees. And I thought I could tell her without her figuring out why.

In other words, I wanted her to dress "poor," so that she would be seen as "deserving." (That the embassy crowd might appreciate a hardworking, successful woman didn't dawn on me. Neither did it occur to me that it was none of my business—and patronizing at best—to suggest how she should dress.)

On the Friday before the event, she came by to plan her talk. As usual, she was beautifully attired, in a dress of her own creation with a beautifully colored scarf around her neck.

"Gauddy," I said. "On Monday, you don't need to dress up if you don't want to."

She said she couldn't imagine *not* dressing up for such an important group.

"Well," I suggested, "you don't need to dress up so *well.* I mean, they want to give money to the refugees and . . ."

Gauddy smiled slyly. And I knew that she had discerned my intention. She carefully undid the scarf around her neck, slowly wrapped

Monastic Humor

Father James Palmigiano is a Trappist priest and an old friend who lives at St. Joseph's Abbey in Spencer, Massachusetts. The Trappists follow the vows of stability (committing to stay in one monastery rather than searching for the "perfect" one), conversion of life (which includes poverty and chastity), and obedience. The monks also live in silence. Recently I asked him about the place of humor in the monastic life. Could humor flourish amid silence? The answer was a resounding (or a quietly resounding) yes:

> Our life grants us ample opportunity to laugh at ourselves, freely and joyfully. We really need to take ourselves lightly, or we would crack up. Our life is built on self-knowledge, coming to recognize our own "woundedness," so that we may see our desperate need for Christ's mercy. One monastic author, paraphrasing St. Bernard, puts it this way, "God does not want my virtue. God wants my weakness." This growing insight into my weakness, what we often refer to as "bitter self-knowledge," engaged with compassionately, allows me to see that fragility is the gateway to Christ's mercy. When I notice my overreaction to the situation, when I notice that I am stuck in a judgmental thought, an angry thought, or a desire to lash out at a brother who has offended me, I try to recognize my foolishness and laugh or at least smile to myself and ask for mercy. For when I get a sense of my sinful folly, then I am more available for Christ's mercy.
>
> A few years ago, for instance, I was at our community bulletin board, and the list of those brothers who would have their feet washed on Holy Thursday [a traditional

part of the liturgy for that day] had been posted. I heard myself grumbling to myself because Brother So-and-So was having his feet washed again, and I had been overlooked—again! I caught myself, was embarrassed, and thought, "Listen to you. How sad that you are upset over something so trivial!" With a bit of effort I was able to smile at myself. Life in the cloister can tend to make us so self-absorbed. When I can imagine it, this kind of gentle interior humor keeps the balance.

There are also more run-of-the-mill incidents that keep us all smiling. We still use some of the traditional Trappist sign language, which was used more extensively when the silences were more extreme. One of the classic signs is the extended middle finger, used to designate the one we call the "president"—the monk who will lead a work detail or lead a mid-morning prayer, which is recited in the workplace. Usually this "president" will be the senior monk. One day an elderly monk, a very sweet man who was obviously the oldest of the group, didn't feel up to leading the prayer, so he gave me the president sign, the extended center finger, implicitly requesting that I lead the prayer in his place. Even though I understood, my knee-jerk reaction was outrage. I almost blurted out, "Same to you, buddy!" Thank God I said nothing! I led the prayer and that was that. Later with a couple of the other monks I retold the story, and we roared with laughter.

it around her head as if she were preparing to work in the fields, made a mock frown, cast her eyes to the sky, held out her hands, palms up, and said, "Like this?"

Then she burst out laughing. "Brother Jim," she said. "I know you very well!"

Her pointed humor was a reminder of a few things. First, she was in control of the situation, even as a relatively poor woman. Second, she could see through my plan with the practiced eye of someone who had seen a great deal of life. Third, we were in this together.

On Monday, she wore her scarf around her neck, made a beautiful presentation, and sold a dozen shirts.

The institution itself benefits when the leaders of religious communities can laugh at themselves. It is an invitation for others to do the same and therefore is healthy for the entire community. Leaders can lead in and with humility.

Once again, for a good example we turn to Pope John XXIII. At one point during his papacy John was giving a formal talk when the microphone went out. When they fixed the mike, the pope said, "Don't worry about not hearing what I was saying. You didn't miss anything. I didn't say anything interesting anyway."

The assumption that a sense of humour and Christian faith are incompatible is totally mistaken. In point of fact, the writers of the great classics of humour—Rabelais, Cervantes, Swift, Gogol—have all been deeply religious. . . . Laughter is indeed God's therapy. Let us then be thankful that, when the Gates of Heaven swing open, mixed with the celestial music there is the unmistakable sound of celestial laughter.

—Malcolm Muggeridge, British author and essayist

It's important for religious leaders to laugh at themselves and realize that, much as they would like to be, they're not perfect, and they're certainly not God.

There are hundreds of stories I could tell about myself that happened within church settings and that brought me down a peg. When I was working in Nairobi, for example, I spent the first few months studying Swahili at a local language learning center. Every day my teacher, a young Kenyan man named Geoffrey, would sit patiently with me and, for two to three hours, review Swahili grammar, vocabulary, and even slang.

Until I learned the language, I needed a translator to help me communicate with the refugees who spoke only Swahili. (East Africa has a welter of languages, but Swahili is the lingua franca.) Happily, Virginia, a sweet-natured Kenyan woman, helped me with these interactions.

Virginia would sit patiently next to me, listen to the Swahili of the refugees, translate what they said into English, and then translate what I said into Swahili. Her opening lines to the refugees were always the same: "*Brother anasema,*" that is, "Brother says." (Not yet ordained, I was referred to by the refugees as "Brother.") For every one of my utterances Virginia would face me, listen carefully, then turn to the refugee, say, "*Brother anasema,*" and launch into the Swahili translation.

This went on for several weeks. Finally, toward the end of my language lessons, I began to feel more comfortable in Swahili. One day, I was speaking to a refugee and I realized that what I wanted to say was fairly simple. It was this: "Please complete the form and return it next week." So I happily said it in Swahili.

Virginia listened and then said, "*Brother anasema,*" and repeated exactly what I had said, again in Swahili. The woman nodded, thanked me, and left.

I turned to Virginia and said, "Why did you say that?"

"Why did I say what?" she asked, surprised.

"After I used Swahili, you just repeated what I said in Swahili again."

"Oh, Brother," she laughed. "No one could understand Swahili as poorly spoken as *that*!"

Humbling humor also reminds us that no one religious group has all the answers. Jesus's disciples, to take but one example, thought they knew what the Messiah would be like, but found out that Jesus was quite different from what they expected. God is bigger than any religion and can upend our human and limited expectations.

There is a story about people from different religious denominations who are traveling on a bus to an ecumenical conference for Christian Unity Week. While singing songs together, they become so distracted that they run off the road and hit a telephone pole, die, and go to heaven.

The crowd meets St. Peter, who welcomes all of them. "Okay," he says. "First the Episcopalians. Welcome to heaven. Since you've all led good Christian lives and enriched us so much liturgically, go into Room Five, but on the way make sure not to look inside Room One." The Episcopalians walk happily over to Room Five.

Then he says to the Baptists, "Welcome Baptists. Thanks for all the great preaching and witnessing you've done during your lives. Why don't you take Room Two, but make sure not to peek into Room One."

Then he turns to another group and says, "Methodists, nice to see you! Thanks for leading such good Christian lives and for all those great hymns. Why don't you all go into Room Three? But make sure not to go into Room One."

Finally, one of the Methodists says to St. Peter, "Can I ask you something? What's in Room One?"

St. Peter says, "Oh, that's where the Catholics are. They think they're the only ones up here."

Humor can keep churches humble. It puts the community in touch with its inevitable limitations as a human organization, and its fundamental reliance on God. That brand of humor leads us to God through the gateway of humility.

In practical ways, humor also helps to lift our spirits in challenging situations in religious institutions. For example, my Jesuit community is populated with some wonderful elderly Jesuits, who serve as terrific role models for the younger men. And the ones who seem the healthiest are those with a lively sense of humor, especially about aging. Humor is a path to an open acceptance of reality.

One of my favorite Jesuits, John, who recently died at age ninety-two, had what a friend called a "darting" sense of humor. He often poked fun at his advanced age. On the day of his ninetieth birthday, I passed him in the hall and suddenly remembered his big day. "Happy birthday, John." I said. "And many more."

John laughed and said, "Oh, I *hope* not!"

One day during Advent a few years ago, John walked into the community chapel for Mass wearing a ratty sweater. Another Jesuit said, "Oh, Father, I see that you're wearing your Christmas sweater." Pause. "Christmas 1943."

Now for a necessary digression—about the abuses and misuses of humor. Humor and laughter, as I mentioned in Chapter 4, help with human relations. And, as I've said in this chapter, those two qualities can help in religious organizations.

Good humor is always informed by love. In that last anecdote, John and the younger Jesuit, who enjoyed ribbing one another, were close friends. Those who overheard their dialogue knew that the joshing was done good-naturedly. We also knew that the younger Jesuit idolized John. We could laugh because we understood the love that lay behind the joke.

But there are times when humor and laughter work to the detriment of human relations and religious institutions, not to mention friendship and families. When used incorrectly, humor tears down rather than builds up.

One of the easiest ways to wound people is to encourage others to laugh at them. All of us experienced the taunts of bullies, bigots, or boneheads when we were young—in the classroom and on the playground. For children especially, mean-spirited comments can devastate, tempting them to doubt their dignity and question their self-worth. Painful memories of cruel words from childhood and adolescence can linger for years.

Mean-spirited humor can be equally devastating to adults. Several years ago a friend described an event that he bitterly regretted. My friend walked into a roomful of people, where he spied an acquaintance—whom I'll call Bob—who had just written a magazine article. Bob was a respected teacher and an occasional author who wrote regularly on the same topic.

My friend sidled up to Bob and said, loudly enough to ensure that all would hear: "Well, Bob, I see that they published your article . . . *again*!" The crowd exploded in laughter, and Bob's face flushed. Normally a garrulous man, he was struck dumb by the unexpected attack and the crowd's mocking laughter. Later, said my friend, he felt so bad over the effects of his "joke" that he apologized to Bob.

But often we don't apologize, and our humor leaves a scar. Pastor Charles Hambrick-Stowe was direct on this topic: "Humor that comes at the expense of another can be sinful or even evil."

I have been guilty of this myself. The temptation to put down others with an Oscar Wildean sally reflects the desire to be considered witty, clever, intelligent, cool, or "better than" the rest of the crowd. Giving in to that temptation can do violence to another. It can be equally harmful for the one who has spoken harshly.

When I was fifteen, I heard a sarcastic comment on a television sitcom about one character's weight. I thought it was hysterical, and the laugh track seemed to confirm this judgment. A few weeks later I was talking one-on-one with a friend who was overweight. I repeated the insult I had heard, hoping to recreate some of the lively banter I had seen on that sitcom. Her face drained of color. Instantly I saw that what was funny in a sitcom was, in real life, cruel. Her parents called my parents, and I was rightly forced to apologize to her.

No doubt she saw it as a stupid remark by a thoughtless adolescent. But I've never forgotten my comment and, most of all, the look on her face. I still regret it, decades later. Used correctly, humor builds up. Abused, it destroys.

Although playful humor invites others to experience God's joy as part of a welcoming community, sarcasm brings sadness and excludes. Knowing where to draw the line is paramount and a requirement for loving interactions: a person may intend a remark to be playful, but the receiver may hear it simply as belittling. The old theological dictum is helpful here. "Whatever is received is received according to the mode of the receiver."*

Err on the side of safety when it comes to sarcasm. Take precautions against offending anyone on sensitive topics. Again, the best brand of humor may be the playful, self-deprecating jokes we tell about our own foibles (so long as we are not using them as an excuse to abase ourselves in an unhealthy way).

Similar pitfalls attend gossip. How tempting it is to make a snarky comment about someone who is not in the room. Once a clever barb is uttered, it lodges there, barnacle-like, on people's consciousness. Once there, it's difficult to remove. A sermon attributed to the nineteenth-century French parish priest St. Jean Vianney (later used to great effect in John Patrick Shanley's Broadway play and film *Doubt*) illustrates this truth. In its essence the tale goes as follows:

A woman confesses to a priest that she has told a malicious lie about another person.

"Well," says the priest, "here is your penance. Go to the top of your building with a feather pillow, slit it open with a knife, and throw all the feathers into the wind."

The next week the woman returns to the confessional.

"Did you do what I asked?" says the priest.

"Yes," she says.

"Now," he says, "go back and pick up all the feathers."

"Oh, but I can't," she says. "By now they're everywhere!"

"And so are your lies," says the priest.

---

* "*Quidquid recipitur secundum modum recipientis recipitur.*"

Malicious humor can spread, with a life of its own, and reaches places you never would have imagined. The Letter of James, in the New Testament, includes a lengthy disquisition about the natural difficulty of reining in this kind of talk:

> For every species of beast and bird, of reptile and sea creature, can be tamed and has been tamed by the human species, but no one can tame the tongue—a restless evil, full of deadly poison. With it we bless the Lord and Father, and with it we curse those who are made in the likeness of God. From the same mouth come blessing and cursing. My brothers and sisters, this ought not to be so.[66]

I'm not sure that I would characterize the tongue as "a restless evil," but the writer makes an important point. Speech can wound.

E-mail and other Web-based and digital communications make this an even more dangerous game. How easy it is to post a snarky comment, engage in character assassination, or, to use an underutilized word, be mean under the easy guise of humor.

Malicious humor is sinful for several reasons. First, it is uncharitable. It is an act that does not proceed from love. Second, it fails to respect the dignity of the person. Third, if done behind a person's back, it steals, in a sense, the person's good name, without giving the person the chance to defend it. (Like those fictional feathers, malicious humor travels to places the speaker cannot have anticipated.)

Jesus of Nazareth, in a passage that is often overlooked perhaps because of an obscure word, once commented on this brand of humor. One translation has it: "If a person calls another person *raca,* then he is liable to the fires of Gehenna."[67] *Raca* is an Aramaic word for "fool." Jesus is saying, in essence, that malicious talk could land you in hell.

Here is an important fact about that short passage. Some Scripture scholars believe that one indication that a phrase came directly from the mouth of Jesus is the preservation of an Aramaic word or phrase. Two familiar examples are *Abba* (Jesus's common way of speaking to God the Father) and *Talitha cum,* his words to a young girl thought dead. ("Little girl, get up!")[68] The words *themselves* were notable enough to become part of the story and may have been preserved by the writers of the Gospels not only for their historicity, but also for what they said about Jesus.

For example, it was probably striking to his contemporaries that Jesus would use the familiar Aramaic term *Abba* to address the Almighty. It is an affectionate way of speaking to a father rather than the more formal way that most Jews of the time addressed God, whose name could not even be uttered. Both of these Aramaic phrases—*Abba* and *Talitha cum*—lend these particular Gospel passages an added level of authenticity; they imply an eyewitness account rather than a story told by someone who heard the story secondhand.

Likewise, *raca* may be one such example of a striking word used by Jesus preserved in its original Aramaic form. Thus, many who read the New Testament carefully and take from it so many specific doctrines, regulations, and prohibitions, sometimes fail to consider this unmistakable prohibition against maliciousness, which most likely comes directly from Jesus's lips.*

We can usually tell when humor crosses the line. Most of us

---

* A vivid description of the harm an insult can do comes in Jane Austen's novel *Emma*. The heroine carelessly mocks, before a crowd, an old family friend: Miss Bates, an unmarried woman with little money. Miss Bates, a timid soul, "did not immediately catch her meaning; but, when it burst on her, it could not anger, though a slight blush shewed that it could pain her." Later Emma's good friend, Mr. Knightley, reproaches her. "It was badly done, indeed!—You, whom she had known from an infant, whom she had seen grow up from a period when her notice was an honour, to have you now, in thoughtless spirits, and the pride of the moment, laugh at her, humble her—and before her niece, too—and before others, many of whom (certainly *some,*) would be entirely guided by *your* treatment of her.—This is not pleasant to you, Emma—and it is very far from pleasant to me."

The Baseball Game

I've been touting self-deprecatory jokes as a way of increasing humility in religious institutions, but sometimes jokes in which the religious figure comes out on top aren't bad.

A group of twenty cloistered nuns receive a special gift of free tickets to a baseball game. The mother superior gives them permission to go to the game and enjoy themselves, a special treat for the nuns. They all sit together in one long row and buy sodas and hot dogs and popcorn and hats and noisemakers. Soon they are enjoying themselves and making quite a commotion.

Behind them sit three grumpy diehard baseball fans, who are annoyed by these ebullient nuns. One of them says loudly enough so the nuns will hear, "This is ridiculous! I'm going to move a few rows ahead, where there are probably only *ten* nuns! Maybe then I can watch the game in peace!"

The embarrassed nuns quiet down. But in a few minutes they are in high spirits and enjoying themselves again.

The second diehard fan says, "I'm going to move to the expensive seats. There are only *five* nuns there!"

The nuns, embarrassed, quiet down again. But in a few minutes they are again having fun.

Finally the third diehard fan says angrily and loudly, "I'm going to the box seats! There are probably only *two* nuns there!"

One nun turns around and says, "Why don't you go to hell? There are *no* nuns there!"

have an internal gauge that tells us when a joke moves from playful to hurtful. Conscience is usually loud and clear on this point. But if you feel that your internal gauge needs some fine-tuning or even an overhaul, you might ask yourself the following questions, slightly adapted from the writings of the popular spiritual leader and New Age icon Krishnamurti (1895–1986). They are the three doors that charitable speech must pass through.

The gatekeeper at the first door asks, "Is it true?" The second gatekeeper asks, "Is it helpful?" The third gatekeeper asks, "Is it kind?"

Good humor is true (it reveals a truth); it is helpful (it helps to increase understanding, to lighten a difficult situation, to self-deprecate); and it is kind (it is neither harmful nor destructive). Those three gates are a good thing to keep in mind whenever we open our mouths for a supposedly funny remark.

Humor also helps in situations in which there is a power differential, often the case in religious institutions. Most people are afraid of offending someone in a leadership role or position of authority, even inadvertently, and so when the one in authority uses humor to defuse a tense situation, it helps others relax.

During my Jesuit novitiate, the New England provincial supervisor, the man in charge of the Jesuits of the region, visited our community. As he was an authority figure, many of us were rather nervous about his visit. To open his discussion he recounted a (true) story that came from the autobiography of St. Ignatius Loyola.

One day, after Ignatius's conversion, he was riding on a mule when he came upon another man on the road also riding on a mule. In the course of their brief conversation, the man insulted the Virgin Mary and then rode off. Ignatius, who was still very much a hothead, waxed furious.

So he started to think about murder.* But, try as he might, he was unable to decide whether he should kill the man or not. At that moment he reached a (literal) fork in the road. Ignatius decided to leave the fate of the blasphemer up to his mule. As he wrote in his

* The saints weren't always saintly, especially in their early years.

autobiography, "If the mule took the village road, I would seek him out and stab him; if the mule did not go toward the village, but took the highway, I would let him be." Fortunately for all concerned, the donkey chose the highway.

After the provincial told us novices this story about Ignatius, he smiled and said, "Ever since then, asses have been making decisions in the Jesuits."

His story was a tiny dig at Jesuit leaders by a Jesuit leader, and it helped the novices relax a bit and laugh. And it made it easier for us to talk to him.

Finally, humor helps the preacher. Pastor Charles Hambrick-Stowe adverted to the necessity of humor in the Protestant churches. "Humor has been important for the preacher of course," he said. "For Protestants it is the pulpit, not the altar, that is the focus. So anything that demonstrates the humanity of the presider is important. American evangelical preachers have to win their audience, and humor helps to humanize a person."

Humor helps in a host of ways in religious institutions. It tells us that God's presence is often communicated through joy. It reminds us that God wants us to laugh from time to time. It invites us not to take our institutions with such deadly seriousness. It fosters a sense of institutional humility. It cautions us that we are not in control. It lifts our spirits. It defuses awkward situations. It reminds us that no religious community has all the answers. If used correctly, it makes for better social relations and work environments.

So why not use it?

And why not enjoy it?

Chapter Seven

I'm Not Funny and My Life Stinks

Answers to the Most Difficult Challenges of Living a Joyful Life

Whenever I speak to groups on the spirituality of joy, I'm usually asked some excellent questions afterward. These questions have prompted me to think more deeply about the topic, so let me share some of the most common—and most challenging—queries with you.

1. Does being joyful mean that I'm supposed to be happy all the time?

No. This is something I would like to underline, since it is a concept that is particularly important to understand in a book on joy. Sadness is a natural response to pain, suffering, and tragedy. It is human, natural, and even, in a way, desirable; sadness in response to a tragic event shows that you are emotionally alive. If you weren't sad from time to time, you would be something less than human. The Jesuit priest and clinical psychologist William A. Barry echoes this: "If you're not saddened by certain things, you're not normal—for example, when a loved one dies or in response to natural disasters. Sadness is part of life."

Although we've discussed, for example, the possibility that Jesus smiled and laughed, the New Testament tells us *outright*—without our having to read between the lines—that Jesus broke down in tears after the death of one of his friends. When Lazarus, the brother of his friends Mary and Martha, died after a brief illness, Jesus traveled to the tomb, and, in one of the simplest and shortest Gospel verses, we are told, "Jesus began to weep."[69] Jesus's weeping is seen as proof of his compassion, of his humanity. "See how he loved him!" say those in the crowd. If Jesus was sad, surely we can be sad.

The notion that you must be cheerful at all times in order to demonstrate belief in God is as ridiculous as it is common. "Get out of the tomb!" one otherwise well-meaning friend said to me when I shared my sadness over my father's death. "Aren't you a believer?" (She was referring to the idea that I was focusing on death rather than resurrection.) But even the saints, those avatars of belief, were downhearted from time to time. Like Jesus, they were occasionally sad because they were human.

Nor do I believe in the "prosperity gospel," which tells people that if they believe in Jesus Christ, their lives will be constantly successful. This is demonstrably false. The twelve apostles believed in Christ, to take one obvious example, and many of them met with difficult, painful, even tragic ends. Does anyone think that St. Peter, who was crucified, had insufficient faith? The Reverend Dr. Martin Luther King, Jr., one of the great religious figures of our time, suffered greatly, was jailed, and was assassinated. Did he not have sufficient faith? Mother Teresa, toward the end of her life, was often in terrible physical pain. She even suffered from a great darkness in her prayer, a "dark night of the soul." Was she unfaithful? Suffering—interior and exterior—is the lot of all people, including believers, including devout believers, and including those who strive to lead joyful lives.

Although the prosperity gospel has a number of important highlights—its focus on joy is a needed corrective in Christian circles; its emphasis on a rock-ribbed faith in God is essential; its encouragement to believe in a God who desires our ultimate joy is an antidote to so many terrifying images of God—its denial of suffering means that it doesn't fully embrace the human condition. This may be one reason why some of its adherents shy away from Good Friday services.

Nor do I believe that people who experience suffering or illness have somehow failed to "think positively." Barbara Ehrenreich (the author of *Dancing in the Streets*) takes aim at that idea in her trenchant book *Bright-Sided: How the Relentless Promotion of Positive Thinking Has Undermined America*. It is often helpful to look on the bright side of life and salutary to strive to be cheerful, but the belief that the sick have failed to "think positively" is monstrous. Such a belief finds its ultimate end in the notion that cancer patients, to take but one of Ehrenreich's examples, are somehow responsible for their illness because of their faulty thinking patterns. That approach only compounds the misery of the sick. Ehrenreich, a cancer survivor herself, writes, "Clearly, the failure to think positively can weigh on a cancer patient like a second disease."

Illness isn't a moral fault or a failure of will. Illness is simply a reflection of our humanity.

On the other hand, a culture of carping and general complaining predominates in some quarters. (I'll leave it up to social critics to ascertain why.) Everyone knows a few champion whiners, always lamenting some new fate that has just befallen them, complaining endlessly about their latest malady, confidently predicting an upcoming calamity, and in general worrying everyone around them. Typically these people are rather self-centered. And unpleasant to be around. I used to know someone who was a full-time hypochondriac (something I am also prone to). I knew better than to ask, "How are you?" lest he told me, in numbing detail, about his latest sniffle.

One of my friends describes it as searching for the drop of red paint in a can of white paint. It's a powerful image. The red represents your one problem. You have an entire can of white paint—let's say, a job, a roof over your head, a loving family—and you choose instead to concentrate on the one tiny red drop—the one thing wrong in your life. Suddenly the whole can turns red; that's all you see.

That is where choice comes into play. Sometimes, when presented with the mixed bag that life hands us, we can choose to focus on what makes us happy, what more readily connects us to joy in our lives. The form of contemporary psychotherapy called cognitive behavioral therapy is also helpful here. As I understand it, this school of psychology starts with the assumption that, since our thoughts shape our experience of the world, unhealthy and inaccurate thinking can lead to an incorrect evaluation of our lives and therefore to unhappiness.

Do not become upset when difficulty comes your way. Laugh in its face and know that you are in the arms of God.

—St. Francis de Sales

For example, if you're the type of person who thinks you're "always" facing some sort of misfortune, when in reality your life is a mixed bag of good and bad, you might end up miserable—not because of your situation, but because of the way you think about it. Once again, I'm not speaking here of a person in the midst of a great tragedy or experiencing real pain. Nor am I denying the need for psychotherapy or professional counseling to deal with serious psychological problems or clinical depression. Rather, I'm speaking about the person who *chooses* to focus only on the negative side of life despite the preponderance of evidence for the positive.

What are the signs that you are doing this? "Global" words are one tip-off. "I *never* get what I want!" "I'm *always* sick!" "*Everyone* hates me!" "I'm the *only* one who has it this bad!" "*No one ever* calls me!" "My boss *always* picks on me!" Remarks like those are indications that you're probably not thinking clearly.

For some, the move toward gratitude can be as simple as deciding, hard as it may seem, to focus more frequently on the positive aspects of life. For others, visiting a counselor or therapist may enable them to see things more accurately. But, once again, this does not mean that tragedy will never happen or that you will never be sad. It simply means fostering a more realistic look at your blessings in life.

A few years ago, for example, I was lamenting to my spiritual director how difficult my life was. So many struggles. So much work to do. So many physical difficulties. So many problems in relationships. And on and on. I told him that I had expressed all of this to God in prayer, and it only made me miserable.

"Are you being honest with God?" he asked.

"Of course I am," I said. "I'm sharing all of my difficulties with God."

"Ah," he said. "But honesty means being truly honest with God about reality. Are you looking at the totality of your life? Both the good *and* the bad? Are you honestly presenting your whole life to God or focusing exclusively on the problems?" That helped me to see how negative I was being, in my prayer and in my life.

So believers must navigate between a grinning, idiotic, false happiness and carping, caterwauling, complaining mopiness. (Notice again that I'm also not speaking of clinical depression here, which is more of a psychological issue.) Overall, believers will be happy and sad at different points in their lives, but joy is possible in the midst of tragedy, since joy depends on faith and confidence in God.

To that end, one of my favorite quotes about religion comes from the Scottish philosopher John Macmurray, who contrasts "illusory religion" with "real religion."[70] The maxim of illusory religion is: "Fear not; trust in God, and He will see that none of the things you fear will happen to you." Real religion has a different maxim: "Fear not; the things that you are afraid of are quite likely to happen to you, but they are nothing to be afraid of." Macmurray's sage observation illustrates the contrast between deep-down joy and evanescent happiness.

Joy can enter into our lives and catch us unawares, in the midst of dark times. Kathleen Norris told me of visiting her sister in a hospital. "I was anxiously watching an oxygen monitor in my sister's hospital room, when a janitor came in with a mop. In a low voice, barely perceptible, she was singing a song I recognized, a love song from a Broadway musical. I commented on it, and she began to sing louder, in a voice more enthusiastic and polished. But small matter. By the time she left the room, my sister and I had been treated to three songs and a significant portion of her life story. Joy is powerful medicine." Norris concluded, "I am convinced that joy is a fruit, because it tastes so sweet."*

Likewise, those in difficult situations can still find humor in their lives and still laugh. Moreover, they can choose to be cheerful around others, not in a masochistic way, but rather as a way of not unduly burdening everyone with their latest complaint. This is not to say that we should never talk about our struggles or burdens. As St. Paul would say, "By no means!" It's important during times of struggle to speak to a close friend, family member, a priest or minister, or a therapist. And it's important to share those struggles with God in prayer. What I'm arguing against is the kind of round-the-clock complaining that many people—including me at times—sometimes engage in.

Lately, I've been trying to be more silent about some of my struggles, that is, not sharing too many personal burdens with people whose lives are already overburdened. Once again, this is not to say that I don't share my struggles with my friends, my spiritual director, or with God in prayer. Rather, it is a gift to offer people your cheerfulness even in the midst of pain. This may be something like what Mother Teresa had in mind when she said, "Every time you smile at someone, it is an action of love, a gift to that person, a beautiful thing."

The ability to do that comes from a deep-down sense of joy even in dark times. Which bring me to the next question.

2. How can I find a sense of joy if I'm unhappy?

Finding joy during times of pain begins with understanding that true joy is rooted in God. Thus, keeping one's relationship with God

---

* This is a wonderful way of understanding St. Paul's listing of joy as among the "fruits" of the Holy Spirit (Gal. 5:22–23).

at the center of one's life is essential to discovering areas of joy, comfort, and solace.

One easy way to recover a sense of joy is to practice, as the saying goes, an "attitude of gratitude." And one technique to foster that attitude is a prayer, popularized by St. Ignatius Loyola, called the examination of conscience.[71] It is a simple five-step prayer in which you review your day from start to finish.

The preface to the examination of conscience is to remind yourself that you're in the presence of God, as one does in all prayer.

The first step is calling to mind the things for which you are grateful. These need not be earth-shattering, life-changing events, but might be simple things that happened during the day: a gentle word from a friend, a task completed, a smile on the face of your son or daughter. Even smaller things can be recalled: your dog's crazy antics this morning, the taste of the pizza you had at lunch, the feel of the warm sunshine on your face as you walked home from work, a good night's sleep.

St. Ignatius invites us to "savor" these events as a way of sinking into gratitude, reminding ourselves of all that "white paint" in our lives. And during times of sadness or unhappiness, nothing connects us to God more quickly than orienting ourselves toward those things for which we are grateful.

Second, review the day and see where God was present and where you might have overlooked God. It's often easier to see God in the past, in retrospect, than it is to see God in the present. So the examination of conscience helps us quickly to find God in our daily lives, even in times of unhappiness, when we are most likely to overlook God.

Third, ask for the grace to see where you might have turned away from God and sinned.

Fourth, ask for forgiveness for any sins you've committed. Perhaps you might want to follow up with a reconciliation with a friend, coworker, or neighbor if this is especially serious or, if you're Catholic, with confession if this is a grave sin.

Fifth and finally, ask for the grace to see God more clearly the next day.

The examination is a prayer of awareness of God, of seeing where God is already active in your daily life. But for the purposes of our discussion the most important aspect is gratitude. Gratitude reminds us of God's gifts in our lives even during times of sadness and can reconnect us with a believing joy. Gratitude reminds us of the underlying joy in our lives.

Father Barry noted that for those who wish to find spiritual joy during a time of sadness, memories are also important. "I often ask people who have difficulties trusting God in these times to begin by looking at some memory," he told me recently. "In times of darkness we tend to forget joyful times. So first try to connect with memories of joyful times. Then you can begin to recognize that sometimes you're caught up in the desire for God and joy. But, first of all, you have to have had some kind of deep spiritual joy in God before the times of sadness."

"Also," said Father Barry, "I've been really surprised over the years at people who are actually grateful for terrible things—alcoholism, depression, cancer. They drifted away, and this brought them back to God. This is not to say that God 'gave it to them.' But the experience itself moved them back to God, which brought them joy."

More specifically, "savoring" is becoming popular in the psychological community. The psychologist Eileen Russell told me, echoing Father Barry's insight, "Savoring and remembering mean that you have access to those feelings and can draw on them when things are difficult." In the past, she explained, psychologists wrote more frequently about anxiety, depression, and other difficult emotional states. Today more are writing about qualities like joy and awe. "Savoring," one of St. Ignatius's favorite practices, is part of these new studies. "Savoring also means that you're *aware* that you're joyful," she said, "which leads to even more expansive feelings of well-being."

Finally, the Episcopal priest Jerome W. Berryman offers a deeply personal approach to adult joy in his book *Teaching Godly Play: How*

Start a Collection

An old book on humor offers some timeless advice for people who tend to focus on the dark side:

> Start a collection of happy and humorous memories. Reminisce about the happy incidents of your childhood. Remember the amusing things that happened at home and at school. Recall the pranks your coworkers played or funny things that occurred. Include any experience that made you laugh or feel good, whether it was an anecdote that someone told, a happy circumstance, or a comical event. Making a list of these cherished happenings is a useful activity. Keep looking for funny experiences to add to your list. Include jokes and stories that you find particularly amusing. Look for constructive and positive humor, which you will find, in the long run, to be more rewarding than anti-ethnic or put-down humor. Return to your list frequently and enjoy recalling the happy times. Tell your funny experiences to your friends, so they will want to share more joy with you, multiplying the laugh for everyone. The triggering of laughter in others and their sharing in your periods of it facilitates the development of a humorous group perspective—the feeling that we can all laugh at ourselves and each other's failings and that we hold amusing experiences in common in this mad world.[72]

to Mentor the Spiritual Development of Children.[73] Berryman's specialty is, as the title of his book suggests, the religious development of children. The second edition of his book, however, begins on a seemingly somber note, as he recounts the homily he gave at the funeral of his wife and collaborator of almost fifty years, Thea. Berryman spoke of meeting her for the first time in 1960, when his life "suddenly went from shades of brown to intense colors." But their life together was not all lightness. "I have been falling in love with her ever since that day, and we have walked together through much sadness and happiness since then."

Once, he said, they hiked together over the "Great Divide," the continental divide, in Colorado, a journey of some twenty-four miles over the high mountains. But they also climbed "up and down the stairs in their own house one last time together, a challenge that was much tougher. Still, being together, as always, was enough to bring great joy."

Berryman asks: "Do you know what you get when you mix lots of happiness with lots of sadness? You get joy, and we had much of that together."

3. I'm not a funny person. How do I learn how to tell jokes? Or, alternately, I'm just not funny. What do I do?

This is a surprisingly common question, perhaps the most common I'm asked. People often think that being joyful means being a stand-up comic or that finding humor in life means you have to be Mark Twain.

Still, it's a fair question. Some of us are simply not jokey types. To quote Karl-Josef Kuschel, we haven't yet developed a "jokological" approach to life. Some of us have a hard time telling a funny story. It's like the story (here comes a joke) that my father used to tell about the new inmate in a prison.

He walks into the dining room, sits down next to an older inmate, and starts eating. Suddenly someone jumps up and calls out, "A hundred and twenty-two!" Everyone bursts into laughter. A few minutes later someone else jumps up and says, "Thirty-eight!" More laughter. Another says, "Three!" Laughter again. Finally the young inmate asks the older one, "What's going on?"

The older fellow says, "We've all been here for so long and know each other so well that we know one another's jokes. Rather than wasting time recounting them, we assign each joke a number. All you have to do is shout out a number, and we all recall the corresponding joke and laugh. You try it!"

"Oh no," says the new inmate. "I don't know any of the jokes."

"It doesn't matter," says the older fellow. "Just pick any number between one and five hundred."

So the new man jumps up and says, "A hundred and seven!"

He is met with silence. No one laughs.

Confused, he sits down next to his friend. "What happened?" he asks.

"Well," says the older fellow, "some guys can tell a joke, and some guys can't."

But you don't have to be a comedian or a comedy writer to find humor in life. Here are a few suggestions if you feel your life is somewhat humorless or joke-challenged.

First, seek out funny people. Even if you can't make jokes, you can laugh at them. And if you can't comment humorously on life's absurdities, or even see life's absurdities, you can appreciate someone else's humorous outlook. One of the great blessings in Jesuit life has been finding so many priests and brothers who have a spectacular sense of humor, who can say funny things at the right moment and reveal life's silliness.

In other words, *you* don't have to make the joke to enjoy life's humor. Remember my friend Mike, whose story about "excessive levity" opened the book? I asked him, "Do people ask you how they can be funny?"

"All the time!" he laughed.

"So," I asked, "how can these people see the humor in life?"

"Enjoy everyone else!" he said. "You don't have to be the one who's funny. You can enjoy the humorous people around you."

My father, who loved to tell jokes, was friends with a neighbor who freely admitted he wasn't a particularly experienced jokester. But he loved to listen to and laugh at my father's jokes. My sister, Carolyn, recalled this recently and said that she often tells her children, "Be a good audience!"

Margaret Silf recently told me that she needs a "laughter fix" at least once a year. "I have one crazy friend who is guaranteed to make me laugh," she said. "It seems to work both ways, so we make sure to go on holiday together every summer for a 'funny fix.' It might seem ridiculous to people around us, but I know it makes a huge difference to me—shakes out all the grumpy bits—changes my perspective on lots of things, and anyway, it's fun! It reminds me of a recent ad I saw encouraging perfectly mature adults to indulge in the kind of chocolate only children are supposed to like. The slogan—Ungrow Up!"

Second, enjoy life's funny moments on your own. You don't have to joke about things publicly, and you don't have to be a professional humorist to appreciate life's absurdities, incongruities, and general ridiculousness. Be content to recognize and appreciate comic incidents on your own. Are there things that tickle your funny bone? Enjoy them! Have you seen any nutty videos on the Web that make you laugh? Watch them again! You don't have to be a stand-up comedian to appreciate the gift of humor.

You don't even have to enjoy jokes per se. One of my closest friends, Paula, simply does not laugh at jokes. Shortly after we first met, I relayed a new joke, and she stared at me blankly. "Yeah," she said, "I don't really get jokes." Never having met anyone who didn't "get jokes," I was dumbfounded. Recently I mustered the courage to ask her about that part of her personality, which was a particular mystery, since her husband was a terrific jokester. "What do you mean you don't get jokes?"

"Well," she said, "I analyze them too much. So when you tell me a joke, I take it apart and think about it, and it doesn't seem that funny. Try one on me."

Bear with Me

A Catholic priest, a Baptist preacher, and a rabbi served as chaplains to the students of a college in the Midwest. The three friends would get together several times a week for coffee. One day, someone commented that preaching to people isn't really all that hard—a real challenge would be to preach to a bear. So they decided to do an experiment. They would venture into the woods, find a bear, preach to it, and attempt to convert it. Seven days later, they gathered again to discuss their experience.

Father Flannery, who had his arm in a sling, was on crutches, and had bandages on his face, went first. "Well," he said, "I went into the woods to find a bear. And when I found him, I began to read to him from the *Catechism*. That bear wanted nothing to do with me and rudely began to push me around. So I grabbed my holy water and baptized him, and he became as gentle as a lamb. The bishop is coming out next week to give him First Communion and to confirm him."

Reverend Smith spoke next. He was in a wheelchair and had one arm and both legs in casts. "Well, brothers, I went out and found a bear as well. And then I began to read to him from God's Holy Word. But that bear wanted nothing to do with me. So I took hold of him, and we began to wrestle. We wrestled down one hill, up another, and down another until we came to a creek. So I quickly dunked him and baptized his heavenly soul. And just like you said, Father, he became as gentle as a lamb. We spent the rest of the day praising Jesus."

The priest and the preacher both looked down at Rabbi Stein, who was on a stretcher. He was in a full body cast. The rabbi looked up and said: "Looking back on it, circumcision may not have been the best way to start."

So I told her one of my father's favorite jokes, about the old man who was hit by a car as he's crossing a street. He's lying in the street, waiting for the ambulance, and a police officer comes up and asks him, "What happened?"

"I got hit by a car," says the man blandly.

"Oh no!" says the policeman. "Are you comfortable?"

"Eh," says the man, "I make a living."

Paula stared at me impassively. "See," she said, "that just doesn't make me laugh. I know that 'comfortable' means well off, so I get the double meaning. It just doesn't make me laugh."

Here's the point: Paula has a wonderful sense of humor nonetheless. She laughs a lot, she sees life's absurdities, and she's a joyful person to be around. She just doesn't happen to be a joke teller or joke hearer. "My brother-in-law is really the life of the party," she told me recently. "And he knows to expect only a wry smile from me." So you don't even have to be the perfect audience to have a sense of humor.

Sometimes your own struggles can make you laugh—or at least your reaction to them can. Have you ever tried exaggerating your woes in an obviously over-the-top way? As a friend of mine likes to say, with mock seriousness, "My life is a *nightmare*!" My funny friend Mike, who teaches a course on religion and comedy, calls that "comic exaggeration." Saying your woes out loud may reveal the frequently ridiculous aspects of a constantly complaining attitude. It may help you to find humor in the last place you might expect to find it.

Third, read authors who highlight life's comic side. Comedians, sitcoms, and movie comedies are terrific for pointing out life's funny moments. But a lesser-known way to refine your sense of humor is to read the work of humorists. And the *ne plus ultra* of this genre, at least to me, is the passage that can make me laugh out loud. Sometimes you can even "savor," as St. Ignatius says, a particular word or phrase, which you might remember for the rest of your life. These help you develop your own sense of humor.

Let me share with you three examples of what is (to me) laugh-out-loud humor. The first is from my favorite humorist, Jean Shepherd. He is best known today as the author of the short stories upon which was based the now-classic 1983 movie *A Christmas Story,* the tale of Little Ralphie's quest to buy a Red Ryder BB gun, which runs incessantly on television stations around Christmastime. But Shepherd is the author of many books, of which my favorite is *Wanda Hickey's Night of Golden Memories and Other Disasters,* a series of hilarious, picaresque, and often ribald short stories about growing up in Depression-era Indiana. Most of his tales include characters who will be familiar to devotees of *A Christmas Story,* including his long-suffering mother, his cantankerous "Old Man," and his annoying little brother, Randy.

The title story refers to his awful high-school prom, which he grudgingly attended with a girl for whom he had little affection. Instead, he pines for another girl, the beautiful and alluring Daphne Bigelow, whom he describes in another story, memorably:

> Her name was Daphne Bigelow. Even now, ten light-years removed from the event, I cannot suppress a fugitive shiver of tremulous passionate dark yearning. Her skin was of the clearest, rarest form of pure, translucent alabaster. She had no "eyes" in the mundane sense, but rather she saw the world, or the world saw her, through twin jade-green jungle pools, mirrors of a soul that was so mysterious, so enigmatic as to baffle ninth-graders for yards around. I hesitate to use such a pitifully inadequate word as "hair" to describe the nimbus of magic, that shifting cloud of iridescence that framed a face of such surpassing beauty that even Buddha would have thought long and hard before staring straight into it.

Jean Shepherd was a true Midwestern wit: wry, generous, drawing on the simple pleasure of seeing the amusing in the ordinary. Is a high-school prom humorous? In Shepherd's eyes it is. Can you find similar absurdities in your own life?

Decades later, Fran Lebowitz published *Metropolitan Life,* which appeared a few years before I moved to New York City. Her book perfectly captured the brittle New York wit and gimlet-eyed view of life that I (along with the rest of the world) came to associate with Manhattan. Her essays and *bons mots* always made me laugh. Here is an excerpt from an essay entitled "A Manual: Training for Landlords," a tongue-in-cheek guidebook for New York landlords, obviously born out of experience:

> *Lesson Six: Roaches.* It is the solemn duty of every landlord to maintain an adequate supply of roaches. The minimum acceptable roach to tenant ratio is four thousand to one. Should this arrangement prompt an expression of displeasure on the part of the tenant, ignore him absolutely. The tenant is a notorious complainer. Just why this is so is not certain, though a number of theories abound. The most plausible of these ascribes the tenant's chronic irritability to his widely suspected habit of drinking enormous quantities of heat and hot water—a practice well known to result in the tragically premature demise of hallway light bulbs.

Even more recent is Bill Bryson, whose writings on travel are peerless. He has written hilariously on his trip to Australia (*In a Sunburned Country*), where he debates with his travel partner on the possibility of drinking his own urine if stranded; on his journey along the Appalachian Trail (*A Walk in the Woods*), where his seriously out-of-shape hiking partner decides to leave behind their water (because it's simply too heavy to carry); on his travels around Great Britain (*Notes from a Small Island*), which includes a terrific description of mangy blankets in a pokey English inn; and on his return to the United States after spending years living in England (*The Lost Continent: Travels in Small-Town America*). Here he is in that book expanding on a visit to Cleveland. Bryson wrote this in 1990, and Cleveland has in fact bounced back. I greatly enjoy my visits there, but, still, this is pretty funny:

> Cleveland has always had a reputation for being a dirty, ugly, boring city, though now they say it is much better. By "they" I mean reporters from serious publications like the *Wall Street Journal, Fortune* and the *New York Times* Sunday Magazine, who visit the city at five-year intervals and produce long stories with titles like "Cleveland Bounces Back" and "Renaissance in Cleveland." No one ever reads these articles, least of all me, so I couldn't say whether the improbable and highly relative assertion that Cleveland is better now than it used to be is wrong or right. What I can say is that the view up the Cuyahoga as I crossed it on the freeway was of a stew of smoking factories that didn't look any too clean or handsome. And I can't say that the rest of the town looked like such a knockout either. It may be improved, but all this talk of a renaissance is clearly exaggerated. I somehow doubt that if the Duc d'Urbino were brought back to life and deposited in downtown Cleveland, he would say, "Goodness, I am put in mind of fifteenth-century Florence and the many treasures therein."

The mental image of the Duc d'Urbino, in his Renaissance finery, contemplating the view of Cleveland and saying, "I am put in mind" is laugh-out-loud funny. At least to me. Of course humor is subjective. You may be like Paula and offer only a wry smile. The point is that, with a little exploration, you can find authors who tickle your funny bone and help you develop your own sense of humor.

These passages also are reminders that you can find humor in even the most prosaic of circumstances. Notice the simple things that gave rise to the comic masterpieces above: a high-school prom, apartment life, a visit to an American city. None of these are extraordinary. A sense of humor depends upon having an eye for the humorous in the ordinary. But even if you never develop into a world-famous comedian, comic actor, or humor writer, the more you spend time with funny people, the more you will find occasions of mirth in everyday life. Humor is within the reach of everyone, because everyone's life is full of absurdity, improbability, and general craziness.

4. What can I do if I live or work in a joyless environment?

First, remember that your environment doesn't define you. One of the most difficult things about living in an environment (home, workplace, religious community) lacking joy is that you may gradually assume that (a) you should not be joyful; (b) you are not naturally joyful, since you're experiencing so little joy; or (c) the world is a joyless place. Joy-free persons sometimes seem to be joy vampires, sucking the happiness out of everyone else's life as well.

In these situations, it's important to remind yourself that (a) it's okay to be joyful; (b) you do in fact experience joy in other areas of your life; and (c) there is joy in the world, though it may be outside of this house, workplace, or religious community. It requires an inner strength similar to what's required in being a believer among those who might scorn your beliefs. Hang on to your joy as you would hang on to your belief in God.

Second, try to find those things for which you are grateful. One of the fastest ways to recover a sense of believing joy is grounding yourself in gratitude. Do you work in an environment with a miserable boss and grumpy coworkers? Perhaps you can call to mind your children and how they make you laugh. Or your upcoming vacation. Or simply being alive. It may not solve all those problems at work, but it may help you to rediscover joy.

Third, learn to laugh about life with someone else. If you find yourself in a difficult situation, a gloomy work environment, or a morose family setting, find someone—inside or outside—with whom you can easily laugh about it. That's not to say you mock anyone in these situations; rather, if you can find someone with whom you can laugh about some of your problems, it will provide you with an escape hatch for a few hours. Just knowing that you have someone to talk with playfully can be a relief. It can also help put things in perspective; you can survive this with a sense of humor.

"Do they have any friends that can help them with this?" asked Father Barry, when I described the situation of individuals trapped in a gloomy environment. "It can be very hard for someone to maintain joy in such an environment—say, when you're young and a parent is dying. But to be able to talk to someone else about it and find out that you can be listened to can lighten the burden."

Especially if your friends have a sense of humor. One of the funniest moments in my life came when I was working at a corporate job in the late 1980s, before I was about to enter the Jesuits. My manager—I'll keep this vague—was a terror. Or at least I felt that way. In any event, I spent a good half hour complaining bitterly to an old friend, John, about my wicked boss. He was terrible. He was an ogre. He was a tyrant. He was the worst boss ever! I went on and on. He listened with a straight face. "What should I do?" I asked plaintively.

John sat silently for a few seconds, as if carefully weighing my comments. Finally he said, "I have some advice for you, Jim."

I eagerly awaited some sage wisdom on how to deal with a difficult manager.

Finally and with great gravity he said, "I think you should kill him."

It was so ridiculous an answer that I laughed for a few minutes. Of course my boss wasn't *that* bad; he wasn't really an ogre or a tyrant or the worst boss ever. I could deal with him. Whenever I thought about my annoying manager, I always remembered John's ridiculous remark and smiled.*

---

* Reader, I did not kill him.

Holding on to a healthy sense of humor in the midst of difficult times can be a double blessing—for yourself and for others. There is something almost inexplicably consoling about being with someone who can smile in the midst of adversity.

The Jesuit theologian Cardinal Avery Dulles suffered at the end of his life from postpolio syndrome, the aftereffects of poliomyelitis he had contracted in his young adulthood. As Avery aged, he lost much of his muscle and neurological control. In his last year, he delivered his final public address at Fordham University. He was so weak that a longtime Jesuit friend, Joseph A. O'Hare, former president of Fordham, had to read his speech aloud for him. Before the talk, Joe playfully asked Avery if he should make any changes to the speech. At this point in his illness all Avery could do was slowly scribble on a piece of paper.

He wrote, "Only if they're improvements!"

After Joe delivered the speech word for word, Avery wrote, "Thanks for the improvements."

Although not as dramatic as some of the martyrs' last words (like St. Lawrence's "This side is done. Turn me over and have a bite"), Avery's gentle humor underlined his faith in God, lightened everyone's burden, and in the process inspired his friends. Not coincidentally, the last words of Avery's final speech were of his faith in God. So the renowned theologian relied on both humor and faith at the end of his life:

> The good life does not have to be an easy one, as our blessed Lord and the saints have taught us. Pope John Paul II in his later years used to say, "The Pope must suffer." Suffering and diminishment are not the greatest of evils, but are normal ingredients in life, especially in old age. They are to be expected as elements of a full human existence. Well into my ninetieth year I have been able to work productively. As I become increasingly paralyzed and unable to speak, I can

> identify with the many paralytics and mute persons in the Gospels, grateful for the loving and skillful care I receive and for the hope of everlasting life in Christ. If the Lord now calls me to a period of weakness, I know well that his power can be made perfect in infirmity. "Blessed be the name of the Lord!"

Fourth, be leaven. Can *you* be the joy? Can you be the bearer of humor or lightheartedness in an otherwise bleak setting?

In my first year in the Jesuit novitiate, the novices were sent to work in various "ministries" in the area. We worked in hospitals, elementary schools, parishes, soup kitchens, and in a retirement home for Jesuit priests and brothers. Once a week we gathered with the novice director to talk about our experiences—particularly where we had found God in our work and among the people.

During one meeting a fellow novice lamented that there were no other Jesuits in the Jesuit high school where he worked. In this era of declining "vocations," with fewer priests, brothers, and sisters, many schools sponsored by religious orders are staffed mainly by laypeople. This is a natural development of the layperson's role in the Catholic Church, but it may still seem odd to outsiders. As it did to my fellow novice.

"Where are the *Jesuits*?" he asked rhetorically. "Where are we? Aren't the Jesuits supposed to be in a Jesuit school?"

Finally the novice director, clearly exasperated, said, "You're there! *You're* the Jesuit!"

His comment stuck with me. If you're looking for joy, can you be the one who provides it? Can you be, as Jesus says, the "leaven"? In one of his parables Jesus compares the kingdom of God to a bit of yeast that a woman kneads into her bread.[74] Only a small portion is needed to make the dough rise. Can you be the leaven of joy in a joyless situation? Perhaps others are waiting for your joyful leaven.

Those are the most frequent questions I'm asked about the difficulties of living a life of joy, humor, and laughter in a world full of challenges. Oh, wait. I'm asked another question frequently. It deserves an answer too.

5. Father Martin, do you want to hear a joke?

Only if it's a good one!

Chapter Eight

God Has Brought Laughter for Me

Discovering Delight in Your Personal Spiritual Life

A diocesan priest, a Franciscan friar, a Benedictine priest, a Trappist monk, and a Jesuit priest are about to start a group retreat together. Since they're going to be sharing some personal matters with one another during their group meetings, they decide to start off by building trust: they will discuss their worst failings on the first day. They will do so in strict confidence, so that everyone can feel free to speak honestly. The parish priest goes first.

"Well, my brothers," he says, "thank God this is confidential, because my sin is so embarrassing. I hate to say this, but I just don't pray. I know it's part of my priestly life, but prayer can be so dry. Oh, I'm so embarrassed. But I'm happy that we can be honest and so glad this is all confidential—I would be horrified if anyone knew!"

Then the Franciscan friar says, "Oh, brothers, my sin is more embarrassing than that. Sometimes when I get a donation for the community, I don't turn it in as I should. I keep it for myself, even though it's against my vow of poverty. I feel better about sharing this, but thank God this is confidential!"

Then the Benedictine says, "Oh, brothers, my sin is far worse. I teach liturgy at our local Benedictine college, but I miss Mass all the time. Sometimes I'm so busy grading papers in the morning that I can't go to Mass. I couldn't imagine what would happen if my abbot knew this. But I feel better for telling you this in confidence."

Then the Trappist says, "Brothers, my sin is far, far worse, and I'm much more embarrassed! We monks are supposed to stay in the monastery all the time, but every few days I sneak out and go to the movies. I'm covered in shame. Thank God this is all confidential."

All the while the Jesuit sits quietly. Finally, one of them says to him, "Father?"

And the Jesuit says, "Oh, brothers, my sin is the worst of all. . . . I just can't keep a secret!"

Here's a secret: joy, humor, and laughter help us to experience God's presence in our daily lives.

A few chapters earlier we looked at the need for humor in the church. Now let's look at three reasons why we need humor in our own personal spiritual life, in our daily relationship with God.

1. Humor leads to poverty of spirit.

As I've mentioned several times,* it's easy for anyone to get puffed up. A famous Jesuit theologian was once asked if he was going to a theology conference. "I don't go to theology conferences," he said, "I *give* theology conferences." Oh, brother.

On a more positive note, the truly holy are truly humble. Reading the lives of the saints confirms this. Over and over, they talk about their own sinfulness, their own limitations, their own humanity, frequently in spite of the fact that those around them speak only of their holiness. Humor is an antidote to spiritual pride.

One of my favorite stories of holy humility comes from the life of

* Repetition is a classic part of the Jesuit educational tradition; early Jesuit educators used repetition as an aid to help students memorize certain facts. It's also part of our spiritual tradition; St. Ignatius Loyola encourages believers to return to a particular Scripture passage in prayer as a way of deepening their understanding and appreciation. So blame any repetitions in this book on St. Ignatius.

Dorothy Day, the founder of the Catholic Worker movement.* Today Catholic Worker "houses of hospitality" carry on her mission to care for the poor and marginalized in cities throughout the United States. The story is told by the Harvard psychologist Robert Coles, in his biography *Dorothy Day: A Radical Devotion*.[75]

In 1952, Coles was a medical student at Columbia University in New York City. One day, he took the subway downtown to the Catholic Worker house to do some volunteer work. The young Coles was filled with excitement over the prospect of meeting the famous Dorothy Day.

When he arrived he found the great woman sitting at a table talking to an unkempt, homeless woman who was obviously drunk and ranting and raving. Dorothy was listening attentively, from time to time asking a quiet question that would only rev the woman up again. Coles remembers thinking, "When would it end?" Finally the woman quieted down, and Dorothy got up, walked over to Coles, and asked, "Are you waiting to talk with one of us?"

She didn't say, "Oh, hello, you must want to see me, the great Dorothy Day." Instead, "Are you waiting to talk with one of us?"

Robert Coles said that with those three simple words—"one of us"—Dorothy Day had cut through layers of self-importance and told him exactly what she, the Catholic Worker, and Christianity were about. All of us are children of God. None is more important than any other. Each of us is as important as everyone else. All of us have equal dignity—woman or man; old or young; gay or straight; ordained or lay; single, married, or vowed—from the pope to the person who cleans the church bathrooms.

This sentiment is similar to what St. Thérèse of Lisieux, the nineteenth-century French Carmelite nun, said when she compared humanity to a garden. "The splendor of the rose and the whiteness of the lily," she said, "do not take away the perfume of the little violet

* I was once at a Mass where the homilist said that "Doris Day" was the greatest Catholic in American history.

or the delightful simplicity of the daisy." The individuality of each flower makes God's garden beautiful. The saints understood this basic truth, which is why they strove for humility.

Cardinal Avery Dulles, whom I mentioned in the last chapter, died in 2008 at the age of ninety. If anyone had the right to be puffed up, he did. A member of a distinguished American family and the son of John Foster Dulles, the U.S. Secretary of State, Avery was a Harvard-educated naval hero and the author of dozens of books and hundreds of scholarly articles. He was widely recognized as the dean of American Catholic theologians and was also the first American theologian and the first American Jesuit to be named a cardinal. But he was an exceedingly humble man who pitched in at his Jesuit community, did his own laundry, tutored college students, and so on.

Once I was asked to accompany Avery on a trip to Boston, where he was scheduled to receive an award. On the train ride from New York, I said, "Are you excited about getting this award?"

And he said, "Well, I haven't done anything to *deserve* it."

I said, "What about all the books and articles, and your teaching?"

And he said, "Oh well, I still feel that I don't deserve it."

Dorothy Day was humble. Avery Dulles was humble. The truly holy are humble because they know their place before God.

But how, with our accomplishments and our egos, especially in a culture that tells us that we have to be on top, to be number one, to be successful, do we keep that humility before us? Self-deprecating humor, as I've mentioned, is one way to do this. Laughing at yourself, not taking yourself too seriously, not making every situation about you, not demanding that life adjust itself to suit your needs, and laughing at yourself when you forget all this are good places to start.

There may be nothing as helpful to our humility as a good friend who can good-naturedly puncture our inflated pride or set us straight when we start to complain too much. A few years ago, I was complaining about some small physical malady to my friend Chris, a Jesuit brother. I said, with mock seriousness, "My life is such a cross!"

The Bridge

After Pope John Paul II dies, he meets God in heaven. God says, "Since you did such an outstanding job as pope, I'm going to grant you one wish. Anything you want on earth, just name it."

John Paul says, "Well, I know what I would like. I've always thought that if there were a bridge between Africa and Europe, a physical bridge that people could drive across, there would be more understanding of the problems of Africa, and Europe could better appreciate the cultural riches of the continent. So I would like you to build a bridge from Italy to North Africa."

God says, "A bridge from Europe to Africa? Well, when you consider how long the bridge would have to be and then how much steel it would take to reinforce the structure because of the wind and the weather, I would say that this is physically impossible. Sorry, but do you have another wish?"

John Paul is surprised that not even God thinks this can be done. So he says, "In that case, how about this? When I was pope, I had a devil of a time figuring out those Jesuits. They were always doing something surprising or unpredictable, and they sometimes gave me *agita*. So here's my second wish. Could you make the Jesuits more . . . manageable?"

God thinks for a bit and says, "How many lanes did you want on that bridge—two or four?"

"Yes," he said without missing a beat. "But for you or for others?"

I burst out laughing. Whenever I am tempted to focus too much on my own problems, I remember Chris's funny, but important, joke.

Well-meaning strangers can do this as well. My friend Jim, a young Jesuit, spent time as an English teacher in China during his Jesuit training. His students asked if they could read a story that they had written about their esteemed teacher. "Jim is very handsome," the story began, to Jim's great delight.

"He is very tall." Jim's pride grew.

"And he is very fat." No one laughed harder at that story than Jim.

"Laughter," as Conrad Hyers writes in *The Comic Vision and the Christian Faith,* "bursts out of the small world of our seriousness and greed and self-importance and allows the water of life to flow freely to all, relieving the dryness and barrenness of our parched spirits."

WHERE DOES HUMILITY LEAD? It leads to poverty of spirit, a sadly neglected spiritual virtue.

Here's a thought experiment. Recall the Beatitudes (mentioned in Chapter 2), that list of "Blessed are . . ." statements in the Gospel of Matthew in which Jesus enumerates the essential characteristics of Christians: "Blessed are the meek. . . . Blessed are the merciful. . . . Blessed are the pure in heart."

What would you say if someone said that you should live the message of the Beatitudes?

You might say, "Yes, I should be meek. Yes, merciful. Yes, pure in heart."

But Jesus also says, "Blessed are the poor in spirit."

Why should you be poor in spirit? That sounds negative. Shouldn't you be *rich* in spirit? What does it mean to be "poor in spirit"?

Johannes Baptist Metz, a contemporary Catholic theologian, reminds us that poverty of spirit, which is another way of talking about humility, is the beginning of the Christian spiritual journey. Without spiritual poverty, we resist admitting our reliance on God, we are tempted to try to do everything on our own, and we are therefore more likely to despair when things do not go the way we had planned. "Poverty of spirit," says Metz, "is not just one virtue among many. It is the . . . ground of every 'theological virtue.'"[76]

Poverty of spirit does not take away joy. On the contrary, it is the gateway to joy, because it enables you to recognize your ultimate reliance on God, which leads to freedom. You have the freedom to say, "It's not all up to me." And the temptation to think or act as if everything is up to you, what I would call "Messiah-ism," is a real one.

When I was working in East Africa with refugees, for example, it took me many months to recognize that I couldn't solve everyone's problems. No matter how hard I worked, no matter how many refugees I helped, many would still face lives of great suffering. This realization could have led to despair, the awful knowledge that even after completing my assignment, their lives might not have changed all that much.

You've probably felt that way at some point in your life. You may have friends whose lives seem utterly chaotic. Your own life may seem a mess. You see so much that needs changing, so much that needs fixing, but you don't seem to be able to change, fix, or even manage it all.

At one point I told my spiritual director in Nairobi how frustrated I was becoming about my work. I couldn't believe how much there was to do! And I was starting to despair that I couldn't do it all. I had to meet with each of the refugees every week, meet with everyone who needed counseling, ensure they all received adequate medical care, advocate for them when they got in trouble with their landlords, plead for them at the UN offices—basically, solve all their problems and fix everything wrong in their lives. "I should be doing all these things," I told my director, named George, "but I don't seem to be able to."*

George said, "Wow, that's a lot to do. Where did you get the idea that you have to do everything?"

And I thought, "What a dumb question." So I said, "That's what Jesus would do, obviously."

George answered, "Well, yes, that might be right. But guess what? I've got some news for you, Jim. You're not Jesus!"

---

* Another spiritual director used to call this "shoulding all over yourself." Say it out loud and the pun becomes obvious.

Or, as my current spiritual director likes to say, "There is a Messiah, and it's not you!"

Once you embrace some poverty of spirit, you're more able to do your best and leave the rest up to God, and you can do so confidently and joyfully. But it begins with humility. And the doorway to that humility is the ability not to take yourself with deadly seriousness. Thomas Merton, the Trappist monk who loved to laugh, felt the same. "I think the main reason we have so little joy," he wrote in 1950, "is that we take ourselves too seriously."[77]

Laughing at yourself reminds you of your essential humanity, of your own foibles, of your own weakness and limitations. To quote the famous last line of *Some Like It Hot,* one of the great movie comedies, "Nobody's perfect!"

Laugh. For this laughter is an acknowledgment that you are a human being, an acknowledgment that is itself the beginning of an acknowledgment of God. For how else is a person to acknowledge God except through admitting in his life and by means of his life that he himself is not God but a creature that has his times—a time to weep and a time to laugh, and the one is not the other. A praising of God is what laughter is, because it lets a human being be human.

—KARL RAHNER, *The Content of Faith*

---

2. Humor reminds us that we're not in control.

If we don't laugh at ourselves, God will remind us to. God invites us to laugh at ourselves and recall our limitations by revealing our own weakness. By recognizing the dumb mistakes we make, the silly things we do, and the pompous attitudes we strike, we can embrace a real poverty of spirit.

Have you ever considered whether the things that make you aware of your limitations may be invitations to live out the Beatitudes? The key is being alert enough to get the joke and see that some of life's most frustrating moments may be invitations to grow in humility. And it happens most often when we're filled with a sense of self-importance. God often takes us down a peg for our own good.

One winter I had an appointment at ten in the morning with my spiritual director, a Jesuit priest named Damian, who works at Fordham University's Manhattan campus, about a twenty-minute walk from my office.

It was an awful morning—cold, wet, and snowy—and I was fighting a miserable cold. After walking through the snow and wind, I arrived at his office promptly at ten and knocked on his door. No one answered.

After waiting for a few minutes, I called his office and could hear the phone ringing inside. But there was no answer. I thought, "What's wrong with him? This is my spiritual direction! Doesn't he realize how important this is?" Standing in front of his office door, I filled with self-importance, pride, and anger.

After waiting about ten minutes I left, walked through the snow again, and returned to my office at ten-thirty. By the time I returned, I was wet and overheated from the walk. A message flashed on my voice mail. "Hi Jim, I'm so sorry. I thought we said eleven, but you're right: it was ten. You can come back now if you want." I was furious!

So I walked back to his office. When I arrived, I was wet and cold and angry. Damian and I talked about it, I got over it, and we had a productive session. But as I walked home, I grew indignant again—how could he have forgotten *me*?

A few days later, after dinner one Monday night, I spent some time working at my desk. (My office and the Jesuit community are in the same building.) When I returned to my room a few hours later, I had a message on my voice mail. It was a young Jesuit, named Carlos, who sees me for spiritual direction.

"Hi Jim," said Carlos on my voice mail. "I'm here. Where are you? Didn't we have an appointment for spiritual direction at eight o'clock? I'm waiting outside your door. It's really cold out here too, but I'll wait!"

Then another message. "Hi Jim, it's eight-thirty, and I'm still waiting. I hope you're there!"

Looking at my calendar, I realized I had forgotten to flip the page for the new week! My calendar was open to last Monday, and I had missed our appointment.

Mortified, I called him to apologize and reschedule. But I also had to laugh at myself. In less than a week, I had done the very thing that I couldn't imagine someone else doing!

This seemed a clear invitation from God to embrace some humility and some perspective. God seemed to be saying, "Get over yourself! You make mistakes like everyone else does." Or "Everyone else makes mistakes too, just like you."

The next time I saw my spiritual director we laughed about it; and the next time I saw Carlos, I again apologized and told him the story. When he laughed, I said, "And one day it will happen to you!"

Perspective is essential for a measure of spiritual and emotional health, and humor sometimes can lead to a more realistic sense of ourselves.

The Reverend David Robb is an assistant minister at All Souls Unitarian Church in New York City and a practicing psychotherapist. Recently I asked him about the psychological benefits of humor. "If people don't have some lightness in their lives," he said, "then they end up taking themselves too seriously and are unable to move outside themselves. And a great deal of spirituality lies in putting yourself in an appropriate place in the universe. Those who can laugh at themselves can also look at themselves critically, but not harshly, a key element of emotional growth."

When things go awry, if they are mostly an inconvenience to you or a threat to your ego, instead of getting furious, can you laugh? Sometimes even the best-laid plans, the most carefully planned events can go awry.

My friend George is a longtime prison chaplain who now works at San Quentin State Prison in California. During his time at a Boston prison he started giving short retreats to the inmates. After all, he explained once, many of the inmates are hungry for God; they have a lot of free time, and some of them, like those in solitary confinement, even have private time for prayer.

Like most prison chaplains, George provided spiritual counseling, ran Scripture study programs, and facilitated group "faith sharing." Often, when the men were about to be released from prison, he led a sharing session in which they reflected on their experiences in prison. At one of these, George asked the men to sit in a circle in the chapel and, one by one, to talk about what lessons they had learned during their prison sentence, no matter what they were, even if they seemed insignificant.

"Well," said one, "I've learned that God loves me no matter what I've done in the past, and I always want to go to him for forgiveness."

And George said, "That's wonderful. Thank you."

Then the next guy said, "I've learned finally to take responsibility for my actions in life."

Another said, "I've learned not to hang out with guys who are just going to be bad for me."

And another, "I've learned that I need to be a good Christian and take care of my wife and my baby."

But one inmate remained quiet. So George asked him what he had learned.

"You're not going to like it," he said.

"Oh, no," said George. "Anything you learned is valuable."

He said, "I've learned that the next time I kill someone, I'm going to hide the body a lot better."

Unplanned occurrences are reminders to check your tendency to think that you're the one in control. In reality, it's someone else.

One of my first homilies after my ordination focused on the story of the Annunciation, the angel Gabriel's visit to Mary, from the Gospel of Luke, where Mary first discovers that she will give birth to Jesus.[78] After spending several days praying, researching, writing, and editing, I came up with what I thought was a fantastic homily.

The story of the Annunciation, I would say in my homily, is like the story of any spiritual experience with God. God works in our own lives the same way God works in the story of the Annunciation. God takes the initiative (as God does with Mary); then we doubt and question (as Mary does); then we are invited to look around us and see signs of God's activity (like the angel asking Mary to consider her cousin Elizabeth); then we say yes; then God brings new life to our lives; and then we are asked to live this out after the experience ends.

Well, I thought, this was just a spectacular homily—completely original. I had never come upon any similar reflections on this passage. I could barely wait to deliver it!

At the end of the Mass, I stood at the door and awaited the inevitable praise. What would the grateful congregation think of my absolutely fascinating insights? I could hardly wait. And what did they say?

"Goodbye, Father."

"Have a nice day."

"Bye."

Not a single person mentioned the homily.

The next week, greatly pressed for time, I wrote—very quickly—what I thought was an exceedingly bland homily. Find God in all things. Look for God in all parts of your life. Blah, blah, blah. Nothing special, nothing new, nothing different.

At the end of that Mass many people approached me with tears in their eyes.

"That was so . . . beautiful!"

"Thank you so much!"

"That was just what I needed to hear today!"

It was a vivid reminder that in ministry, no matter how hard you work, ultimately it's God's work, not yours. All this puts our work in perspective.

ACCEPTING THAT YOU'RE NOT in control is a reason not only for humility—but for more joy. You can work hard and leave the rest up to God. Pope John XXIII once said that when he woke up in the night, worried about the future of the church, he would relax by asking himself a question. "Giovanni," he would say to himself. "Why are you so worried? Who is in charge of the church—you or the Holy Spirit? The Holy Spirit! So go back to sleep, Giovanni!"

You are not God. And if you forget this, God will remind you. So we need to lighten up about life and ministries. Not that our work and family and religious lives are not important. But we're ultimately not the one who brings about results.

Recently my friend Joe, a newly ordained priest in Seattle, told me that he gave a homily at a funeral about grieving, in which he said that in times of loss we all want a simple recipe for getting through the grief. He told a story about his mother's bread, which she had taught him how to make when he was younger. There were some basic ingredients—flour, water, yeast. But today when he baked, Joe added some of his own ingredients. Grieving is similar, he said. There are some standard ways of doing it—gathering together as a community of faith, retelling stories about the one who has died, and trusting in the Resurrection. But we each have to take that basic "recipe" and add to it, so that we can be "fed" by God in our sorrow.

Joe was, he admitted, inordinately proud of his homily.

Afterward, a woman came up to him and said, "Father, I can't remember a word you said, but it was very comforting!"

Joe and I both howled when he told me that.

"Well," said Joe, "it was a good reminder of who was in charge."

* * *

Children are particularly adept at reminding you that you're not in control. A few years ago I was home for a weekend with my mother and my sister's family, in Philadelphia, where I grew up. That Sunday I was invited to celebrate Mass at my home parish. I thought, "Well, how fortunate for the parish! They would get to see one of their own, a local boy made good, here to celebrate Mass! Lucky them!" I was filled with self-importance and vanity.

In the congregation was my family, including my two nephews, Charles, then age ten, and his younger brother Matthew, age three. At the time, Matthew was quite religious. He liked to read picture books about Jesus, enjoyed going to Mass, and even sang hymns around the house. What Matthew liked best, though, was making the sign of the cross during grace at meals. Before we would say a blessing over the meal, Matthew would begin: "In the name of the Father and of the Son and of the Holy Spirit." That was his role at family dinners. And woe unto the person who didn't let Matthew begin the grace.

In any event, at the beginning of that Sunday Mass I processed up the main aisle filled with self-admiration, turned toward the crowd, and started with the traditional blessing: "In the name of the Father and of the Son and of the . . ."

Suddenly there came a piercing scream from the front pew. "Stop! That's my part! Shut up, Uncle Jim! Uncle Jim said my part!" It was impossible not to laugh.

Can you see such moments as invitations to humility, gateways to poverty of spirit? As the Protestant theologian Reinhold Niebuhr said, "What is funny about us is precisely that we take ourselves too seriously."

3. Levity is a sign of God's presence in your life.

Recall some of our insights from our earlier examination of humor and the life of Jesus of Nazareth. As I noted before, the life of Jesus of Nazareth was filled with joy. Think of what happens when people are healed by Jesus. They give voice to joy and amazement. "We have never seen anything like this!" Think of how happy Jairus is when his little daughter is made well. How happy the father is when his epileptic son is healed. Think of how the blind man's joy leaps right off the page. When they ask the man what happened he says, "One thing I do know, that though I was blind, now I see."[79]

Joy is also a welcome companion to many characters in Jesus's parables. Remember our discussion of the parable of the prodigal son, in which the father exclaims, "Put a ring on his finger and sandals on his feet. . . . Let us eat and celebrate!" When the older son doesn't want to celebrate, the father explains his desire for joy, now that his younger son has returned. "We had to celebrate and rejoice," he says.

Here is the father, and implicitly Jesus, reproaching the elder son in the parable for not being joyful *enough*. The elder son, who refuses to enter the house (thus, according to custom, insulting the father) and reconcile with his brother is consumed with resentment. The father's joy is sharply contrasted with the elder son's bitterness. "This brother of yours was dead and has come to life; he was lost and has been found." Rejoice, says the father to the son. Rejoice, says Jesus to his listeners.

Joy brackets Jesus's life on earth. At the beginning of his life, after the Annunciation, Mary goes to Elizabeth. What happens? John the Baptist leaps for joy in Elizabeth's womb. And what does Mary do? She sings a song of praise. "My soul magnifies the Lord, and my spirit rejoices in God my Savior." At the end of Jesus's earthly life, after the Resurrection, the Risen Christ is grilling some fish on the shore. Peter sees him from a boat and leaps into the water for joy.

Joy also kicks off Jesus's public ministry. What is traditionally called his first miracle happens in Cana, where Jesus miraculously turns water into wine, thus making sure that the party will continue. Joy is an essential element of the life and ministry of Jesus. So should it be for any of his followers.

In *Laughing with God,* Gerald Arbuckle uses the terms "divine incongruity," "divine humor," and "divine illogicality" to describe the "totally unexpected, surprising ways" that God relates to humanity and "God's pursuing and forgiving love of fickle humankind." Joseph Grassi, in *God Makes Me Laugh,* notes that in the Old Testament, "God's plans, working through weak human beings, seem so surprising and impossible to achieve that they cause people to laugh in astonishment." As God did for Sarah.

In the Old Testament, God is constantly forgiving men and women who break the covenant established between God and Israel.* Abraham's persistent bargaining in Genesis with God to save the town of Sodom from destruction is comic even today. (God declares that he will save the town if he can find fifty righteous people in it. By the end of the negotiations, Abraham gets him down to ten.) Rabbi Daniel Polish described the Old Testament to me as "earthy." Humor is a piece of this earthiness.

In the New Testament, says Arbuckle, the contrast between "human expectations of how the creator should act and what actually happens is dramatic." The Messiah is a simple Galilean peasant. "Is not this the carpenter's son?" asks an onlooker in the Gospels. Think of the images Jesus uses to describe God's love. The shepherd who leaves behind ninety-nine sheep to find only one lost sheep? The father who welcomes back his selfish son? The woman who spends an entire day sweeping her house to find one coin? Crazy!

Both the Old and New Testaments are shot through with not only the confounding of expectations and the often topsy-turvy nature of the divine, but also of God's playfulness. Richard Clifford, S.J., points to that story of Abraham bargaining with God to save

---

* Arbuckle notes that the very idea of God entering into a covenant is, at the very least, ironic: "Judged from a purely human perspective this is surely a humorously incongruous situation: God freely entering into a contractual relationship with people he has created!"

Sodom in the Book of Genesis, saying: "There's a humor there, because it's like two peasants bargaining over a sheepskin."

David Robb links God's playfulness with creativity. "Creativity," he says, "has a great deal to do with the 'play' of imagination." Think of someone like Johann Sebastian Bach, Robb suggested, who created glorious music from a set number of notes and harmonies. God's creativity is like that—imaginative, diverse, playful.

Does he feel that God is ever playful with him?

"My whole life sometimes seems like one big joke!" laughed Robb. "God is full of surprises! I hit a wall and wonder what I've done wrong, and then something totally unexpected happens. That's God's playful creativity."

Mother Teresa, Stand-Up Comic

As we saw in Chapter 3, many of the saints had a great sense of humor. Some could even laugh about the idea of being a saint. During his time as pope, between 1978 and 2005, John Paul II was known for canonizing an unprecedented number of saints. Around that time, as a bishop recounted the story to me, Mother Teresa was asked by one of her sisters how she could become a saint. The sister most likely was expecting a pious answer on living a holy life, serving the poor, and praying frequently. Instead, Mother Teresa laughed and said, "If you want to be saint, die now. The pope is canonizing everyone!"

Considering all these instances of humor and laughter in the sacred Scriptures and in others' lives, you might ask yourself: Does *my own* spiritual life always have to be so gloomy? Can I see joy, humor, and laughter as signs of God's presence in my life?

Many of the saints and spiritual masters did. I've already told the stories of several saints who lived life with zest. Joy is vital, as Rebbe Nachman of Breslov said.*

Being close to God fills people with joy. Why hide it? In his book *Living with Wisdom,*[80] a biography of Thomas Merton, the author Jim Forest tells the story of how he and another young man from the Catholic Worker house in New York traveled all the way from New York, by hitchhiking, to Merton's monastery in Kentucky. The two were anxious to meet the famous monk and talk to him about peace and nonviolence.

After they arrived, dog tired after many hours of traveling, the two were shown their rooms in the monastery. Jim Forest went to the chapel to pray, and his prayer was interrupted—by laughter. Forest hadn't expected laughter at a Trappist monastery. He left the chapel to look for the source of the laughter, and here is how he tells it:

> The origin, I discovered, was [my friend's] room. As I opened the door the laughter was still going on, a kind of gale of joy. The major source was the red-faced man lying on the floor wearing [the Trappist habit], his knees in the air, hands clutching his belly. . . . I realized instantly that the man on the floor laughing with such abandon must be Thomas Merton. . . . And the inspiration for the laughter? It proved to be the intensely strong smell of feet that had been kept in shoes all the way from the Lower East Side to [the monastery] and were now out in the open air.

Thomas Merton, one of the great Christian spiritual masters of our time, was on the floor, laughing at stinky feet.

A few years ago, I spoke with an elderly monk who had been one of Merton's novices. He told me that most of the new novices, when

* Here is the rest of Rebbe Nachman's prayer. "Let me always be happy—truly happy with all my heart and soul. Put pure joy within my heart so that I will always only be happy. Help me also to bring others to happiness."

they entered the monastery, were initially unable to identify Merton, despite his being the most well-known monk in the country. (At the time, there were almost two hundred monks in the monastery.) He said, "If you had asked me which one he was, he would have been the second to last one I picked."

I asked, "Why?"

And he said, "He was always laughing! And I had an idea that a monk should be very serious."

What use would there be in hiding what joy we had?, as St. Teresa of Ávila said. "Let each of us humbly use this to cheer one another."

Can you see joy as a sign of God's presence among you?

"Besides," said Professor Martin Marty, "how can you talk about Christian joy, if you never have an impulse to dance or play or do funny things? If you are inundated with God's grace, you should be liberated and free to dance, to laugh, and to smile!"

A Study in Joy: 1 Thessalonians

You would think that the book that many Scripture scholars agree to be the oldest in the New Testament would garner a great deal of respect and attention. You would think that a document written around 50 AD—only seventeen years or so after the death and resurrection of Jesus—would be pored over by all Christians. You would think that most Christians would know even the smallest verses of this document by heart.

Well, you would be wrong. St. Paul's First Letter to the Thessalonians isn't all that well-known by many Christians.

Still, by common consent, it is the earliest of Paul's letters, and therefore the earliest writing in the entire New Testament. Scholars say that 1 Thessalonians was most likely written from Athens or Corinth around 50 AD. As such, it predates the four Gospels and the Acts of the Apostles. And buried in the letter is a remarkable phrase from St. Paul that upends the popular conception of Paul as a cranky, grumpy, depressive prude.

First, a little history. Paul is writing to the church (that is, the Christian community) that he had founded in Thessalonica, located in the Roman province of Macedonia, on the northern shore of the Aegean Sea. (Today the town is Thessaloniki in northern Greece.) In this relatively brief letter he encourages his fellow Christians to have confidence in the "Second Coming" of Jesus, which they thought would happen in their lifetime. (Many Christians of the time believed that the Second Coming was imminent.)

Unlike in some of his other letters, here Paul is not responding to any heated theological debate raging within the Christian community in the region. Nor is he scolding his fellow Christians for some litany of horrible sins. Instead, he is mainly encouraging them to lead holy lives. The beginning of the letter, in fact, contains fulsome praise of the conduct of the Christians in Thessalonica, who he says are an example to other churches in the region. This may account for his gentle words. First Thessalonians, says one commentator, is "pastoral, warm in tone, and affectionate throughout."[81]

Now back to that remarkable phrase. Toward the end of his letter, Paul offers a triad of Christian practice: "Rejoice always, pray without ceasing, give thanks in all circumstances; for this is the will of God in Christ Jesus for you." You could spend a lifetime meditating on that one sentence. Actually, you could spend a lifetime meditating on just the words "rejoice always."

But is it possible? Realistically, what would it mean to "rejoice always"?

First of all, it does not mean that you cannot be sad about suffering or that you have to ignore the tragedies in the world around you. But at first blush, Paul's words seem to imply that. In his book *Chasing Joy: Musings on Life in a Bittersweet World,* the Reverend Edward Hays, a Catholic priest and popular spiritual writer, notes that Paul's words are challenged not only by sadness in our own life, but also by injustice in the world. Rejoicing always may seem not only impossible, but offensive.

"To do this in our present world is extremely difficult," says Hays, "since the daily headlines overflow with the bad news." Isn't injustice in the world something to lament, not smile about?

"To confront evil with joyfulness instead of outrage," he says, "feels like the cowardly complicity of silence."

But Thessalonica in the time of St. Paul was no paradise either. Under the heel of imperial Rome, many in the town lived as slaves. Those who were free may have been poor, illiterate, and unable to obtain what we would consider many of the basic necessities of life.

Serious (and untreatable) illnesses and an early death would have been the lot of many. The Thessalonians would have known the meaning of suffering. And the Christians there would have also known "persecution," something that Paul alludes to in the first few lines of his letter.

So how could Paul ask them to turn a blind eye to the realities of life? He wasn't. Instead, he was pointing to something deeper. It's easy to be joyful when you're happy or in those fleeting moments when the world seems like a fair and just place for everyone. But how can you be joyful in sad times and in the face of injustice? Hays offers a suggestion, "To live in joy is to abide in God who is love, and being an authentic prophet requires loving who and what you denounce."

Here I think of the example of the great African American spirituals. There is not enough space here for a long exegesis on that rich topic, but we can say, in brief, that one of the most lasting signs of the great faith of African American Christians is the legacy of their spiritual hymns, pieces of joy born in the midst of deep suffering. These are signs of confidence in God. As the African American theologian James Cone notes, "Far from being songs of passive resignation, the spirituals are black freedom songs which emphasize black liberation as consistent with divine revelation."[82]

The joy of those songs, forged in the fire of suffering, continues. One of the most vivid memories I have as a Jesuit novice is being invited to a predominantly black church in the Roxbury section of Boston. Before this I had never been in such a church. Yet from the moment the choir began singing "Lead Me, Guide Me," I felt swept away in a chorus of joy. Years later I experienced that same ebullience in the songs of the choirs in the churches of the slums of Nairobi, where Kenyans would be packed shoulder to shoulder (literally) as they sang out the words to Swahili hymns. What these two groups had in common (the descendants of slaves and East Africans) was not simply the color of their skin, but their abiding confidence in God.

Joy, deeper than happiness, is a virtue that finds its foundation in the knowledge that we are loved by God. For Christians, the knowledge that Jesus has been raised from the dead is a cause for rejoicing, even in tough times. This does not mean that suffering does not bring sadness. Of course it does. But suffering is not the last word—in Jesus's life nor in ours. And that knowledge can lead us to a deep joy.

Just as I was writing this chapter, in fact, I received some unpleasant medical news: I would have to have some minor surgery. Nothing life-threatening or terribly serious, but something that I would rather not have to do. And when I was praying about it the next morning, right before I was about to write on joy, I realized that I wasn't feeling especially joyful.

But gradually, as I prayed, I realized that God would be with me through this small malady; and that God would give me the strength and intelligence to deal with it, to figure it out, and to live with it. As God had done in the past. That put me in touch with not only peace, but joy. I can't say that I was *happy* or that I wouldn't have wished for different news, but I felt joy. This may be part of what it means to rejoice "in all circumstances."

As I've said, sadness is an appropriate and natural response to suffering. God desires, I believe, that we be honest about our sadness and share it, in prayer, with God. But even in the midst of great tragedy, knowing that God accompanies us can lead us to a deep-down joy that can carry us through difficult, and sometimes unbearable, times.

Likewise, "rejoice always" does not mean that we should simply "look on the bright side" in the face of injustice. The anger that rises in you over an unjust situation may be a sign that God is moving you to address that injustice. That is, God may be speaking to you through your outrage at what you see, through your disgust over what you have read, or your shock over what someone has told you. (How else would God move people to action?) This is particularly the case when it is the injustice visited on *another* person, since anger over an injustice to ourselves (rightful though the anger may be) may be tinged with selfishness and a sense of wounded pride.

For example, let's say you saw a homeless person sitting on the sidewalk in front of a fancy restaurant out of which were coming diners who, having spent hundreds of dollars on their meal, failed to give the man even a glance, let alone a few dollars or a kind word. You might be angry or sad. You'd probably be moved to give him some of your own money and even spend time with him. But you certainly wouldn't say to yourself, much less to him, "Be happy!" Witnessing the injustice, you would try to lessen it. Out of such strong emotions and righteous anger are born great works of charity.

Where is the joy, then? It comes from a loving trust in God, in the awareness that God is working through the compassion you feel, in the knowledge that God desires a just world where the poor are treated fairly, as well as in the trust that God will help those who heed his voice to help bring about justice.

It's important to see that all three parts of Paul's triad of Christian practice—joy, prayer, and gratitude—are intimately bound together. Joy, prayer, and gratitude are connected. Let's consider how.

First, joy springs *from* gratitude. When we recall things, events, or people for which or for whom we are grateful, joy increases. Second, prayer supports the other two virtues. A contemplative awareness of the world and an attitude of prayerful attentiveness make it easier to see life's blessings. Finally, joy moves us *to* gratitude. Our gratitude over good news can lead to joy. Joy can also move us to pray. In our joy, we want to be with God, to share our joyful life, gratefully, in prayer—just as we would share joy with a friend.

Each virtue supports the others. Prayer awakens gratitude. Gratitude leads to joy. And joy moves us to prayer. In this way, we are able to follow Paul's gentle advice to the Thessalonians of almost two thousand years ago.

Many modern believers think of St. Paul not as the Apostle of Joy, but as the Apostle of Gloom. He is usually (and unfairly) characterized as a stern moralizer, intent only on frustrating authentic human emotions and obsessed with tamping down human sexuality, rather than as an encouraging friend inviting us into a world of joy. But here is Paul, in his earliest letter, doing just that. There were other Christian communities that needed to hear sterner words. But to the Christians at Thessalonica, and to Christians today, the Apostle Paul advises three things, and the first of these is joy.

1 Thessalonians 5:12–28

But we appeal to you, brothers and sisters, to respect those who labor among you, and have charge of you in the Lord and admonish you; esteem them very highly in love because of their work. Be at peace among yourselves. And we urge you, beloved, to admonish the idlers, encourage the fainthearted, help the weak, be patient with all of them. See that none of you repays evil for evil, but always seek to do good to one another and to all. Rejoice always, pray without ceasing, give thanks in all circumstances; for this is the will of God in Christ Jesus for you. Do not quench the Spirit. Do not despise the words of prophets, but test everything; hold fast to what is good; abstain from every form of evil.

May the God of peace himself sanctify you entirely; and may your spirit and soul and body be kept sound and blameless at the coming of our Lord Jesus Christ. The one who calls you is faithful, and he will do this.

Beloved, pray for us.

Greet all the brothers and sisters with a holy kiss. I solemnly command you by the Lord that this letter be read to all of them.

The grace of our Lord Jesus Christ be with you.

Chapter Nine

Rejoice Always!

Introducing Joy, Humor, and Laughter into Your Prayer

How might a friend show delight in you? One way is simply by telling us outright. "Boy, it's great to see you!" a friend might say. Or, in the middle of doing something enjoyable—say, taking a vacation together or enjoying a night out—"Isn't this fun?" God does the same, though in different ways. God shares delight through church services, nature, music, relationships, and play in all sorts of exterior ways.

God does so through our inner lives too, filling us with delight at seeing our children enjoy themselves at a birthday party, the happiness we feel when we arrive at our favorite vacation spot, or our glee at seeing the first sign of spring after a long winter. One of my mother's most longed-for moments usually comes around March. "I saw my first robin today!" she'll say, with elation.

One of my favorite lines in film comes in the 1981 movie *Chariots of Fire,* based on the stories of the competitors in the 1924 Olympics. One athlete, based on a real-life Scotsman who was later ordained, is a devout Christian who is also a runner. "When I run, I feel his pleasure," he says of God. That's a marvelous way of talking about an inner moment of delight.

Another way that a friend takes delight in us might be through playfulness. One of the most enjoyable things about a friendship is joking around with someone. My own friends, for instance, like to tease me about many things, particularly how much I write. My friend George, who entered the Jesuits the year before me, always brings me down to earth with his humor. Sometimes when we're together with friends, say over a burger, and I say, "Boy that was delicious!" he'll say, "Really? Are you going to write a book about it?"

Parents, as I mentioned, are also playful with their children. When my father used to come home from work in the late 1960s, he would regularly keep his hat on while he sat at the dinner table, which would prompt gales of laughter from my sister and me.

"Daddy!" we would say.

"What's wrong?" he would ask with mock innocence as he sat at table with his gray fedora on.

"Daddy! Your *hat* is still on!" Playfulness is part of being a good parent.

To please God . . . to be a real ingredient in the divine happiness . . . to be loved by God, not merely pitied, but delighted in as an artist delights in his work or a father in a son—it seems impossible, a weight or burden of glory which our thoughts can hardly sustain. But so it is.

—C. S. Lewis, *The Weight of Glory*

So if one way to think about our relationship with God is as a friendship, and friends are playful; and if one way of thinking about God is as parent, and parents are playful, then you might ask yourself: "How is God playful with me and how am I playful with God?"

At one point during my stay in Kenya, I fell ill with mononucleosis. That meant four weeks of rest in bed. But the refugees with whom I was working suspected something much worse—that I had meningitis, typhoid, or another of the many serious or deadly diseases prevalent in East Africa. While I was sick, they would often visit me at the Jesuit community in which I lived, though I was utterly fatigued. In Kenya, as I discovered, the thoughtful person visits a sick friend and helps clean the house. So during my recuperation refugees would drop by and sweep the floor, while I tried in vain to stay awake.

In a few months I was well enough to return to work. The first day I was driving my beat-up jeep through one of Nairobi's slums when three refugees spotted me. They waved frantically and motioned for me to pull over. I rolled the window down, and the three thrust their hands through the window to shake mine.

With a huge smile, one said, "Brother Jim, we are so happy you are not dead!"

Hearing that, I laughed aloud. And that spontaneous laughter felt as though it gave voice to many things: my joy that I had recovered after a long illness, my gratitude for the refugees' affection for me (which I hadn't heard expressed so vividly before), and my delight over the sheer unexpectedness of their comment.

But something else struck me about that funny comment. Taken together, all of this made me think that it might be a sign of God's playfulness.

Such playful moments communicate truth in an unmistakable way. Remember how Rabbi Daniel Polish's encounter with the "Sabbath queen" invited him to experience a new kind of intimacy with God? Yet too often we dismiss these moments of God's playfulness. We tend to think, that *couldn't* be God. It's not *serious* enough.

God's playfulness may carry a serious message. Late last winter, I was wondering if I really needed two woolen caps. Shouldn't one suffice? Maybe I should give one to the poor. Foolishly, I kept debating about whether I should give one away. On the way out of a barber shop one day I reached into my pocket to pull out my hat, and it wasn't there; I realized it had fallen out. I turned around and saw a homeless man putting it on his head. Well, I thought, that settles that. Was this God playfully telling me what I should have done in the first place? Was the comment from the refugees a reminder that I needed to trust in God more?

We tend to overlook, ignore, or simply reject these lighthearted moments, forgetting the possibility of God's sense of play, which is well documented in Scripture. It reminds me of the story of the fellow looking for the parking space. He's the best man at his friend's wedding, and he's late for the ceremony. So he's frantically driving around the church parking lot. Not a religious sort, he nonetheless prays, "Oh God! Please help me! If you open up a parking space, I'll go to church every Sunday, I'll pray every night, and I'll be kind to everyone I meet!" Suddenly a spot opens up. And the guy says, "Oh, never mind, God. I found one."

Don't overlook, ignore, or reject possible signs of God's playfulness in your daily life. Or in your prayer life.

The Face of God

All this talk about God's playfulness might make you wonder how I know that God is playful. Well, as I mentioned in this chapter, the funny things that happen to us seem to me signs of this divine quality. But of course none of us knows exactly what God is like. To paraphrase St. Thomas Aquinas, if you can define "it," then it's not God. Which reminds me of one of my favorite jokes.

A Catholic sister is teaching finger painting to her first-grade art class. The sister walks up and down the aisles looking at what each of her students has painted. She stops over the desk of one little boy. "What are you painting, Billy?" she asks.

Billy looks up and answers, "I'm painting the face of God."

"But that's impossible," says the sister. "No one has seen the face of God."

Billy turns back to his drawing and says, "They will in five minutes!"

One of my favorite suggestions for a meditation is Anthony de Mello's statement: "Look at God looking at you . . . and smiling." De Mello's image is essentially an invitation into a prayer of joy and contentment, into what you might call private, one-on-one time with a smiling God, into seeing the world the way that God does.

But before we talk about incorporating joy into your prayer, let's talk a little about prayer. First of all, what is it?

Briefly put, you could say that prayer is the conversation that happens in a relationship with God. Our relationship with God is of course lived out in our daily life. But, as in any relationship, there needs to be some one-on-one time with God, intentional time when we are quietly sitting (or walking, or kneeling, or whatever works best) and just being with God.

To put it in the language of a friendship, what kind of friendship would you have if you never spent any one-on-one time with your friend? Think of how enjoyable it is to have some lighthearted time with a friend and what a break it can be from the difficulties of life. Can you think of prayer in that way—an invitation to allow God to lighten your heart?

There are many different ways to pray, but no "best" way. What is "best" is what works best for you. Even the physical positions differ from person to person. Some sit in a comfortable chair, some like to kneel, some walk, and some like to write out their prayer as if they were writing a letter. God meets you where you are, in both your daily life and your prayer life.

So by way of framing our discussion on joyful prayer, here are just a few means of private prayer (as distinguished from communal prayer in worship services):

Rote prayers. These are traditional prayers in a standard format. The most common are the Our Father or Lord's Prayer, the Hail Mary, the Shema in Judaism, or any of the traditional daily prayers of Islam. Many Catholics use rosary beads and Muslims prayer beads to help them recall their prayers. Even the most familiar of rote prayers can lead to a deep connection with God. The mother of one

Being with God

In his book *Armchair Mystic*, Mark Thibodeaux, a Jesuit spiritual writer, distinguishes between four stages of prayer. The first is *talking at* God (which includes petitionary prayer, that is, asking for help). The second is *talking to* God (which includes expressing your feelings and emotions, frustrations and hopes to God). The third is *listening to* God (a more contemplative way of reflecting on what is going on in your daily life as well as being attentive to the inner movements of your soul during prayer). The final way is *being with* God (this is closer to "centering prayer," a prayer of presence). Joy can find its way most easily into the three final stages.[83]

friend said to her son, "When I pray the Rosary, I look at God and God looks at me."

Lectio divina. Drawn from the monastic tradition, the term means "sacred reading." Here you slowly meditate on a particular passage from Scripture, asking questions like "What is going on in this passage?" "What is God saying to me in this passage?" "What do I want to say to God about this passage?" In this way you encounter the text in a meditative way.

Ignatian contemplation. Here you imagine yourself in a scene from Scripture, trusting that God can work through your imagination. As you imaginatively place yourself in a passage from the Bible, you ask yourself: "What do I see?" "What do I hear?" "What do I smell?" "What do I taste?" "What do I feel?" As you enter more deeply into the scene, imaginatively, you notice what insights and emotions arise as you spend time with, for example, Jesus or the apostles.

Centering prayer. You "empty" yourself as far as possible, moving away from distractions and toward your "center," where God dwells. Often this involves a "prayer word" like "God" or "love" or "peace," which helps to center you. This is primarily a prayer of emptiness and quietly resting in God's loving presence.

The examination of conscience. Here you remember the events of the day, trying to notice where you may have encountered God. You begin with what you're grateful for; then review the day; then notice where you may have moved away from God and sinned; then ask for forgiveness from God or resolve to reconcile with the one you've hurt (or, alternately, resolve to go to confession); and then ask for grace for the next day. It is a prayer of awareness of God's presence during your day.

Prayer is not simply talking to yourself. Rather, it implies an active listener: God. It also implies that *you* are listening. And by listening I mean not hearing voices in a physical way, but listening to the places where God is active in your daily life and, particularly in prayer, in terms of what arises by way of insights, memories, feelings, emotions, and desires.

Now add joy, humor, and laughter to the mix of what can happen in prayer. If prayer is the conversation that happens in a friendship between you and God, and if friendships bring us joy, and if friendships are brightened with laughter, and if sacred Scriptures contain humor, then why not consider joy, humor, and laughter as important aspects of your prayer life?

This is not to deny the awesome nature of God. Being joyful in prayer does not diminish your respect for and humility before God.

A stance of respectful awe before what the theologian Rudolf Otto called the *mysterium tremendum et fascinans,* the mystery that both makes us tremble and fascinates us, is an essential part of one's spiritual life. The Creator of the universe should be approached in a spirit of deep reverence. But awe does not negate joy.

To use the model of a parent, one can have a profound respect for a mother, a father, a grandmother, or a grandfather and still be joyful in their company. To use the model of the wisdom figure, one can still be in awe of a person's position and incorporate humor into the relationship. Finally, to use the model of friendship, one can respect one's friend while at the same time laughing with him or her.

For Christians, the idea of laughing with God may be even simpler to explain. The disciples must have laughed and enjoyed themselves when in Jesus's company. Why should Christians, then, not do the same in prayer?

Laughter and lightheartedness in another's company are signs of the depth of one's friendship. We laugh loudest and longest when we are around those we love and treasure. And if we treasure God's love, why can we not smile during our times of prayer or meditation?

It makes little sense to omit joy, humor, and laughter from prayer. So let's consider three ways to incorporate joy into your prayer life.

In the beginning [of the spiritual life], then, we should strive to be cheerful and unconstrained; for there are people who think it is all over with devotion if they relax themselves ever so little.

—St. Teresa of Ávila, *Autobiography*

---

1. Be joyful with God.

We often approach God in prayer in times of distress. It's a human instinct to turn to God in times of trouble. How could we *not* cry out when we are in pain or are worried or stressed? The lament psalms express this deeply human language. "How long, O Lord?" begins Psalm 13. "Will you forget me forever?" Asking for help from God in troubling times is as old as humanity.

But this is not the only time to turn to God. Pain and sadness are not the sole motivations for prayer. Comparing prayer to a personal relationship, it would be as if you spoke to a friend only when you were in distress.

Likewise, we often come to God to ask for a special favor. When I was young, for example, I used to see God as the Great Problem Solver, who would fix my problems if only I prayed hard enough, used the right prayers, or repeated them in the right sequence. God, in my adolescent mind, was like a cosmic gumball machine. If you placed the correct prayer into the right slot, out would pop your good fortune.

This too is a limited notion of friendship with God. We all need help from time to time. And if it's natural to ask our friends for help, it's natural to turn to God as well. Jesus encouraged his followers to pray this way. "Give us this day our daily bread" is in fact petitionary prayer.

But there is more to a relationship than that too. Praying solely in this way would be like having a friendship whose only purpose was to enable you to ask for things. So besides lamenting to God and asking God for things, there is another way of being with God—and that is joyfully. This may mean something as simple as sitting joyfully with God in prayer and imagining God sitting joyfully with you. Or it could mean bringing to God not only the difficult parts of your life, but the enjoyable, exciting, and funny parts too. For example, has anything happened recently that made you laugh or made you laugh at yourself?

The story in the last chapter about my nephew yelling out during Mass, "That's my part!" seemed, at least to me, an indication of God's playfulness. That night in prayer, I smiled about the incident with God. God may have been gently cutting me down to size and reminding me not to take myself so seriously.

Are there similar times in your life that you can share with God?

When you spend time with God during your private prayer, you might imagine telling God something funny that happened during the day, something that made you smile, or something that made you laugh at yourself. This is one way of being joyful with God.

2. Recall what gives you joy and share your grateful heart with God.

St. Ignatius Loyola's greatest gift to believers is his classic text *The Spiritual Exercises,* written in the sixteenth century. Essentially, it's a manual for a four-week retreat, or time of prayer, that invites us to see ourselves as taking part in various Gospel stories, imaginatively following Jesus through his life, death, and resurrection.

Gratitude suffuses the *Spiritual Exercises.* At both the beginning and end of the four-week period, St. Ignatius invites us to think about the ways God has blessed us. Toward the end of the retreat, for example, Ignatius invites us to think of God's blessings in four ways. First, he says, "Ponder with deep affection how much God our Lord has done for you" and "how much he has given you of what he possesses." That is, think of all the individual blessings in your life.

Second, says Ignatius, think about the way that God "dwells" in his creatures. To the rocks and minerals, God has given existence. To the plants, he gives life. To animals, he gives sensation. And to us, God gives "existence, life, sensation, and intelligence." You might consider how God sustains your life and "dwells" in you.

Third, consider how God "labors" in creation. Thinking about God constantly creating has always been a deeply moving image for me. God gives the creatures "their existence, conserving them," helping them to grow and be themselves. God makes the sun shine, the rain fall, the plants grow, the animals eat, and on and on.

Fourth, says St. Ignatius in a beautiful image, think of how these gifts—and others like justice, goodness, and mercy—come down from God "as the rays come down from the sun, or the rains from their source."

These are just a few ways of thinking of our blessings. Typically during such retreats, people find that the primary response to all these blessings is gratitude.

Gratitude is one of the keys to a healthy spiritual life. A grateful heart means not only that one is aware of the blessings in life, but that one is aware of the source of these blessings: God. Indeed, for St. Ignatius Loyola *ingratitude* was the "most abominable of sins" and "the cause, beginning, and origin of all sins and misfortunes."

Gratitude prompts us to say "thank you" to God. Thanking God is as important as saying thanks to a friend. And expressing gratitude to a friend moves you beyond a feeling of gratitude—it is also an action that can deepen the relationship. It's similar in prayer. Being able to say thanks to God deepens your relationship, because it encourages you to more consciously identify the source of your joy.

If you find those notions too abstract, you might ask yourself what brings you joy. Here is a list of suggestions, in case you feel especially unjoyful:

Consider *individuals.* Think of people who give you joy: spouses, children and family members, boyfriends or girlfriends, friends, work colleagues, fellow members of your church, synagogue, or mosque.

Consider *experiences.* Include big things like having a child, enjoying a good friendship, or being part of a loving family. But don't overlook more ordinary events like a refreshing vacation, a good night's sleep, even a fun night out with a friend.

Consider *ways you are invited to grow.* Perhaps you are grateful for something that educated or challenged you, like a provocative book, film, or play. Perhaps you saw a television documentary that helped you understand something in a new way.

Consider *explicitly religious things.* Can you be grateful for your faith, for the presence of God in your life, for your religious community, for time out to pray?

Consider *very small blessings of daily life.* Bring to mind a pleasant meal you had recently, an unexpected phone call that lifted your spirits, or a sunny day you enjoyed.

Consider *things you take for granted.* Do you have a place to live? Do you have enough to eat? Do you have a job? Do you have friends? That's a lot more than many people have. Can you be joyful for these things?

Consider *what makes you laugh.* Your young child did something silly or just told his first joke. You went around the house looking for your glasses when they were on your face the whole time. You watched a funny television show or movie or play that you're still smiling about.

Thinking explicitly about the things that make us joyful leads to thankfulness and instills in us the "attitude of gratitude." Living from a grateful center means that we are more likely to be joyful throughout the day.

One of the most effective ways of grounding ourselves in gratitude comes from the work of Martin Seligman, a professor of psychology at the University of Pennsylvania, and one of the founders of the field known as cognitive psychology, which I mentioned earlier.* In his book *Authentic Happiness,* he describes a practice suggested by one of his students called "Gratitude Night." As Seligman describes it, class members would "bring a guest who had been important in their lives, but whom they had never properly thanked. Each would present a testimonial about that person by way of thanks, and a discussion would follow each testimonial."

---

*Just as a refresher, cognitive psychology looks at how our thoughts, particularly inaccurate ones, affect our emotional life.

For both the givers and receivers of the gratitude it was a powerful moment, unlike anything they had ever experienced. "There was literally not a dry eye in the room," writes Seligman, as one woman spoke about the deep gratitude she had for her mother. Seligman recognizes that we rarely explicitly thank those whose presence in our lives makes us happy, even joyful. "Even when we are moved to do so," he says, "we shrink in embarrassment." All the more reason for a conscious orientation toward gratitude. But even if you never participate in a "Gratitude Night," gratitude remains an essential element of a joyful spiritual life—and can ground you during difficult times.

Recently I was talking to a Jesuit friend named Steve about gratitude. Steve mentioned that one of his favorite passages in the whole New Testament, and one he used frequently in his work as a Jesuit high-school president, was on being grateful.

In the Gospel of Luke is a story of Jesus healing ten "lepers" (a catchall term in the Bible for any serious skin condition):[84]

> On the way to Jerusalem Jesus was going through the region between Samaria and Galilee. As he entered a village, ten lepers approached him. Keeping their distance, they called out, saying, "Jesus, Master, have mercy on us!" When he saw them, he said to them, "Go and show yourselves to the priests." And as they went, they were made clean.

Jesus asks them to present themselves to the priests since, according to the Book of Leviticus, they alone could certify their new "cleanliness" and restore them to the larger community. Those healed would have been exceedingly grateful, because they were healed from a fatal illness, they were now permitted to enter the city, and they could be reunited with their family and friends, perhaps after years of separation.

Yet only one of them, a Samaritan, returns to thank Jesus, to express gratitude. Now, the other nine might have had their reasons (or excuses). Perhaps they thought they were following Jesus's advice by visiting the priests, as he said, and that nothing more was required. Perhaps they rushed to their families to share their good fortune. Perhaps, as many of us think, there's no need to express our gratitude to God, since God knows all things.

Perhaps, however, they were simply lazy. Even Jesus is noticeably taken aback. "Were not ten made clean?" asks Jesus. "But the other nine, where are they? Was none of them found to return and give praise to God except this foreigner?" Then Jesus said to the one man who expresses thanks, "Get up and go on your way; your faith has made you well."

The healing, said Steve, was not complete until the gratitude had been expressed. " 'Thank you,' " he said, "is when the healing happens fully."

Why did he think that was so?

"When you say 'thank you,' you're acknowledging that you can't do it alone, that you need someone else, that you need God," said Steve. "Expressing gratitude indicates ego strength and also highlights one's sense of humility. In the relationship between Jesus and the leper, the expression is central to the leper's healing—he knows he can't heal himself."

Unlike the other nine, over whom Jesus utters a blanket healing ("Go and show yourselves to the priests"), the grateful man is addressed directly by Jesus. His gratitude not only leads him to joy, but into a closer relationship with God, who speaks with him directly. Gratitude is an essential part of any relationship, even a relationship in prayer with God.

You might also remember things that have surprised you. I asked earlier about whether the funny or unexpected events that happen in your day might be signs of God's playfulness in your life. Can you thank God for those surprises?

And here's a provocative question: Can you surprise God? Admittedly, that's a complicated philosophical notion. If God is all-knowing, then God knows the past, present, and future. On the other hand, I like to think that, as in any relationship, both parties can be surprised. And after all, God has given us the free will to make decisions in life. In that case, can you surprise God in your prayer and in your life? Can you do something out of character (say, lie on your back in a field and enjoy the sunshine, draw a picture with crayons to express your creativity, or sing a hymn aloud) that might, just might, surprise God? Perhaps God wants to be surprised from time to time. And delighted.

3. If you are a Christian, imagine yourself laughing with Jesus.

This type of prayer comes from the *Spiritual Exercises,* in which St. Ignatius encourages people to imagine themselves alongside Jesus. It's different than imagining yourself with God, who is often imagined more as a "presence." Imagining yourself with Jesus means something more specific.

As a Jesuit novice, when I first heard about this kind of prayer, I thought it sounded ridiculous. Imagining something in prayer? Wouldn't I just imagine what I wanted to happen? Did that mean that everything that happened in my imagination was somehow a message from God? It seemed absurd. But my spiritual director, named David, asked me a few questions that put my mind at rest.

I told David, "This is ridiculous! Imagining myself with Jesus sounds too much like making things up in my mind, like a childish fantasy. And this kind of prayer seems to go against type too. Aren't Jesuits supposed to be rational?"

He answered, "Jim, do you think that God can work through your daily life, through your relationships and experiences?"

"Sure," I said.

"What about your inner life? Your emotions, your desires, your intellect?"

"Sure," I said.

"So why couldn't God work through your imagination too?"

David asked. "Isn't your imagination a gift from God, like your intellect or your memory or your emotions? And if it is, can't it be used to experience God?"

Using your imagination isn't so much "making things up" as trusting that your imagination can draw you closer to the one who created it: God. That didn't mean that everything I imagined during prayer was coming from God. Rather, from time to time God could use my imagination to communicate with me.

We cannot really love anybody with whom we never laugh.

—Agnes Repplier, American essayist

Can you imagine yourself sitting with Jesus himself and laughing about something silly that happened? Imagining yourself with Jesus can take a variety of forms.

For some reason, I've long imagined myself sitting with Jesus at a rough-hewn table under a grape arbor in Nazareth, just outside his carpentry workshop. It may sound hokey, but it's an image that once came to me in prayer. Many people like to imagine Jesus sitting in an armchair across from them. One Catholic sister spent a few days on retreat imagining herself sitting with Jesus on a wooden bench by a stream. And a young Jesuit from the Midwest who came to me for spiritual direction told me that he liked to imagine himself with Jesus around a campfire—a new image for me. Another Jesuit I know thought of Jesus walking beside him through the streets of New York City. You could use a favorite place in your own life or perhaps a scene from the New Testament (in a fishing boat, by the shore of the Sea of Galilee, walking along a dusty road).

When you're doing this kind of prayer, try to imagine your surroundings as vividly as possible. As you place yourself in the scene and imagine yourself with Jesus, use all of your senses. What does each part look like, sound like, feel like, and so on.

After you have "composed" the scene in your mind, you can share your joy with Jesus. Tell him something that made you laugh today. Tell him things that you're joyful about. As we've seen, Jesus must have been someone who, during his earthly life, enjoyed joy. Share yours with him.

God has brought joy into your life. Share yours with God.

Conclusion

Get Ready for Heaven

By now I hope you can see why "excessive levity" is not to be feared, as that elderly priest told my friend Mike all those years ago, but to be welcomed. And—it's worth mentioning again—this is not to say that one should ignore the reality of suffering and sadness. But too many religious people overemphasize these aspects of life while downplaying the more mirthful ones. This book has tried to balance things out a bit. Joy, humor, and laughter are virtues necessary for a healthy spiritual life.

Those virtues also point us beyond our earthly lives. And that's the last thing I would like to speak about before we end our discussion.

This is not the place for a long disquisition about heaven—especially since I just indicated that I was wrapping things up.[85] But in many religious traditions, one way of looking at our earthly life is as a preparation for heaven. In that case, excessive levity may be one way to ready ourselves for the future. Rabbi Visotzky said, "Laughter and humor are ways to prepare oneself for the ecstasy in the world to come. In fact the Talmud says that in the world to come we will dance a *hora*[*] with God in the middle!" Margaret Silf, in a letter to me, said, "What a difference it would make if we thought that we might be headed for a sphere of being where laughter, not judgment, would be the norm!"

I'm not sure what heaven will be like; everyone has their own idea. My own vision is one of endless joy, good-natured humor, and abundant laughter. One woman who sees me regularly for spiritual direction pictures heaven as an endless library with an infinite number of books and an eternity to read all of them. For another friend it's the place that you can eat all you want without gaining any

---

* A traditional and joyful Jewish dance.

weight. Obviously, our visions of heaven are as different as we are.

But if our lives on earth provide us with a taste of heaven, as I believe they do, then we may assume heaven includes laughing with friends and families, finally relieved of any of the painful burdens of our physical bodies, sharing our happiness with the saints, in the company of our loving God, who has prepared a place of eternal joy for us. God awaits us in joy with joy.

Preparation for heaven forms the basis of a great deal of Christian theology. Life, in this understanding, is not so much a test as it is a rehearsal. And one way of preparing for something is by *doing it.* You get ready for a Little League tryout by practicing your pitching, batting, and fielding. You practice for a concert by playing your instrument at home. You prepare for a wedding with a rehearsal the night before.

In that case, why couldn't earthly joy, humor, and laughter be a way of preparing for a lifetime of happiness? Why not allow yourself to enjoy a little heaven on earth? Engaging in those virtues, then, is not simply a way to live a fuller spiritual life now, but to orient yourself to your future.

So be joyful. Use your sense of humor. And laugh with the God who smiles when seeing you, rejoices over your very existence, and takes delight in you, all the days of your life.

For Further Exploration

Here are several books on joy, humor, and laughter that have informed this one. You'll enjoy all of them. Some of them might even make you laugh:

Arbuckle, Gerald A. *Laughing with God: Humor, Culture, and Transformation*. Collegeville, MN: Liturgical, 2008.

Barry, William A. *God and You: Prayer as a Personal Relationship*. Mahwah, NJ: Paulist, 1992.

De Mello, Anthony. *The Song of the Bird*. Garden City, NY: Image, 1982.

Eco, Umberto. *The Name of the Rose*. New York: Everyman's Library, 2006.

Ehrenreich, Barbara. *Dancing in the Streets: A History of Collective Joy*. New York: Metropolitan, 2007.

———. *Bright-Sided: How the Relentless Promotion of Positive Thinking Has Undermined America*. New York: Metropolitan, 2009.

Fesquet, Henri. *Wit and Wisdom of Good Pope John*. Trans. Salvator Attanasio. New York: Kennedy, 1964.

Grassi, Joseph A. *God Makes Me Laugh: A New Approach to Luke*. Wilmington, DE: Michael Glazier, 1986.

Gritsch, Eric W. *The Wit of Martin Luther*. Minneapolis: Fortress, 2006.

Häring, Bernard. *Celebrating Joy*. Trans. Edward Quinn. New York: Herder & Herder, 1970.

Hays, Edward M. *Chasing Joy: Musings on Life in a Bittersweet World*. Notre Dame, IN: Forest of Peace, 2007.

Hebert, Victoria, and Judy Bauer. *Wit and Wisdom of the Saints: A Year of Saintly Humor*. Liguori, MO: Liguori, 2002.

Hyers, Conrad M. *The Comic Vision and the Christian Faith: A Celebration of Life and Laughter*. New York: Pilgrim, 1981.

Jamison, Christopher Abbot. *Finding Happiness: Monastic Steps for a Fulfilling Life*. Collegeville, MN: Liturgical, 2008.

Kuschel, Karl-Josef. *Laughter: A Theological Essay*. Trans. John Bowden. New York: Continuum, 1994.

Lebowitz, Fran. *The Fran Lebowitz Reader*. New York: Vintage, 1994.

Marty, Martin E., and Jerald C. Brauer, eds. *The Unrelieved Paradox: Studies in the Theology of Franz Bibfeldt*. Grand Rapids, MI: Eerdmans, 1994.

Paul VI. *Gaudete in Domino* ("On Christian Joy"). 1975.

Rahman, Jamal. *The Fragrance of Faith: The Enlightened Heart of Islam*. Bath, U.K.: Book Foundation, 2004.

Rahner, Hugo. *Man at Play*. Trans. Brian Battershaw and Edward Quinn. New York: Herder & Herder, 1972.

Rahner, Karl. "Laughter," in *The Content of Faith: The Best of Karl Rahner's Theological Writings*. Ed. Karl Lehmann and Albert Raffelt. Trans. Harvey D. Egan. New York: Crossroad, 1993.

Samra, Cal. *The Joyful Christ: The Healing Power of Humor*. San Francisco: Harper & Row, 1986.

Seligman, Martin E. P. *Authentic Happiness: Using the New Positive Psychology to Realize Your Potential for Lasting Fulfillment*. New York: Free Press, 2002.

Sypher, Wylie, ed. *Comedy: "An Essay on Comedy" by George Meredith and "Laughter" by Henri Bergson*. Baltimore: Johns Hopkins Univ. Press, 1980.

Trueblood, Elton. *The Humor of Christ*. New York: Harper & Row, 1964.

Türks, Paul. *Philip Neri: The Fire of Joy*. Trans. Daniel Utrecht. New York: Alba, 1995.

For Further Exploration

The following books on the broader topics of the Bible, spirituality, and church history were also helpful in my research and are highly recommended for further study.

Barclay, William. *The Mind of Jesus*. New York: Harper, 1961.

Bergant, Dianne. *People of the Covenant: An Invitation to the Old Testament*. Franklin, WI: Sheed & Ward, 2001.

Brown, Raymond E. *An Introduction to the New Testament*. New York: Doubleday, 1997.

Brown, Raymond E., Joseph A. Fitzmyer, and Roland E. Murphy, eds. *The New Jerome Biblical Commentary*. Englewood Cliffs, NJ: Prentice-Hall, 1990.

Cates, Diana Fritz. *Aquinas on the Emotions: A Religious-Ethical Inquiry*. Washington, DC: Georgetown Univ. Press, 2009.

Chadwick, Henry. *The Early Church*. The Penguin History of the Church, rev. ed. New York: Penguin, 1993.

Dahood, Mitchell. *Psalms II: 51–100*. Anchor Bible, vol. 17. Garden City, NY: Doubleday, 1968.

Di Monte Santa Maria, Ugolino. *The Little Flowers of St. Francis of Assisi*. Trans. W. Heywood. New York: Vintage, 1998.

Dodd, C. H. *The Founder of Christianity*. London: Collins, 1971.

Downey, Michael, ed. *The New Dictionary of Catholic Spirituality*. Collegeville, MN: Liturgical, 1993.

Harrington, Daniel J. *Jesus: A Historical Portrait*. Cincinnati, OH: St. Anthony Messenger, 2007.

———. *How Do Catholics Read the Bible?* Lanham, MD: Rowman & Littlefield, 2005.

Hopcke, Robert H., and Paul A. Schwartz, trans. *Little Flowers of Francis of Assisi: A New Translation*. Boston: New Seeds, 2006.

Johnson, Elizabeth A. *Consider Jesus: Waves of Renewal in Christology*. New York: Crossroad, 1990.

Johnson, Luke Timothy. *The Gospel of Luke*. Sacra Pagina Series. Collegeville, MN: Liturgical, 1991.

Kamenetz, Rodger. *The Jew in the Lotus: A Poet's Rediscovery of Jewish Identity in Buddhist India.* San Francisco: HarperSanFrancisco, 1994.

Komonchak, Joseph A., Mary Collins, and Dermot A. Lane, eds. *The New Dictionary of Theology.* Wilmington, DE: Michael Glazier, 1987.

Levine, Amy-Jill. *The Misunderstood Jew: The Church and the Scandal of the Jewish Jesus.* San Francisco: HarperSanFrancisco, 2006.

Marshall, Alfred, trans. *The Interlinear Greek-English New Testament.* London: Samuel Bagster, 1966.

Mays, James L., ed. *HarperCollins Bible Commentary.* San Francisco: HarperSanFrancisco, 2000.

McCahill, Bob. *Dialogue of Life: A Christian Among Allah's Poor.* Maryknoll, NY: Orbis Books, 2001.

Meier, John P. *A Marginal Jew: Rethinking the Historical Jesus.* Vol. 1, *The Roots of the Problem and the Person.* New York: Doubleday, 1991.

Nolan, Albert. *Jesus Before Christianity.* Maryknoll, NY: Orbis Books, 2004.

O'Collins, Gerald. *Following the Way: Jesus, Our Spiritual Director.* Mahwah, NJ: Paulist, 2001.

Pieper, Josef. *Leisure: The Basis of Culture.* Trans. Alexander Dru. San Francisco: Ignatius, 2009.

Richardson, Cyril C. *Early Christian Fathers.* New York: Touchstone, 1996.

Saliers, Don E. *The Soul in Paraphrase: Prayer and the Religious Affections.* Akron, OH: OSL, 2002.

Schüssler Fiorenza, Elisabeth. *In Memory of Her: A Feminist Theological Reconstruction of Christian Origins.* New York: Crossroad, 1989.

Senior, Donald. *Jesus: A Gospel Portrait.* Rev. and exp. ed. Mahwah, NJ: Paulist, 1992.

Smith, Jonathan Z., and William Scott Green, eds. *The HarperCollins Dictionary of Religion.* San Francisco: HarperSanFrancisco, 1995.

Throckmorton, Burton H., ed. *Gospel Parallels: A Comparison of the Synoptic Gospels.* Nashville: Nelson, 1992.

Acknowledgments

JOY SPRINGS FROM GRATITUDE, and I'm immensely grateful to a number of people who helped me with this book. To begin with, I want to thank the scholars and friends (and scholar-friends) who read drafts of this book in its early stages and helped with suggestions, emendations, and, very often, corrections. So abundant thanks to Daniel J. Harrington, S.J., Thomas J. Massaro, S.J., James Keane, S.J., Christopher Ruddy, Grant Gallicho, David van Biema, Robert Ellsberg, James D. Ross, Carolyn Buscarino, and Maureen O'Connell.

I would also like to thank Sister Edith Prendergast and her colleagues at the Los Angeles Religious Education Congress, a gathering of Catholics that takes place every year (improbably, not in L.A., but in Anaheim). This book had its genesis in lectures I was invited to present there over the years.

For the scholarly material in this book, I would like to thank the scholars and experts upon whom I called to talk about joy, humor, and laughter. So joyful thanks to Daniel J. Harrington, S.J., Richard J. Clifford, S.J., Harold Attridge, Amy-Jill Levine, the Reverend Martin Marty, Rabbis Daniel Polish and Burton Visotzky, and Sheik Jamal Rahman as well as those who work "in the trenches," including Pastor Charles Hambrick-Stowe of the United Church of Christ, the Reverend Ann Kansfield of the Dutch Reformed Church, and the Reverend David Robb of the Unitarian Church.

Thanks also to the following people who helped me on additional areas of inquiry specific to their fields of expertise, including Lawrence S. Cunningham, Jordan Friedman, James Palmigiano,

O.C.S.O., and Michael O'Neill McGrath, O.S.F.S. Thanks to Cal Samra, the editor of *The Joyful Noiseletter,* for his list of joyful verses in the New Testament; to Drew Christiansen, S.J., for pointing me to selections from St. Thomas Aquinas on the emotions (as well as to the work of Donald Saliers); to Tom Beaudoin, for pointing me to Karl Rahner's marvelous essay on laughter; to Thomas Fitzpatrick, S.J., for alerting me to the theme of joy in Nehemiah; to Paul Pearson, for reminding me of the tale of Thomas Merton laughing; and to Robert Ellsberg, for unearthing the tale of Blessed Jordan of Saxony. And for my discussions on the psychology of joy, humor, and laughter, I would like to thank William A. Barry, S.J., and Eileen Russell.

Thanks also to Roger Freet, Julie Burton, Michael Maudlin, and Mark Tauber at HarperOne for their enthusiasm for this project; to my literary agent, Donald Cutler, for his sage advice; and to Carolyn Holland and Ann Moru, for their terrific edits; and to Heidi Hill, the world's greatest fact-checker. Thanks to Chris Keller and P. J. Williams, who helped me with the typing when my carpal tunnel syndrome flared up (which is to say, almost every week).

Most of all, thanks be to God. As Mary said, "My spirit rejoices in God my Savior."

About the Author

James Martin, S.J., is a Jesuit priest, the culture editor of the Catholic magazine *America,* and the author of many books, including *The Jesuit Guide to (Almost) Everything* (a *New York Times* bestseller), *A Jesuit Off-Broadway, Becoming Who You Are, Searching for God at Ground Zero, In Good Company, This Our Exile,* and *My Life with the Saints,* which was named one of *Publishers Weekly*'s "Best Books" of the Year. Father Martin has written for a variety of religious publications, including *Commonweal, The (London) Tablet,* and *U.S. Catholic* as well as for the *New York Times, The Wall Street Journal,* The Huffington Post, and Slate.com. He is a frequent commentator on religion in the media and has appeared on all the major television and radio networks and in venues as diverse as CNN, BBC, Vatican Radio, the History Channel, NPR's *Fresh Air with Terry Gross,* PBS's *Newshour with Jim Lehrer,* Fox News's *The O'Reilly Factor,* and Comedy Central's *The Colbert Report.*

Notes

1. Phil. 2:12.
2. Quoted in Wylie Sypher, ed., Comedy.
3. *The Catechism of the Catholic Church,* #1676.
4. Qur'an 53:43.
5. *Sahih Muslim,* vol. 1, 365.
6. *Sahih al-Bukhari,* vol. 1, 770.
7. Mark 15:16–20.
8. Thomas Aquinas, *Summa Theologica,* II–II, 28.1.
9. Ps. 42:7.
10. Eph. 5:4. In one translation Paul inveighs against "foolish talking or jesting" (Alfred Marshall, trans., *The Interlinear Literal Translation of the Greek New Testament*).
11. Matt. 7:3.
12. John 13:1–11.
13. Matt. 14:22–33.
14. Matt. 16:18.
15. Num. 22.
16. James L. Mays, ed., *The HarperCollins Bible Commentary.*
17. Pss. 119:1; 98:4; 100:2; 126:1–2.
18. Neh. 12:43.
19. Mark 2:16.

20. Gerald O'Collins, *Following the Way.*
21. John 20:30.
22. Luke 10:21; 13:17; John 16:22; 16:24; Luke 24:41; John 20:20.
23. 2 Cor. 7:4; Rom. 14:17; 12:12; Phil. 4:4; Gal. 5:22–23.
24. Matt. 5:3–12; also Luke 6:20–23.
25. Matt. 25:14–30.
26. Matt. 11:18–19.
27. Luke 5:34.
28. John 1:43–51.
29. Luke 19:1–10.
30. Acts 20:7–12.
31. Luke 24:13–35. The story is often called the "Road to Emmaus" or the "Supper at Emmaus."
32. Matt. 8:28–34; Mark 5:1–20; Luke 8:26–39. The name "Gerasene" comes from the place that the "demoniac" resided. In Mark and Luke it is the "country of the Gerasenes"; in Matthew, the "country of the Gadarenes."
33. Raymond E. Brown, Joseph A. Fitzmyer, and Roland E. Murphy, eds., *The New Jerome Biblical Commentary.*
34. Elizabeth Johnson, a Catholic theologian, expands upon the traditional double model of patron and companion in her marvelous book on the saints, *Friends of God and Prophets* (New York: Continuum, 1998).
35. Susan M. Garthwaite, Ph.D., refers to the saint's "playful teasing of God" in an article in *Spiritual Life* (Spring 2009) entitled "The Humor of St. Teresa of Ávila in *The Life.*"
36. 1 Cor. 4:10: "We are fools for the sake of Christ . . ."
37. Mark 3:21.
38. Ugolino di Monte Santa Maria, *The Little Flowers of St. Francis of*

Assisi. Another good translation is the one by Robert H. Hopcke and Paul A. Schwartz.

39. Paul Türks, *Philip Neri: The Fire of Joy*.
40. Robert Ellsberg, *All Saints* (New York: Crossroad, 1997).
41. I am indebted to Rabbi Daniel Polish for pointing me to this traditional story.
42. Jamal Rahman, *The Fragrance of Faith: The Enlightened Heart of Islam* (Watsonville, CA: Book Foundation, 2004).
43. Karl Rahner, "Laughter," in *The Content of Faith*.
44. Prov. 26:17.
45. Matt. 22:15–22.
46. He adapted this fable from a tale he found in Jamal Rahman's *The Fragrance of Faith*.
47. Isa. 62:4.
48. Cardinal Joseph Ratzinger, *God and the World: A Conversation with Peter Seewald* (San Francisco: Ignatius, 2002).
49. Gen. 17:1–17; 18:1–15; 21:1–7.
50. Luke 9:5.
51. Luke 1:42.
52. Doris Kearns Goodwin, *Team of Rivals: The Political Genius of Abraham Lincoln* (New York: Simon & Schuster, 2005).
53. Daniel Goleman, "Humor Found to Aid Problem-Solving," *New York Times,* August 4, 1987.
54. Blaine Greteman, "I Laugh, Therefore I Am," *Utne Reader,* August 2009.
55. Thomas Aquinas, *Summa Theologica,* II–I, 33.1.
56. Luke 15:32.
57. 1 Sam 2:1–10.
58. Luke Timothy Johnson, *The Gospel of Luke*.

59. Robert J. Karris, "The Gospel of Luke," in Raymond E. Brown, Joseph A. Fitzmyer, and Roland E. Murphy, eds., *The New Jerome Biblical Commentary*.
60. Walter Kasper, *An Introduction to Christian Faith* (London: Burns & Oates, 1980).
61. Gen. 9:20–27.
62. Matt. 23:9.
63. Herbert J. Thurston and Donald Attwater, eds., *Butler's Lives of the Saints,* vol. 4.
64. Matt. 6:16.
65. Matt. 23:11.
66. James 3:7–10.
67. Matt. 5:22, NAB.
68. Mark 5:41.
69. John 11:35.
70. John Macmurray, *Persons in Relation* (London: Faber & Faber, 1967).
71. Also called the *examen,* from the Spanish. A more complete explanation of the daily examination of conscience can be found in my book *The Jesuit Guide to (Almost) Everything* (San Francisco: HarperOne, 2010).
72. Laurence J. Peter and Bill Dana, *The Laughter Prescription* (New York: Ballantine, 1982).
73. Jerome W. Berryman, *Teaching Godly Play: How to Mentor the Spiritual Development of Children* (Nashville: Abingdon, 1995).
74. Matt. 13:33; Luke 13:20–21.
75. Robert Coles, *Dorothy Day: A Radical Devotion* (Reading, MA: Addison-Wesley, 1987).
76. Johannes Baptist Metz, *Poverty of Spirit* (Mahwah, NJ: Paulist, 1998).

77. From his journals, February 5, 1950. I'm indebted to Jim Forest, author of the Merton biography *Living with Wisdom,* and Paul Pearson, director of the Thomas Merton Center at Bellarmine University in Kentucky, for tracking down this quote.

78. Luke 1:26–38 (discussed in "A Study in Joy: The Visitation").

79. Mark 2:12; 5:35–43; 9:14–29; John 9:1–34.

80. Jim Forest, *Living with Wisdom: A Life of Thomas Merton* (Maryknoll, NY: Orbis Books, 1991).

81. Edgar M. Krentz, "First Thessalonians," in Harold Attridge, ed., *HarperCollins Study Bible, New Revised Standard Version* (San Francisco: HarperSanFrancisco, 2006).

82. James Cone, *The Spirituals and the Blues* (Maryknoll, NY: Orbis Books, 1991).

83. Mark Thibodeaux, *Armchair Mystic: Easing into Contemplative Prayer* (Cincinnati, OH: St. Anthony Messenger, 2001).

84. Luke 17:11–19.

85. But a fun place to start is Lisa Miller's book *Heaven: Our Enduring Fascination with the Afterlife* (New York: Harper, 2010).

Index

References to Biblical chapters and verses appear in italics.